ROBERT DOUGLAS-ꜰᴀɪʀʜᴜʀꜱᴛ

Look Closer

How to Get More Out of Reading

FERN
PRESS

1 3 5 7 9 10 8 6 4 2

Fern Press, an imprint of Vintage, is part of the
Penguin Random House group of companies

Vintage, Penguin Random House UK, One Embassy Gardens,
8 Viaduct Gardens, London SW11 7BW

penguin.co.uk/vintage
global.penguinrandomhouse.com

Penguin
Random House
UK

First published by Fern Press in 2025

Typeset in 11.75/15pt Adobe Garamond Pro by
Six Red Marbles UK, Thetford, Norfolk
Printed and bound in Great Britain by Clays Ltd, Elcograf S.p.A.

The authorised representative in the EEA is Penguin Random House Ireland,
Morrison Chambers, 32 Nassau Street, Dublin D02 YH68

A CIP catalogue record for this book is available from the British Library

ISBN 9781911717317

For my students

Contents

How to Find Your Way Around

How to Keep Your Head

How to Get Involved

How to Read Between the Lines

How to Move On

Prologue

LEARNING TO READ

IT IS EARLY IN the evening and my bedroom is full of rabbits. I'm probably four or five years old, and in my hands is a copy of Beatrix Potter's *The Tale of Peter Rabbit* that my mother is helping me to read. I've already experienced a familiar jumble of emotions that includes curiosity, confusion and the quiet glee that comes from knowing not everyone is safely tucked up in bed with a well-thumbed picture book. Now I turn the page and my pulse quickens as the story takes a darker turn. Peter Rabbit is in trouble.

After entering a kitchen garden, he has gorged on lettuces, French beans and radishes until he feels sick, but finally his luck appears to have run out. Trying to escape from Mr McGregor, who is shown angrily waving a rake and has a beard that makes him look a bit like my father, Peter has got tangled up in a net of some kind, snagged by the shiny brass buttons on his new blue jacket.

I have a lot of sympathy for Peter, especially when I try to make out the words that sit alongside the book's soft-edged illustrations, because already his story is turning out to be as full of snares and booby traps as any imaginary garden. Now I stumble my way through another sentence, half deciphering it and half remembering what happened last time we went on this particular adventure: 'P-ee-ter, Peter, g-ave, gave, h-im-self, him-self, up for l-oft, oh, l-*ost*, lost, and sh-ed, shed (is there a shed because they're in the garden?), big t-e-ars, tears (has he torn his coat?), oh, *tears* . . . ' I am still finding it hard to organise the letters into meaningful clumps of sound, and occasionally I watch in frustration as some of the words squirm away from me or play a game of hide-and-seek on the page. Even when I have carefully spelt them out, there are sentences that remain as mysterious as messages written in code, like the friendly sparrows who fly down to Peter and 'implored him to exert himself'. I have no idea what this means.

What will happen next? I'm fairly confident Peter will escape, slipping out of his jacket and running home to his mother, because that's what he's always done when we've read this story before, but I can't be absolutely sure he'll pull off the same trick again. Perhaps someone sneaked into the book when I was asleep last night and rearranged the words on the final page, like the contents of the doll's house that Tom Thumb and Hunca Munca turn upside down in *The Tale of Two Bad Mice*. There's always a chance that *The Tale of Peter Rabbit* will behave like its hero and succeed in wriggling free.

It seems that not everyone shared my early struggles with reading. Indeed, some writers claim to have acquired what Patrick Leigh Fermor describes as 'the miracle of literacy' with the mysterious speed of a magic spell. Doris Lessing recalls how she 'began reading at seven, off a cigarette packet, and almost at once progressed to the books in my parents' bookcase'. Growing up in pre-war Berlin, Judith Kerr used to point to 'shop signs, posters, anything with letters on it', asking her mother 'What does that say?', until 'one day something must have clicked, and I found I could read'. Suddenly a previously mute world had come alive and was talking to her.

It's tempting to think that these writers' memories may have confused learning to read with the sudden transformations that many children enjoy reading about, from Kipling's *Just So Stories* ('How the camel got his hump', 'How the elephant got his trunk') to superhero comics in which a teenage boy can acquire a spider's web-slinging powers, or a female lawyer can receive a blood transfusion that turns her into a muscle-bound green giant capable of smashing up her surroundings. Actually, it's a lot more complicated than that.

Studies of how children learn to read have drawn attention to the multiple cognitive processes involved, and in particular to the new neuronal pathways that are gradually formed in the brain until it can recognise a word like 'rabbit' and know that it refers to a furry creature with a tail like a puff of cotton wool, rather than to a type of biscuit or a brand of hairdryer. A few milliseconds of reading time results in an astonishingly complex set of connections being made between the different areas of the brain that deal with vision, memory, information processing, thought and feeling: billions of neurons dancing to the sound of a single word. These specialised adaptations of the brain's basic physical structures are also involved in some important stages of behavioural development, as the child's growing ability to enter into the consciousness of a fictional character like Peter Rabbit or Mr McGregor encourages them to discover who they are, and who they can imagine being, through the ongoing process of compare and contrast that occurs whenever we read about figures who are like us in some ways and unlike us in others.

Yet the physiological and intellectual changes that happen when we read don't stop when we are no longer children. According to the neuroscientist Maryanne Wolf, the adult human brain continues to be altered by the same means. 'Much of how we think and what we think about', she writes, 'is based on insights and associations generated from what we read.' Her conclusion?

'Reading changes our lives, and our lives change our reading.' And like anything else that involves practice, such as playing a musical instrument or perfecting a new golf swing, the more we read the better we are likely to get at it. We might be tempted to think that reading is a skill we acquire once and then perform almost automatically, like learning how to ride a bicycle or tie a pair of shoelaces, but as the literary critic I. A. Richards pointed out in 1942, the truth is that 'We are all of us learning to read all the time.'

That certainly matches my own experience. As far back as I can remember, books have formed some of the most important stepping stones of my life. I still vividly recall scrambling on board the Puffin Club boat that was moored in Greenwich for Roald Dahl to sign my newly purchased copy of *Charlie and the Chocolate Factory* (1964), an encounter that for a seven-year-old boy with thick glasses and a greedy imagination felt a bit like meeting Father Christmas. Many years later, as a graduate student in America, there was the summer I spent sitting on the hot paving slabs outside Princeton's Firestone Library, reading Proust and feeling like a stranger in two countries at once. Books have shown me how to fall in (and out of) love and how to examine the world around me with more curious, searching eyes; they have helped me to think more clearly and feel more deeply.

I have also been lucky enough to turn a lifelong passion into a career. For more than twenty years, I have taught some of the world's greatest literature to some of the world's brightest students at the University of Oxford, and if you walked into my office today you would see books everywhere: tatty paperbacks on shelves that reach from wall to wall and floor to ceiling; chunky hardbacks piled up on the carpet like stalagmites. I sometimes think that if you cut into me I would bleed ink, rather as the scholar Casaubon in George Eliot's *Middlemarch* (1871–72) is described as being so obsessed with his work that if you put a drop of his blood under a magnifying glass it would be 'all semicolons and parentheses'. Yet I still experience each new book I open as a fresh challenge to my literary assumptions. Even as I am trying to teach my students how to be better readers, I am learning how to do the same thing myself.

Why should this matter? There are as many answers to that question as there are readers in the world, but when we consider what reading does to help people get through life – whether by glossing it with pleasure or sharpening it with extra meaning – some common factors emerge. That's particularly true when it comes to our reading of imaginative works like novels, short stories, poems and plays, which can act like lenses to refocus the world around us or kaleidoscopes to twist it into bright new patterns. 'Reading is to the mind, what exercise is to the body', Joseph Addison claimed at the start of an essay he wrote for his periodical *The Tatler* in 1709, and anyone who has followed the adventures of fictional protagonists like Isabel Archer or Holden Caulfield will know exactly what he meant. When we feel involved in a story, we do more than merely observe its characters from a distance. We are invited to get inside their heads and have a look around; we work out where their thoughts end and our own begin. And when we finally close the book, we are likely to know more about ourselves as well as about these imaginary people made from paper and ink.

For many readers this is a process that begins early. I remember the same thing happening when I had outgrown Beatrix Potter and moved onto slightly more challenging authors like A. A. Milne (who was the first to make me realise that books were allowed to be funny) and Enid Blyton (who wasn't always easy to love but was almost impossible to escape). Walking to my local library and taking a book off the shelf felt like picking up a bottle that had washed up on the shore, and discovering a message that someone had put there especially for me to find.

Reading the book helped me to understand this other person, while feeling that I too was understood.

This is also why psychologists continue to stress the importance of reading for adults. Even if we think we know who we are, reading a piece of imaginative literature can temporarily release us from the invisible constraints of selfhood. It can give us new personalities to try on and new worlds to try out, allowing us to be simultaneously ourselves and someone else, or to be living here (this bedroom, this train, this waiting room), and elsewhere (New York, Narnia, The Ocean at the End of the Lane) without having to move a muscle.

But if reading can be a form of escapism, helping to distract us from our lives, it can also work in the opposite direction, introducing us to aspects of experience that we were only half conscious of until we saw them being assembled and organised on the page. This is one of the reasons why people send each other love poems that were originally written for someone else, like Shakespeare's 'Shall I compare thee to a summer's day?' or Keats's 'Bright Star'. Here are pieces of writing that express feelings we recognise as our own but could not have formulated on our own. The same is true of larger literary works. They too can be read as instruction manuals or guidebooks for life, filtering the world to make it more understandable or encouraging us to look at it in new ways through a borrowed pair of eyes.

Yet as we get older, often we don't read with the same level of attention we once devoted to books, or comics, or anything else that successfully held our attention as children. We are more easily distracted; when we are faced with blocks of print we are more likely to find ourselves skimming rather than lingering. There are simply more demands on our time, more things (and more people) that come between us and the words on the page.

This sense that we are reading with less concentration is partly a consequence of just how much printed matter now exists and partly down to how much of it we become exposed to over the course of our lives. In 2006, the critic John Sutherland calculated that approximately half a million different novels were available to purchase online, which at a conservative estimate (he imagined spending three hours on each book, and working a forty-hour week for forty-six weeks of the year) would take roughly 163 lifetimes to get through. Since then the flood of print has risen even higher – and that's before we factor in the potentially infinite offerings of the Internet.

In Douglas Adams's most famous novel, we are introduced to a device that looks like 'a largish electronic calculator' featuring many flat buttons and 'a screen about four inches square on which any one of a million "pages" could be summoned at a moment's notice'. It's known as 'The Hitchhiker's Guide to the Galaxy', and it has the words 'DON'T PANIC' printed in 'large friendly letters' on its plastic cover, chiefly in response to the head-spinning fact that 'if it were printed in normal book form, an interstellar hitchhiker would require several inconveniently large buildings to carry it around in'. When *The Hitchhiker's Guide to the Galaxy* was first published in 1979, this device would have seemed as laughably implausible as the earth being demolished by Vogons to make way for a new hyperspace bypass. Today it sounds perfectly reasonable. After all, it's a device many people carry around with them in their pockets or handbags, and refer to as a mobile phone rather than a guide to the galaxy. Given that it can now be used to summon far more than a million 'pages' simply by pressing a few buttons – including the complete works of Douglas Adams – the original guide's advice seems more relevant than ever. DON'T PANIC.

In 1926, Virginia Woolf gave a speech entitled 'How Should One Read a Book?' that pointed out how many novels, poems, memoirs and other kinds of writing 'jostle each other' for our attention. 'Where are we to begin?' she asked. 'How are we to bring order into this multitudinous chaos and so get the deepest and widest pleasure from what we read?' The following pages try to offer some answers.

I have divided my suggestions into a series of short chapters, each of which gives a cross section of the materials that writers use when building an imaginary world for us to inhabit. In each chapter, I also look closely at a single example that concentrates some broader ideas and literary techniques, a bit like applying a magnifying glass to a piece of embroidery to reveal how it is stitched together. (The English word 'text' comes from the same Latin root as 'textile', so this isn't as far-fetched a comparison as it might sound.) Finally, I offer a few thoughts about how paying careful attention to these texts might also help us to become better readers of the world of words that surrounds us, from news stories to adverts and social media posts. And that's because becoming a better reader isn't only a question of reading more; it also means learning how to get more out of the writing we encounter every day.

There's no assumption that you will already know the material I will be discussing, but hopefully the examples I've chosen will intrigue you enough to go and investigate their contexts. Unavoidably there are some plot spoilers, but I've tried to choose pieces of writing where knowing what happens won't stop you wanting to learn more about how and why it happens. Many of these passages are drawn from short stories and novels, which tend to be the works most people choose to read in their spare time; some are from poetry; a few are from plays and other genres. Most of the time I refer to them all as 'books', which should be seen as a word that bundles together online texts, and in some cases audio recordings, in addition to traditional forms of publication. I should probably stress that they don't form any sort of literary canon. As you'll see from the fragments of autobiography

I've included, they reflect my own history as a reader and are also part of the jigsaw puzzle of experiences that have shaped my life outside the library. But I do think they all reward careful reading, or – if you already know them – rereading.

What I won't be spending much time on are fiddly metrical patterns, experimental narrative time schemes and all the other technical flourishes that critics sometimes treat as the real stars of the show. That's partly because describing how such things work rarely helps us understand why they matter, but also because the best pieces of writing are always exceptions to the rules they have helped to form. When William Empson, then in his late sixties, was asked to contribute an essay to a book published in honour of the eighty-year-old I. A. Richards, one of his university teachers, he observed that the trouble with getting old is that everyone becomes the same age. Similarly, one danger with knowing what a form such as a Petrarchan sonnet should look like, and then spotting a few, is that they all become the same poem, whereas good writers are escapologists who are forever squeezing their way out of the forms that try to box them in. They might pretend to be Mr McGregors, but at heart they are all Peter Rabbits. That's why I will mostly be dealing in literary examples rather than rules. It's also why some readers may want to quarrel with my conclusions and substitute their own examples for mine. And that's just as it should be. Criticism is neither pure art nor pure science but an ongoing conversation between the two, so it always relies on discussion, debate and dissent.

One of the most obvious things that separates an experienced literary critic from other readers is *speed*: whereas someone who is reading a novel for pleasure might stop and start, pause over certain passages or flip back a few chapters to remind themselves of a key plot detail, someone who is assessing it with a more professional eye might power through it in less than half the time, pinpointing familiar allusions and drawing fresh conclusions on every page. But if we are to get more out of books, one of the first things we may all need to do is s-l-o-w d-o-w-n.

A good deal has been written in recent years about the various movements that have emerged to help people get more out of life by taking it at a less frantic pace: slow food, slow work, slow parenting, slow travel, slow sex. Slow reading sounds rather different, the sort of thing that might evoke pity or scorn in anyone who associates it with stupidity, but it also has supporters who recognise that it can help to break the bad habit many of us have fallen into of reading texts only for information – on the page as well as online – in an uneven rhythm of scanning and skipping. By contrast, we might think of slow reading as a way of patiently allowing the words to do their work, or reveal their possibilities for play, in a fashion many of us still remember from the time we first encountered the world of print. No doubt this is what the philosopher Friedrich Nietzsche meant when he described himself in his 1881 book *Daybreak* (*Morgenröthe*) as 'a teacher of slow reading'. In an age of work, he wrote, 'that is, of haste, of unseemly and immoderate hurry-scurry, which is so eager to "get things done"', what is needed is an approach that will teach us 'how to read well, that is, slowly, profoundly, attentively, prudently, with inner thoughts, with the mental doors ajar'.

That's what this book tries to offer: an approach to reading that recognises how, when we pick up a book, we aren't only trying to lose ourselves in it. We might also find ourselves there, if we are willing to look closely enough and leave our mental doors ajar.

How to Begin

Chapter 1

Welcome

A FEW DAYS AGO YOU bought a book. It's a second-hand copy of the fat nineteenth-century novel *Paul Clifford*, and it probably caught your eye because its title reminded you of many other stories you've enjoyed that were named after the central protagonist, from Charlotte Brontë's *Jane Eyre* to Stephen King's *Carrie*, each of which made you feel that you were being introduced to a stranger who might became a good friend if only you were to spend enough time in their company. Since then it's been waiting patiently on a bookshelf in your living room, but this afternoon you finally pick it up and settle down in your favourite armchair. It's time to start reading.

Perhaps you have a cup of coffee and a plate of biscuits on the table next to you; perhaps there's a cat snoozing on your lap.

The author, Edward Bulwer-Lytton, isn't someone you know a great deal about, but you have heard that he was one of Dickens's rivals and the inventor of popular phrases such as 'the great unwashed' and 'the pen is mightier than the sword', so you're feeling optimistic. This is probably his most famous novel, and it certainly sounds exciting, with its focus on a fashionable man about town who enjoys a secret double life as a highwayman. It sold out on publication day in 1830, and launched a whole new genre of crime fiction in which the hero moonlighted as a law-breaking rogue.

With a growing sense of anticipation, you find the first chapter, skip past a long verse epigraph, and begin:

It was a dark and stormy night;

Feeling a bit puzzled, you lift your eyes from the page. Aren't most nights dark? Then you return to the opening sentence and discover that it goes on. And on.

> the rain fell in torrents – except at occasional intervals, when it was checked by a violent gust of wind which swept up the streets (for it is in London that our scene lies), rattling along the housetops, and fiercely agitating the scanty flame of the lamps that struggled against the darkness.

Again you lift your eyes from the page, and this time you decide not to return to it. Overwrought, under-thought, and emptily straining for significance, it's a piece of writing that's hard to read without your fingers itching to pick up an editor's pencil and get to work. Disappointed, you reflect that Bulwer-Lytton's style hasn't aged well (posterity can be a cruel judge of talent), and add his novel to a pile destined for the charity shop.

Today *Paul Clifford* is commemorated by the annual Bulwer-Lytton Fiction Contest, established in 1982 to celebrate the 'best worst' opening to an as yet unwritten novel. The 2021 Grand Prize was awarded to 'A lecherous sunrise flaunted itself over a flatulent sea, ripping the obsidian bodice of night asunder with its rapacious fingers of gold, thus exposing her dusky bosom to the dawn's ogling stare', with a Dishonourable Mention for 'It was a dark and stormy night; the rain fell in Torrance, but not in nearby Rancho Palos Verdes, which was unusual given the two towns' proximity.' All the entries are supposed to be funny, but when I first read about this contest I also experienced a more serious tug of memory. And after looking through my surviving school notebooks, I discovered why.

It turns out that when I was about twelve years old I was fond of writing equally tempestuous openings for my English homework assignments. One story begins 'A bolt of lightning streaked through the sky, ripping open the heavens with a malicious CRACK!' (The title I chose for this piece of look-at-me prose was 'The Storm'.) Another begins 'Outside the cave, the thunderstorm raged.' (I called this one 'The Cave'; clearly I was a rather literal-minded child.) I hadn't yet heard of Edward Bulwer-Lytton, but I had certainly read the *Peanuts* comic strips in which would-be novelist Snoopy tries to show off his literary skill. In one he is seen typing 'It was a dark and stormy night' on top of his doghouse, and Linus responds, 'Your novel has a very exciting beginning.' (Snoopy looks suitably pleased with himself.) Then Linus hands back the manuscript: 'Good luck with the second sentence.' (Snoopy arches his eyebrows knowingly at the reader.) In another comic strip, Lucy tells Snoopy that 'It was a dark and stormy night' is a terrible opening to a story, and he should instead begin with 'Once upon a time'. (Snoopy thinks for a moment, and then types 'Once upon a time, it was a dark and stormy night.') I don't think I fully got these jokes at the time, but the impulse to write in a way that would satisfy my own readers was perfectly sincere. Even if I was trying to produce spine-melting, nerve-twanging horror stories, whenever anybody opened one I wanted them to feel at home.

Many writers never outgrow this impulse. Martin Amis began his final book, the autobiographical novel *Inside Story* (2020), by telling his readers 'Welcome! Do step on in', before metaphorically taking their coats and offering them a drink. He recognised that on reading the first sentence of any story we cross a threshold, entering a world we may share with the author for several hours or more. There will probably be some house rules to learn, and there will almost certainly be a few domestic quirks we will have to get used to, from the style of the building to how it has been furnished, but if we have an experienced host they will quickly help us to settle in.

Sometimes it takes only a sentence for us to work out how to occupy our temporary new home. Humbert Humbert, the charming but amoral narrator of Vladimir Nabokov's *Lolita* (1955), introduces himself with 'Lolita, light of my life, fire of my loins', and already it is clear that he prefers to create a storybook version of the girl he will later abduct and rape, ignoring her real existence (her name is Dolores, not Lolita) so that he can attach her to a rickety romance plot like a butterfly pinned to a board. Jane Austen's *Northanger Abbey* (1817) offers us 'No one who had ever seen Catherine Morland in her infancy would have supposed her born to be an heroine' – a description that mostly comes from a neutral narrator, but also dips into Catherine's mind to reveal how she sees the world, as an unwritten story just waiting to arrange itself around her.

Although the title of *Northanger Abbey* seems to promise us a Gothic tale full of bleeding nuns and rattling chains, gradually we are shown that its physical setting is in fact a modern family home full of humdrum social problems such as stupidity and greed. And this is another common pattern in fiction, where the novelist performs a piece of narrative misdirection by making us think we are getting one kind of story and then giving us something quite different.

Take the opening paragraphs of George Orwell's *Nineteen Eighty-Four* (1949):

> It was a bright cold day in April, and the clocks were strik-ing thirteen. Winston Smith, his chin nuzzled into his breast in an effort to escape the vile wind, slipped quickly through the glass doors of Victory Mansions, though not quickly

enough to prevent a swirl of gritty dust from entering along with him.

The hallway smelt of boiled cabbage and old rag mats. At one end of it a coloured poster, too large for indoor display, had been tacked to the wall. It depicted simply an enormous face, more than a metre wide: the face of a man of about forty-five, with a heavy black moustache and ruggedly handsome features. Winston made for the stairs. It was no use trying the lift. Even at the best of times it was seldom working, and at present the electric current was cut off during daylight hours. It was part of the economy drive in preparation for Hate Week. The flat was seven flights up, and Winston, who was thirty-nine and had a varicose ulcer above his right ankle, went slowly, resting several times on the way. On each landing, opposite the lift shaft, the poster with the enormous face gazed from the wall. It was one of those pictures which are so contrived that the eyes follow you about when you move. BIG BROTHER IS WATCHING YOU, the caption beneath it ran.

Where *does* a novel like *Nineteen Eighty-Four* begin? If we're reading it as a traditional printed book, there's quite a lot to get through before we reach that famous opening sentence. The cover of my old Penguin edition warns the reader what sort of fictional home they are about to enter, featuring an illustration of a shadowy helmeted figure speaking into a bright red megaphone, with a watchtower and razor wire lurking in the background. Opening this cover, the title page includes 'A NOVEL' printed in small letters underneath 'NINETEEN EIGHTY-FOUR' in large block capitals, reassuring us that even though in the following pages Orwell will be keeping one foot in the world of plain chronological fact, he will be keeping the other in the more elastic world of fiction.

Our memories tend to work in a similar way – every time we try to recall what happened to us in the past, we are part historian and part storyteller – so it's probably not surprising that whenever I open my battered paperback copy it reverberates with more personal echoes too. *Nineteen Eighty-Four* was one of the first 'serious' books I was required to study at school, and I still find it impossible to read these opening paragraphs without overlaying them with memories of my fifteen-year-old self slouching up the concrete steps to a classroom that did indeed smell of boiled cabbage and old mats. Here we waited for our English teacher to step through the door: a man in his late twenties who had a beard as well as a thick moustache, and a booming voice that seemed capable of demolishing buildings at a hundred paces. We were all fascinated by him, but my feelings were a little more complicated than that. I feared and worshipped him in roughly equal proportions. He appeared to know everything about everyone – including me – and whenever I handed in my essays I vaguely understood that I hadn't only been writing them *for* him. I had been writing them *to* him. They were critical love letters to a man I didn't remotely fancy, but whose recognition and approval I craved. He was my very own Big Brother.

Writing about this novel at school was probably the first time I felt the stirring of a new critical appetite, so the clock striking thirteen marked a fresh start for me too. I had also recently discovered that Orwell faced an even more difficult challenge. In personal terms, when he wrote *Nineteen Eighty-Four* he was waiting for an end rather than a beginning. Suffering from the last stages of tuberculosis, he had already spent several months in a private sanatorium in the Cotswold hills, and in September 1949, three months after this novel was published, he moved to a private room at University College Hospital in London. Four months later a blood vessel in his lung ruptured and he rapidly

the idea that *Nineteen Eighty-Four* is also a tale of two cities, with the difference that in this novel the two cities occupy just one place: the London of 1949, when Orwell first published his novel during a grim post-war period of rationing and power cuts, and the London of an imagined future. This is significant, because the novel's opening is littered with details that for British readers just after the Second World War would have sounded strangely familiar, from bad food to propaganda posters and the name of Winston (Churchill rather than Smith), although the unexpected twist Orwell gives to these details might have made his readers question how far they could trust their own understanding of the world around them.

In his essay 'Why I Write', published shortly before he started to work on *Nineteen Eighty-Four*, Orwell argued that writers should try to describe this world without getting too much in the way: 'Good prose is like a window pane.' However, in these opening paragraphs his narrative voice shifts between looking through Winston's eyes ('It was no use trying the lift' hints at the resigned shrug this character has learned to internalise rather than risk open dissent) and seeing life with the all-knowing authority of Big Brother. And as a result we are also left unsure how far we can we rely on what we are being told.

The best example of how *Nineteen Eighty-Four* disorientates us is also the easiest to miss. 'It was a bright cold day' – a far more restrained description than 'It was a dark and stormy night' – is presented as a straightforward statement of fact, just one tiny stitch in the larger fabric of Orwell's narrative. It also establishes a key aspect of his style. The phrase 'It was' appears on more than 500 further occasions in *Nineteen Eighty-Four* – so often, in fact, that it simply disappears before our eyes, being as ordinary and invisible as little connecting words like 'and' or 'but'. Even in the short second paragraph there are four more examples: 'It was no use . . . it was seldom working . . . It was part of . . . It *repetition of phrases e.g. "It was" = mind [unclear]*

was one of those . . . '. Yet as Winston is gradually broken down
by the political forces ranged against him, tortured and brain-
washed until he accepts that '2+2 = 5', the basic meaning of 'It
was' is stretched so far that when we reach the end of the novel
its repetition has become the final piece of evidence that he can
no longer think for himself. 'But it was all right', we are told, 'He
loved Big Brother.' It is like a grammatical acknowledgement
of Winston's recognition that he is doomed from the moment
he chooses to rebel. 'The end is contained in the beginning', he
resignedly thinks to himself.

The way we have been approaching these opening paragraphs of Orwell's novel – isolating individual words, thinking
about their implications and seeing how the writer weaves them
together into larger narrative patterns – can be duplicated with
almost anything else we might read. But such close attention
is especially rewarded by literary beginnings, because these are
the places that help us to organise our thoughts about how we
will try to make sense of the pages to come. A beginning can
be the first piece in a jigsaw puzzle, as is the case with a work of
detective fiction, or a domino we push to start a toppling chain
reaction, as is the case with a romantic comedy, but it's also a
seed. The author plants it and, sometimes visibly and sometimes
out of sight, it starts to grow. And if we want to see how it does
this, often the simplest way is to consider how often certain
words or ideas are repeated.

To take another example, as we read this passage from *Nineteen Eighty-Four* our eyes may alight on a common word that
will later be used in many other contexts. As a result it sets up
shockwaves that reach forwards through the rest of the novel, but
also backwards and sideways as it starts to establish a network
of associations in our minds. Thus, the fact that it is 'a bright
cold day' may sound as neutral as a weather forecast, but 'bright'
will later be returned to when we encounter a woman who turns

'bright pink' with excitement during the Two Minutes Hate, the 'bright red streak' of blood caused by a bomb blowing off somebody's hand, and one of Winston's colleagues telling him how much he enjoys public hangings when he gets to see the victim's tongue sticking out and 'blue – a quite bright blue'.

We may not be consciously aware of these echoes as we read, but they set up subterranean connections in our mind between propaganda and violence like a smouldering fuse that occasionally bursts into life. Such connections also remind us of one of the great satisfactions of reading: an ability to join together isolated fragments of knowledge into a meaningful whole. For if life is where things happen, a book is where they usually happen for a purpose; events succeed one another in a way that replaces a loose 'and then' with a tighter and more controlled 'because'. To open a novel like *Nineteen Eighty-Four* is to enter a world that willingly discloses its hidden patterns.

Drawing more general conclusions from this specific example isn't straightforward, because every work of literature operates in a particular way. Even a poem that is written in the same form as thousands of others is likely to have something that makes it distinct – a sharp turn of phrase here; a crafty rhyme there. This is what makes it something other than a photocopy. But it's also why reading an author like Orwell can feel less like peering down a tunnel at events that were written about a long time ago, and more like a conversation between ourselves and the author, as he tells us what he is thinking and we respond in our heads with approving comments ('beautifully put', 'I completely agree') or criticisms ('I'm not sure that's the most elegant way of expressing it', 'oh come *on*'). And paying him this sort of close attention, down to the level of discovering which words he is most drawn to, can help us to become even better listeners.

This isn't necessarily what we're used to. Most of the time when we read we are simply trying to make sense of what is presented to us, word by word and sentence by sentence, whereas the sort of close reading we've been attempting in this chapter does something rather different. As well as encouraging us to pay attention to individual words and think about their effectiveness, it reveals how the work as a whole is put together. Reading in this way is a bit like the experience many of us have when going on holiday. We make our way through the airport, inelegantly hopping as we remove our shoes for the security scanner, we drift through the duty-free shop spritzing ourselves with samples of perfume we have no intention of buying, and finally we board our plane and settle into our seat with a relieved sigh. Then, as the plane takes off, we look out of the window and see the world below us being transformed into an orderly collection of tiny buildings and neat lines of tarmac. Suddenly all those ground-level distractions are put into perspective.

So too, when we read a work like *Nineteen Eighty-Four*, we might start by noticing individual words – their sounds, their shapes, their edges of meaning – but eventually we come to see how they fall into certain patterns. And after we notice these, the work no longer seems to be made out of separate lines of words, but instead resembles something more like a giant spider's web. Touch it at any point and the whole structure instantly quivers into life.

Chapter 2

It's the Little Things

WE SAW IN THE LAST chapter that in his essay 'Why I Write' Orwell claimed that good prose should work like a windowpane, but – as we also saw – the closer we get to an author's writing, the more their fingerprints on the glass start to show.

In any piece of writing, certain details are likely to stand out. These can be small moments that reverberate far beyond their immediate context, such as the unexpected clang of 'thirteen' in the opening sentence of *Nineteen Eighty-Four*, but there are a number of other words in the rest of the passage that are more quietly surprising. For example, when we read that the oversized poster of Big Brother tacked to the wall in Winston's hallway 'depicted simply an enormous face, more than a metre wide: the face of a man of about forty-five, with a heavy black moustache and ruggedly handsome features', the word 'simply' sticks out – not only because it isn't grammatically necessary (the sentence would make perfect sense without it), but also because it could be understood in several different ways. It tells us about the crude design of the poster, and it imagines the reactions someone like Winston might have towards it, ranging from awe (it is simply *enormous*) to an impotent shrug (it is, simply, enormous), both of which are attitudes that Big Brother seems keen to cultivate. (Later Winston thinks that 'the truly characteristic thing about modern life was not its cruelty and insecurity, but simply its bareness, its dinginess, its listlessness', and on three separate occasions we are told that anyone who went against the Party 'simply disappeared'.) That is, the more carefully we read Orwell's writing, the more aware we are that 'simply' can, somewhat paradoxically, become a complex word in his hands, touching on important ideas that ripple out into the rest of the novel. Knowing this, when we reread those opening paragraphs we may admire Orwell's skill at recreating the textures of ordinary life – gritty streets, cooking smells, the small indignities of middle age – but as soon as we reach 'simply' the scene quietly rearranges itself in our heads around this one descriptive detail.

Sometimes our attention can be snagged by details that are so tiny we might not even notice them under normal circumstances. Consider a snowflake. We all know that snow changes the appearance of the world, cladding and confusing the outlines of familiar objects so that they look increasingly strange. My own awareness of this fact was thrown into sharp relief the same year I read *Nineteen Eighty-Four*, when I went on a school trip abroad for the first time. It was the opposite of a luxury holiday. We were going to stay in a youth hostel in a French ski resort, where every day we would be provided with a packed lunch consisting of a bread roll, a silver puck of soft cheese and two slices of vividly pink ham, and until we reached our destination everything was depressingly familiar. For more than twelve hours, fifty boys were packed into the wheezing school coach, where we filled the time by boasting about our (completely imaginary) sex lives or staring out of the window in an atmosphere that was thick with deodorant spray and stale farts. It felt a bit like being put in a day-long detention. Then we arrived, and everything changed. Cars and gateposts were reduced to soft-focus outlines, yet the snow gave the illusion of revealing the true essence of everything it was helping to conceal. The sound of our footsteps was deadened, but when we spoke our voices were somehow brighter and clearer.

Using the word 'snow' can produce similar effects in a literary text. Here is the opening stanza of Christina Rossetti's poem 'A Christmas Carol' (1872), better known today as the hymn 'In the Bleak Midwinter':

> In the bleak mid-winter
>   Frosty wind made moan;
> Earth stood hard as iron,
>   Water like a stone;
> Snow had fallen, snow on snow,   *repetition*
>   Snow on snow,   *resembles*
> In the bleak mid-winter   *snow*
>   Long ago.   *falling*

These are lines that have been dulled by familiarity over the years. In a way that's appropriate, because they beautifully capture the steady drift of snowflakes that at first sight are as indistinguishable from each other as repetitions of the word 'snow'. 'Snow had fallen, snow on snow, | Snow on snow': words as figurative snowfall. At the same time, Rossetti's lines remind us that when we are thinking about the words on a page, we need to consider how each word fits into its surroundings. And this in turn asks *relation between* us to engage in a type of literary anthropology, observing how *words – what does it do?* words behave in each other's company rather as an anthropologist might observe the social interaction of different members of a family or gang.

Our reading also involves recognising that words, like people, can behave in ways that express not only their private intentions, but also the forces of habit and convention. The poet and critic

Adrienne Rich explains how this might work in practice when she describes what it feels like to write a poem:

> Words are being set down in a force field. It's as if the words themselves have magnetic charges; they veer together or in polarity; they swerve against each other. Part of the force field, the charge, is the working history of the words themselves, how someone has known them, used them, doubted and relied on them in a life.

For a reader, this is likely to involve recognising two things. The first is that the force field of words in any piece of writing can be compared to the writer's visual field: some things will be focussed on directly and at length, while others will only be caught, as it were, out of the corner of their eye. The second is that most texts – which work rather like textiles, as I suggested in the Prologue – are woven out of a series of vocabularies from different areas of life, so that another of the reader's tasks is to disentangle each colour of thread and trace out their points of contact.

James Joyce provides a remarkable example of this textual weaving in his collection of short stories *Dubliners* (1914). The book was one he intended to be a 'nicely polished looking-glass' in which the ordinary citizens of Dublin could have a 'good look at themselves', and the images he provides of them are hardly flattering. The social issues he addresses include poverty, child-beating, drunkenness, bullying, suicide, sexual exhibitionism and several varieties of exploitation. Many of these narra-tive strands are brought together in 'The Dead', the last story in *Dubliners*, as the illusions of the main character, a vain and insecure teacher named Gabriel Conway, are ruthlessly stripped away. Joyce's title is partly an allusion to a character who never appears: Michael Furey, who died at the age of seventeen when

Gabriel's wife was passionately in love with him, creating a hole in her heart that her husband has been unable to fill. After she is 'overcome by emotion' when talking about her dead lover, Gabriel realises that his marriage to her has been a pitiful sham. Now he has to face up to his future in a country that seems to him little more than an echo chamber of secrets and lies.

Here is the final paragraph:

A few light taps upon the pane made him turn to the window. It had begun to snow again. He watched sleepily the flakes, silver and dark, falling obliquely against the lamplight. The time had come for him to set out on his journey westward. Yes, the newspapers were right: snow was general all over Ireland. It was falling on every part of the dark central plain, on the treeless hills, falling softly upon the Bog of Allen and, farther westward, softly falling into the dark mutinous Shannon waves. It was falling, too, upon every part of the lonely churchyard on the hill where Michael Furey lay buried. It lay thickly drifted on the crooked crosses and headstones, on the spears of the little gate, on the barren thorns. His soul swooned slowly as he heard the snow falling faintly through the universe and faintly falling, like the descent of their last end, upon all the living and the dead.

The first time I read this, encouraged by my English teacher with the booming voice and bristling facial hair, I was confused by the fact that it seemed to work more like a prose poem than a standard piece of narrative. It imagined a journey but didn't itself appear to be going anywhere in particular; instead of moving from one event to another, it kept brooding and backtracking. Of course, I blamed Joyce for not knowing what he was doing, and it took me a while before I realised that my confusion was actually a response to his decision to squash several different styles into one compact paragraph. For example, we might notice how he blends a set of adverbs that are soothingly unfocussed (softly, thickly, slowly, faintly) with a set of adjectives that are flatly matter-of-fact (dark, lonely, crooked, barren), as if his language was engaged in a private struggle between the forces of romance and those of realism. We might also notice that this language seems unsure whether it is more on the side of the living or the dead, as it switches between newly minted turns of phrase ('silver and dark' snowflakes, or 'mutinous' waves) and clichés that are shuffled around to see if they still have anything to say to us ('falling softly . . . softly falling').

However, we might start by noticing something much simpler. Two useful questions we can ask about any moment in a literary work are: why did the writer choose *this* word rather than another word; and why did they put it *here*? The first question can sometimes be answered by blanking out the word in question and seeing what difference it makes if something else is introduced in its place. For example, it's easy to imagine a creative-writing teacher wincing at Joyce's inclusion of so many repetitions of the same ordinary words: 'snow . . . snow . . . falling . . . falling softly . . . softly falling . . . falling . . . snow falling faintly . . . faintly falling'. This seems to go against many of the rules of good writing, which usually assumes that the best way of maintaining a reader's interest is to be as specific as possible, and ideally to come up with a set of words that seem freshly created for each new idea.

So, if Joyce had been in this teacher's class, we can imagine that he might have been encouraged to try out a few alternatives. Instead of this sentence –

It was falling on every part of the dark central plain, on the treeless hills, falling softly upon the Bog of Allen and, farther westward, softly falling into the dark mutinous Shannon waves.

– perhaps he could have come up with something like this:

> It was silently tumbling on every part of the dark central plain, on the treeless hills, peacefully settling upon the Bog of Allen and, farther westward, slipping quietly into the sea.

Or, more elaborately, this:

> It was falling like a squad of tiny parachutists onto every part of the dark central plain, on the treeless hills, swirling and twirling onto the Bog of Allen and, farther westward, seeking the final embrace of the pitch-black Shannon waves.

Joyce's actual word choices seem far more predictable, as if his prose has finally been taken over by the paralysis that several other stories in *Dubliners* identify as a central problem in Irish life. And that is precisely his point. The layering of a substance that gradually smothers and muffles life echoes what Joyce saw as the deadening effects of social and religious conventions on the lives of Ireland's citizens, and his own words – written in what he described as 'a style of scrupulous meanness' – mimic this process as they slowly pile up on the page.
• Once we start to recognise this, noticing the frequency with which Joyce returns to something as ordinary as the word 'falling' can encourage our ears to detect another sort of frequency. It is like turning the dial on an old-fashioned short-wave radio until its hiss and static fades out, and we start to hear the acoustics of his unique voice on the page. On rereading *Dubliners* we hear a variation on it as early as the first story, 'The Sisters', where the narrator visits a dead priest and remembers the 'constant showers of snuff which gave his ancient priestly garments their green faded look', despite the man's attempts 'to brush away the fallen grains' with a red handkerchief. Later we hear it again in

the story 'Grace', where an argument about 'the infallibility of the Pope' is accompanied by 'The light music of whisky falling into glasses', and the chime of 'infallibility . . . falling' sets claims of spiritual perfection against the kind of spirit that might get you agreeably drunk. By the time we reach the climax of 'The Dead', the sinking cadences of Joyce's final sentence, as it moves from swooning, to falling, to a descent, to the dead, have begun to tug on the reader's voice with all the hidden force of gravity.

Just as we can rework Joyce's prose to see how it is put together, so we can imagine how another kind of writer might have tackled its ideas. A newspaper columnist could make many of the same arguments about the danger of society falling into bad habits; someone giving a political speech could urge their audience not merely to accept the status quo. The difference in Joyce's case is that he doesn't ever mount his soapbox and announce what he thinks. Instead, he encourages us to alight on these ideas ourselves, by using the details of his writing to give us everything we need to place ourselves alongside his characters and experience what it *feels* like to live like them, with all their dreams and memories and tragicomic struggles to get through each ordinary day. In his writing, as in the lives of his Dubliners, it's the little things that count.

This is usually referred to as *showing* rather than *telling*, a distinction that can be traced back to the Russian writer Anton Chekhov explaining in a letter to his brother that when writing a natural description 'one must seize on small details', and then assemble them in such a way that if the reader closes their eyes they will get the whole picture without any extra guidance. 'For instance, you'll have a moonlit night if you write that on the mill dam a piece of glass from a broken bottle glittered like a bright little star, and that the black shadow of a dog or a wolf rolled past like a ball.' Few later writers are as good as Joyce at *showing* what he means, as we have seen with his passage about falling snowflakes in 'The Dead'. This does more than round off *Dubliners* with a burst of beautiful, lyrical prose. It provides us with a final warning about how some people see the world, as they use the same old words to blot out the realities of life rather than using language to make these realities sharper and clearer, and in doing so it shows us how to approach the same task very differently ourselves.

Chapter 3

One Moment

ISOLATED EVENTS CAN SEEM especially important if we later come to think of them as turning points or crossroads in our lives. My own mobile phone is full of ordinary moments that have been snatched out of time: birthday parties and book launches; smiling groups of friends; one of my cats unwittingly doing something hilarious. They are life's flotsam, fragments of experience that have survived time's ceaseless wreck. But I also hang on to a few photos that are far more significant to me. One captures a weekend in Paris with someone who was then a fairly new boyfriend. We are wet through after being caught in a thunderstorm, and we are both stupidly grinning at the camera, full of cheap wine and recently discovered love. Another shows a plastic bag full of strawberry-pink goo that is about to be dripped into a vein in my arm, capturing the final stage of a stem cell transplant I underwent a few years ago in the hope that it would prevent my multiple sclerosis from getting any worse. When I look at these photos now, both are far more than just slivers of my past. They create little whirlpools of memory that exert a gravitational pull on everything else that was going on around them at the time they were taken.

Some writers have tried to produce similar effects on the

page. Many of the stories in *Dubliners* revolve around what Joyce described as 'epiphanies': moments of clarity or unexpected insight that can suddenly emerge from that slow drift of ordinary experience. Similar to Gabriel's realisation in 'The Dead' that his marriage has been a colossal mistake, these epiphanies often involve feelings of loss or regret. In 'Araby' a young boy goes to the fair to buy a present for the girl he is infatuated with, and when faced by the banal reality of the stalls there he understands how vain and stupid he has been; in 'Eveline' a young woman longs to escape her abusive father and leave Dublin with the man who loves her, but eventually has to accept that she is not strong enough to sever her ties with the past.

Joyce's contemporary Virginia Woolf was similarly drawn to what she called 'moments of being': a phrase that captured how we usually experience life, as a series of fleeting instants, but also how some events can turn out to be of lasting significance – momentous as well as momentary. And writers have a number of resources to help us understand this process. As we saw with *Nineteen Eighty-Four*, although published narratives appear to be printed evenly across the page, they can use their own linguistic patterns to dramatise how some moments are charged with far more significance than others. The same effect is central to the workings of a popular whodunnit like Agatha Christie's *Murder on the Orient Express* (1934), where the reader is encouraged to examine a murder from many different angles until it can be reconstructed in crisp three-dimensional detail in their head.

Poems can be even better at revealing how we hold on to certain memories, by singling out individual moments in a structure that clings and coheres around them. Here is a famous poem that William Wordsworth first published in 1807 as one of several he grouped together as 'Moods Of My Own Mind':

I wandered lonely as a Cloud
That floats on high o'er Vales and Hills,
When all at once I saw a crowd
A host of dancing Daffodils;
Along the Lake, beneath the trees,
Ten thousand dancing in the breeze.

The waves beside them danced, but they
Outdid the sparkling waves in glee:—
A Poet could not but be gay
In such a laughing company:
I gaz'd – and gaz'd – but little thought
What wealth the shew to me had brought:

For oft when on my couch I lie
In vacant or in pensive mood,
They flash upon that inward eye
Which is the bliss of solitude,
And then my heart with pleasure fills,
And dances with the Daffodils.

Wordsworth later added an extra verse and fiddled with some of his original phrasing, and over time the poem gradually inserted its hooks into the memories of its readers. In Britain it often features in lists of 'The Nation's Favourite Poems' – in a 1995 poll conducted by the BBC it came fifth, just after Stevie Smith's 'Not Waving but Drowning' – and it remains a popular choice in other literary anthologies, which is especially appropriate given that 'anthology' literally means 'a collection of flowers' (from the Greek *anthos*, 'flower'). Perhaps that's why it has also become so stale for many readers: a poem that our eyes tend to graze over without pausing. The fictional schoolboy Nigel Molesworth probably speaks for many when he scoffs at poetry as the sort of writing where 'Weedy people say la and fie and swoon when they see a bunch of daffodils.' Actually, Wordsworth's poem is far more interesting than that – and far stranger.

Just as we saw in the last chapter that often we can work out why a writer chose a particular word by trying a few alternatives ourselves, so we can discover more about their style by imagining what another writer might have done with the same raw materials of experience. In this case that's a straightforward task, because although Wordsworth may have wanted his readers to think that he spent his time wandering around the Lake District 'lonely as a cloud', on this occasion – 15 April 1802 – his sister Dorothy had accompanied him. This wasn't unusual; their contemporary Thomas De Quincey noted that from childhood onwards the pair were 'constantly together; for Miss Wordsworth was always ready to walk out – wet or dry, storm or sunshine, night or day', and on this occasion they had stumbled across the daffodils while walking home from a nearby village where Dorothy had been visiting some friends. That night they stayed in an inn, where they drank glasses of warm rum and water, and Dorothy wrote in her journal about what they had both seen earlier:

> It was a threatening, misty morning, but mild. We set off after dinner from Eusemere. Mrs Clarkson went a short way with us, but turned back. The wind was furious, and we thought we must have returned. We first rested in the large boathouse, then under a furze bush opposite Mr Clarkson's. Saw the plough going in the field. The wind seized our breath. The lake was rough . . . We got over into a field to avoid some cows – people working. A few primroses by the roadside – woodsorrel flower, the anemone, scentless violets, strawberries, and that starry, yellow flower which Mrs C. calls pile wort. When we were in the woods beyond Gowbarrow Park we saw a few daffodils close to the water-side. We fancied that the sea had floated the

seeds ashore, and that the little colony had so sprung up. But as we went along there were more and yet more; and at last, under the boughs of the trees, we saw that there was a long belt of them along the shore, about the breadth of a country turnpike road. I never saw daffodils so beautiful. They grew among the mossy stones about and above them; some rested their heads upon these stones, as on a pillow, for weariness; and the rest tossed and reeled and danced, and seemed as if they verily laughed with the wind, that blew upon them over the lake; they looked so gay, ever glancing, ever changing.

This is a more detailed piece of nature writing than her brother's poem, although as we might expect from a diary entry that uses 'I' far more sparingly than 'we', there are several overlaps between their accounts. Both try to make themselves feel at home by imagining flowers that dance and laugh like cast members in a crowd scene; both celebrate the world's natural patterns by finding hidden connections between their own words, whether that's in the poem's rhymes or in the journal's more concealed echoes: 'rested . . . and the rest . . . danced . . . glancing'. (Such overlaps may not be entirely coincidental: during this spring, Wordsworth wrote of his sister that 'She gave me eyes, she gave me ears', and when he came to write the poem that would later be known as 'Daffodils' it's possible that he used her journal to refresh his own powers of recall.) But then the poem goes a stage further, by showing how some moments can be stored up in our minds and later returned to when we need a particularly rich memory to nourish us in the leaner times to come – a psychological phenomenon that in his long autobiographical work *The Prelude* (1850) Wordsworth described as the creation of 'spots of time'.

When it was originally published, 'Daffodils' was part of Wordsworth's much larger project to encourage us to think differently about homely or neglected bits of the world, by inviting us to see what they looked like after they had been filtered through his imagination. That's why in this poem he shifts to the present tense of 'dancing Daffodils' and, in the final line, 'dances with the Daffodils', as a way of showing how something that happened in the past is still happening inside his head. Wordsworth's punctuation echoes this sense of time passing, with the colon he places at the end of the second stanza working like a little doorway from the past back into the present, as he lies on his couch at home and once again conjures up the sight of daffodils bobbing and swaying.

But his most effective strategy for revealing how human memory works is to use some words that are quickly set aside ('wandered'), and combine them with other words that are lingered over ('gazed – and gazed') or repeated with only small variations ('dancing . . . danced . . . dances'). That's one reason why Wordsworth's vocabulary seems so much more restricted than his sister's: whereas she recalls how some daffodils 'rested' while others 'tossed and reeled and danced', he recalls them 'dancing' and again 'dancing' – not because he has failed to consult a thesaurus, but because since it happened this event has become part of a mind that itself dances whenever he summons the memory of it. If we think of it as a 'key' moment, that is because it unlocks a door in his mind through which the past can flood in unchecked.

We all recognise something similar in our own lives. Ask someone what they did today and you are likely to be given a first-this-then-that catalogue of events and impressions: 'I woke up at 6 a.m. and had a shower, then I got dressed and went downstairs, fed the dog, ate some cereal, scrolled through a pile of messages on my phone, and replied to one from my girlfriend telling me to phone her for a chat about something.' Ask them what happened last week, and they are likely to filter most of these things out and arrange the rest into a cleaner line of narrative: 'It was an ordinary morning until I phoned my girlfriend and learned that she had been having an affair with my best friend.' Later still they might realise that one particular event was crucial, and their memories will be pulled into a pattern around it like iron filings around a magnet: 'A single phone call changed my life forever.'

For many of us certain photographs fall into this category. It is why the photo of me and my nearly new boyfriend in Paris is one he keeps in a silver frame in our living room, rather than any of the hundreds of other images he could have chosen. It isn't a particularly good photograph: technically it is amateurish, and if we both look a bit shiny-faced and blurry-eyed, that can probably be put down to the second bottle of wine rather than the fact that we were in the city of love. But like the more recent image of my frozen stem cells being dripped back into my body, it is a narrative snapshot that has come to represent a whole hidden back story.

If literary works can describe this process – the way that we grasp some moments and let others go – they can also show us how it works. A poem like 'Daffodils' seems very simple at first, and it certainly presents few challenges to most readers hoping to discover *what* it means. But as we have seen, *how* it creates that meaning, and *why* it matters, is slightly more complicated. Unlike Dorothy Wordsworth's journal entry, her brother's poem has all the resources of verse to draw upon – quietly pulsing rhythms, neatly aligned rhymes and so on – and these do more than just create attractive mosaics of language. They reveal how the poet's memory has started to arrange his thoughts around a single event. And when we read Wordsworth's poem, we do something similar. We put ourselves in his shoes as he sees the daffodils for the first time, and then we come to realise that he is showing us how our minds can reshape certain experiences into stories that we too will hold on to in the years to come. Or, as he puts it in *The Prelude*, 'what we have loved | Others will love, and we will teach them how'.

Chapter 4

What do you Mean?

SOMETIMES LIFE'S KEY MOMENTS are far harder to pin down, either in our minds or in words. There's a suggestion of this in Wordsworth's poem when he first comes across the daffodils and describes them as 'a crowd | A host'. If 'crowd' implicitly compares the flowers to a group of ordinary people, 'host' suggests a divine presence hovering somewhere in the background (angels as the heavenly host), and perhaps also adds a hint of hospitality, as if the sight of all these laughing daffodils had made Wordsworth feel somehow more at home in the world. Spread across two lines, the change from 'crowd' to 'host' is the poetic equivalent of a double take, as Wordsworth captures the experience of stumbling upon a beautiful field of flowers and then reaches for the right word to describe it.

The ambiguity of 'host' shows how a similar double take can be built into individual words, and if we examine Wordsworth's poem closely we see that he does this elsewhere too. For example, the fact that the daffodils are dancing in 'glee' is largely because they appear so joyful, but there may also be hints of wealth, bright colour and beauty in their appearance, all of which are included in the dictionary as older senses of the word.

In real social interactions, usually we try to avoid ambiguity if there's a danger of leaving people unsure about our intentions. There was a notorious example of this in the 1952 murder trial that revolved around the words allegedly used by Derek Bentley – an illiterate nineteen-year-old with an IQ of 77 – in a bungled burglary attempt. 'Let him have it, Chris,' he was reported to have said shortly before his accomplice, sixteen-year-old Christopher Craig, shot a policeman dead. The prosecution's case was that he meant 'Shoot him, Chris.' The defence's case was that, even if he did use these words, he meant 'Give him the gun, Chris.' The jury sided with the prosecution, Bentley was found guilty of murder under the legal principle of joint enterprise and after he was refused clemency by the Home Secretary he was hanged.

On the other hand, ambiguity can be useful when we don't feel that we can commit to an idea, or want to leave people unsure about our true opinions. There are many stories about theatregoers attending the first night of a terrible new production put on by their friends, and afterwards trying to find a way of sounding positive without technically lying. 'I'm speechless,' they might tell the cast, or 'Good isn't the word.' (I've sometimes been guilty of this myself when giving feedback to my students on their essays. 'You've done it again' and 'You never fail to surprise me' have both proven to be helpfully open to interpretation.) Writers can be equally slippery when offering a pat on the back that upon closer inspection proves to be a slap in the face, as when T. S. Eliot once sent a letter of thanks to someone who had complimented him on his work. 'I don't think you could have done it better', he wrote levelly. Was this a generous burst of praise? (I don't think you could have done it *better*.) Or was it a lightly disguised insult? (I don't think *you* could have done it better.) We simply cannot be sure. It is like a secret his writing continues to keep.

Verbal uncertainty is also important to certain kinds of comedy, as when somebody makes a pun that allows them to say one thing and something else at the same time. The dirty postcards that were for decades sold in British seaside resorts provide dozens of examples, allowing readers to entertain naughty thoughts while using the ambiguity of what was printed as a form of moral alibi. In one postcard, an anonymous speech bubble floats up from behind a bush ('I beg you Florence – don't break it off!') while a scandalised matron in the foreground blushes and clutches at her handbag. In another, an astonished couple listen as a bikini-clad woman tries to put up a windbreak on the beach: 'It's too soft Fred – it won't stay in – shall I hit it with the mallet?' Many of these postcards play on the referential vagueness of 'it', which depending on the context can point in as many different directions as a weathervane spinning in a gale. Such examples do more than encourage readers to snigger at someone else's misunderstanding of a perfectly innocent remark. They reveal how thin is the membrane between areas of life we usually try to keep distinct.

Yet ambiguity can serve more serious ends. The critic William Empson's brilliantly quirky *Seven Types of Ambiguity* (1930) was the first book-length attempt to outline some of the psychological and social functions of ambiguity in writing. He points out that it can be a way of negotiating between the demands of different types of reader, as well as acknowledging the mixed feelings that an individual may have. It can keep ideas in a state of balance, inviting us to weigh up alternatives without having to choose between them, or it can hold them in suspense, as flexing the ambiguity in one word twitches the dormant sense of an earlier or later word into life.

Sometimes this process turns out to be more than a linguistic game. In the previous chapter I slid over a couple of lines in Wordsworth's poem without comment: 'A Poet could not be but gay | In such a laughing company.' At the time he was writing, and for a long time afterwards, 'gay' meant merely cheerful and carefree, but it's much harder to read the lines today without the question of sexual identity raising its head. Perhaps children are far more generous now than they were at my school when we stumbled across this line in a sixth-form lesson, at which point most of the boys started sniggering and an ex-girlfriend looked pointedly in my direction. Clearly that meaning wasn't Wordsworth's intention, although it's an inevitable result of the living nature of any language, as old words go off on new adventures and acquire additional layers of significance. But something similar can happen to words that circulate within a single period, as different social groups use them to carve out distinct identities for themselves, which is why 'sick' might mean something very different to a teenager (for whom it will probably be associated with what is fun or outrageous) and their grandparents (for whom it is more likely to involve staying in bed with a packet of paracetamol). Similarly, ambiguity can allow the members of a social group to identify themselves to each other without announcing their presence to anyone else who happens to be listening.

Historically, this has been an important way in which someone looking for a same-sex encounter could approach a stranger without leaving themselves open to rejection or physical assault. Even Christopher Isherwood, whose early fiction celebrated the permissive atmosphere of 1930s Berlin, later declaring that 'To Christopher, Berlin meant Boys' (Isherwood often wrote about his younger self as if he were someone else), was aware that away from the dozens of gay clubs and bars operating in the city a degree of caution was necessary. In his novel *Mr Norris Changes Trains* (1935), the narrator finds himself being delicately sounded out by the 'fishy and suave' Baron von Pregnitz in conversations that looked at from one angle are full of coded references to a shared gay subculture, ranging from favourite holiday destinations to possible pick-up spots, and from another are just innocent chit-chat between two people trying to pass the time:

'Excuse me. Do you know Naples?'
'No. I've never been there.'
'Forgive me. I'm sorry. I had a feeling that we'd met each
  other before.'

'Excuse me, you were in London?'
'Part of the time, yes.'
. . . 'And, excuse me, how are the Horse Guards?'
'Still sitting there.'
'Yes? I'm glad to hear this, you see. Very glad . . . '

Different versions of this game continue to be played today. A few months after the awkward 'A Poet could not be but gay' lesson at school, I was on a family holiday in Spain where I tried to pick someone up by telling him he looked like David Bowie. (He didn't.) 'Cheers,' he said with a puzzled frown, and moved his sun lounger a few feet further away. Something similar can be found whenever freedom of expression is restricted by legal censorship or fear of persecution, as the author presents an idea that one reader might understand in one way, and another reader might understand very differently. In this context, ambiguity can be a way of smuggling in ideas that cannot be said out loud. Not here, not yet.

Few writers were as good at this game of literary peekaboo as the poet A. E. Housman, who spent decades working in Cambridge as a classical scholar for whom the most interesting long-term relationships were with the dead rather than the living. 'Nothing very remarkable has happened', concludes one of his early letters, and the curdled regret and relief in that phrase continued to echo throughout his later life, where he appears to have taken some care to ensure that nothing very remarkable ever happened. Occasionally, details surface that suggest a rip tide of hidden passions – a list of male prostitutes in Paris or information about a gondolier in Venice – but these usually turn out to be biographical dead ends. The fact that one of his earliest biographers was named Percy Withers merely adds a comic gloss to the little we know about his private life. He was the laureate of repression.

In this context, perhaps it's appropriate that the most important event of Housman's life was one that didn't quite happen. As a student at Oxford, he met a hearty athlete named Moses Jackson, and if Housman's later poetry gives us any clues ('I shook his hand, and tore my heart in sunder, | And went with half my life about my ways'), at some point he told his friend that he wanted to be more than just friends. He was unsuccessful. And for Housman, it seems, first love was the only kind that really mattered. His lopsided romantic friendship with the man he called 'Mo' (so near and yet so far from *amo*, the Latin word for 'I love') drifted on but got him nowhere, producing awkwardly bantering letters in which he occasionally peeped out from behind his usual mask of irony to confess that although he was now a successful academic, 'I would much rather have followed you round the world and blacked your boots.' If this is painful to read, one can only imagine what it must have been like to write.

However, what destroyed his chance of personal happiness turned out to be the making of him as a poet. News that Jackson was to travel to India spurred Housman into a purple period of creativity, and in 1896 he published the results as a slim volume of poems: *A Shropshire Lad*. It was a curious literary hybrid. Seen from one angle, it was a late flowering of Romanticism, full of passionate country folk who were forever coming to grief; seen from another angle, it was as spare and taut as an experimental piece of modernism. The poems were almost wilfully limited in range – 'May, death, lads, Shropshire' was Virginia Woolf's brisk summary – and were crammed with glimpses of things that couldn't quite be put into words.

> The street sounds to the soldiers' tread,
>   And out we troop to see:
> A single redcoat turns his head,
>   He turns and looks at me.
>
> My man, from sky to sky's so far,
>   We never crossed before;
> Such leagues apart the world's ends are,
>   We're like to meet no more;
>
> What thoughts at heart have you and I
>   We cannot stop to tell;
> But dead or living, drunk or dry,
>   Soldier, I wish you well.

In the last chapter we considered how Wordsworth's 'Daffo-dils' might encourage us to think about how we make sense of past events, by remembering key moments and putting them into perspective. Housman's poem does this too, and by using similar literary resources, as he takes the raw mate-rials of history and arranges them into three neat stanzas, a bit like a story that has a beginning, a middle and an end. Also like Wordsworth, Housman treats his stanzas like a set of picture frames that give a sense of order and control to what-ever is being depicted inside them. But then he goes a stage further. Whereas Wordsworth wants to show us how we can keep returning to the same event in our memories, Housman is more concerned with showing us how we can look at it from several different angles. And he does this by exploiting the most obvious difference between poetry and prose, which is that whereas prose writers usually have to delegate to a publisher the task of where each line of print ends, this is something that poets get to choose.

Let me explain what I mean by this. The English word *verse* comes from the Latin *vertere*, meaning 'to turn', indicating how a poem loops and curves as it proceeds down the page, like a plough moving in a straight line before turning when it reaches the edge of a field. You may remember that in Chapter 2 I suggested that the easiest way to work out what a particular word is doing in a particular place (why *this* word and not *that* word; why *here* and not *there*) is to try out a few alternatives. Similarly, if you want to work out what impact a particular form is having on what is being said, one good tactic can be to strip it out and see what difference this makes.

For example, here is the first stanza of Housman's poem rearranged as prose:

The street sounds to the soldiers' tread, and out we troop to see: a single redcoat turns his head, he turns and looks at me.

In this version we are presented with a straightforward set of events: the speaker is one of several people who hear a group of soldiers coming, and when he goes out to see them an individual soldier glances in his direction.

Without changing any of the words, adding a line break after 'see' and another after 'turns his head' changes this situation in several ways, adding a sense of uncertainty and an extra element of drama to the scene:

The street sounds to the soldiers' tread,
And out we troop to see:

A single redcoat turns his head,
He turns and looks at me.

[handwritten annotation: · what does the line break do? what does the last word and/or punctuation do]

Now, when we read 'see', our eyes dart from right to left and settle on 'A single redcoat' as if we were singling him out in a crowd; then we read 'turns his head', and again the turn of the line mimics the action being described, before we are given a more detailed, perhaps more charged version of the same event: 'He turns and looks at me.'

We might summarise these changes by saying that the prose version describes what happens, and the poetic version shows someone trying to make sense of it. Yet while Housman's pronouns stage a teasing, elusive drama, as 'he' and 'me' revolve enquiringly around each other, the look itself is expressively blank. Is it just a neutral acknowledgement of the speaker's presence, or is it the first move from a 'single' man who understands the choreography of cruising? (The idea that an attractive person could 'turn heads' had been available in the English language for a number of years when Housman wrote his poem.) Alternatively, is it a more hostile response to someone who is willing to 'troop' outside to watch a group of soldiers marching past but not to enlist? Like other moments in the poem, such as the reference to the soldier as 'My man', this turn of the head invites us to construct loving narratives and then smiles at us for getting ahead of ourselves. And that is because it resists any attempt to determine precisely what it means. In common with many examples of printed ambiguity, it offers itself as a question that has more than one answer. However the encounter might have resolved itself in real life, on the page it can remain full of different possible outcomes. Here the two men will forever be looking at each other, and if the speaker will never be accepted he will also never be rejected. It is like a latent flirtation that has been frozen in time.

The ambiguity of Housman's poem is hardly unusual. In some ways it reflects how often we find ourselves trying to think two different – and potentially irreconcilable – thoughts at the same time. William Empson suggested in a note to one of his own poems that 'Life involves maintaining oneself between contradictions that can't be solved by analysis', and it isn't difficult to think of examples that support his claim. Nineteenth-century American citizens saw it in the case of politicians who passionately defended the Declaration of Independence but decided that the part about all men being created equal and having the unalienable right to 'Life, Liberty and the pursuit of Happiness' didn't apply to slaves; we see it today in the case of men who proudly claim to be feminists but also think that their contribution to the household chores should be limited to taking the bins out. A similar kind of mental division can occur when we think about many other events, although usually we have to make a decision. You are at a party and catch someone's eye. Should you tell him he looks like David Bowie? What if he says 'Cheers' and moves a few feet further away? A whole series of sliding doors opens and shuts in our heads in a fraction of a second, and in the end we have to choose which path to go down. (Even doing nothing is a choice that may have consequences.) The clock can't be turned back. Not so when reading a poem, where we can follow one line of interpretation, then double back and start again, and repeat the same literary manoeuvre any number of times.

'What is this life', asks William Henry Davies in his popular poem 'Leisure', 'if, full of care, | We have no time to stand and stare'. What makes a poet like Housman so fascinating is that in a lyric like the one we have been looking at in this chapter he doesn't only describe someone standing and staring; he encourages a similar response from his readers. We discover a soldier locking eyes with someone and, for as long as we want them to, their encounter holds our gaze as well.

How to Look . . . and Listen

Chapter 5

PICTURES

SOME BOOKS ASK US 'to stand and stare' by using more than words alone. They build these invitations into their own physical appearance through the inclusion of illustrations, which freeze the action at a certain point in the narrative. This makes them particularly attractive to readers who like seeing stories come to life in a different form, rather as they might enjoy seeing a TV or film adaptation of the same work. However, the choice of illustration can also leave those involved open to criticism – and even ridicule.

For example, when A. E. Housman was sent a batch of pen and ink drawings by the artist Lovat Claud Fraser in 1920 for a proposed new edition of *A Shropshire Lad*, his reactions ranged from grudging approval ('Good', 'Good enough') to outright scorn. His note for poem XVII, which Fraser had illustrated with a man wearing a top hat and holding a cricket bat tucked under his arm, read 'Lunatic at large', while the image suggested for poem XXXVII led to Housman grumbling about a farm-worker's 'enormous boots'. Some of Housman's prickliness was the result of a simple dislike of Fraser's antiquated visual style, arguing in one letter that 'To transpose into the 18th century a book which begins with Queen Victoria's jubilee is the act of a rhinoceros. I should look like a fool if I allowed the book to appear with these decorations.' But it appears an even more fundamental reason was that in many cases Fraser hadn't captured what was in Housman's own mind as he wrote.

Housman was particularly scathing about Fraser's response to his lines describing the redcoat turning and looking at the speaker (it is poem XXII in the sequence), which Fraser had tried to capture in an image that appeared close to a comic double take. The fact that Fraser's illustration allowed this look to be held forever meant that it could be scrutinised far more closely than any counterpart in real life, and according to Housman, 'The soldier was not so much astonished and horrified as all that.'

Although Housman was disappointed that *A Shropshire Lad* hadn't been depicted exactly as he had imagined, he probably shouldn't have been surprised. One of the crucial differences between books and other art forms, such as painting or theatre, is that whenever we read a description of somewhere like Housman's Shropshire we do not just enter a world that someone else has already constructed. We use the clues provided by the author to create this world for ourselves. The same is true of fictional characters, which is one of the reasons why trying to find an actor to play a role like James Bond on screen is so difficult. Everyone who reads the descriptions of Bond's slim build, 'cruel' mouth, 'blue-grey' eyes, and 'comma' of dark hair falling across his forehead in Ian Fleming's novels is likely to conjure up a slightly different set of images, creating a hero in their mind's eye who is as unique as a set of fingerprints.

This creative element in reading is especially important when we are just starting to encounter printed stories. My memory of the Beatrix Potter books I read as a child is that when I arrived at one of the original illustrations it was like stumbling across a clearing in the tangled thicket of words, a place where suddenly everything made sense. But I much preferred the pictures I made up for myself, whether I was wondering if the 'fir-tree' where

Peter Rabbit and his family lived might be made from real fur, or creating a whole wardrobe of different styles for Peter's blue jacket with the brass buttons.

For older readers, too, illustrations that sit alongside the author's words can play an important role. Sometimes they work like a set of visual footnotes to the main text, showing us one way we might choose to interpret it, and sometimes they freeze the action at a particularly tense moment, as if the story was visibly holding its breath. And because they are wordless, they can draw our attention to what else is present but silent in the text, such as ideas that the author may be fascinated by but is unwilling to express out loud.

Take Lewis Carroll's *Alice's Adventures in Wonderland*. Since the book's original publication in 1865 it has reached into almost every area of culture, largely thanks to the familiarity of characters like the Hatter (incidentally, he is never referred to by Carroll as the Mad Hatter) and narrative set pieces like the tea party where nobody ever gets any tea. Moreover, Wonderland is an imaginary universe that is still expanding. Alice's adventures have been reproduced in dozens of films, in translations ranging from Afrikaans to Zulu, in the form of a Disneyland ride featuring brightly coloured spinning teacups, and as a giant bronze statue in New York's Central Park. We don't even have to leave home to be reminded of Alice falling down a rabbit hole into a world that is both alluring and alarming, because these days it's possible to do something similar whenever we glance at the screens on our mobile phones: for many of us, Wonderland has become www.onderland.

Yet despite the rich cultural afterlife of Carroll's story, many younger readers still first enter its strange underground world via John Tenniel's original illustrations, like the one that shows Alice pulling back a curtain to reveal a mysterious door that opens onto Wonderland. Some of these illustrations have become almost as famous as the scenes they were drawn to accompany, including Alice picking up a bottle labelled 'DRINK ME', and later getting so squashed by the frame of Tenniel's picture when she is in the White Rabbit's house that she appears on the verge of outgrowing her own story.

Tenniel's illustrations draw our attention to an unavoidable tension in any literary work that includes more than words alone: one between image and text. And that's because an illustration slices out a moment in narrative time and fixes it on the page, which means that it is always going to be somewhat at odds with the way a narrative gradually unspools in the reader's head. When Alice explores Looking-Glass Land in the sequel Carroll wrote a few years later, she exclaims, 'Things flow about so here!' Mostly she is alluding to the way that objects in this dream-world never appear to stay still for long: knitting needles turn into oars in her hands; rushes live up to their name by melting away as rapidly as snow. But she is also reminding us that this is what happens when we read any story, as we enter a world where one thing happens after another, and we bring this world flickeringly to life in our minds as our eyes move from one word to the next.

This is especially noticeable in a book like *Alice's Adventures in Wonderland*, where characters are forever changing their minds, their bodies and even a sense of their own identity. At the heart of this slipperiness is Alice herself. When the Caterpillar asks her 'Who are *you*?' she doesn't seem quite sure. 'I – I hardly know, sir, just at present,' she replies, 'at least I know who I was when I got up this morning, but I think I must have been changed several times since then.' Her confusion is understandable, because over the course of her adventures she's variously mistaken for a housemaid, a serpent, a flower, a volcano and a monster; she grows as tall as a tree, and shrinks as small as a mouse. She reminds us that one person has the potential to be many different things – especially in Wonderland, a place she has conjured up in her sleep that is full of unpredictable lurches in situation and tone from one episode to the next.

Tenniel tried to gesture towards these changes in his illustrations. For example, he depicted the Cheshire Cat perched in a tree on one page, and in an identical pose but with its body fading away on the next, so that simply by turning the page a reader could create an effect like a modern film dissolve. Now you see it, now you don't. But more often he chose to freeze the action at a moment of transformation, such as the episode when Alice rescues a baby from the violent clutches of the Duchess and her saucepan-hurling cook, and then holds on to it as it gradually turns into a pig:

> Alice caught the baby with some difficulty, as it was a queer-shaped little creature, and held out its arms and legs in all directions, 'just like a star-fish,' thought Alice. The poor little thing was snorting like a steam-engine when she caught it, and kept doubling itself up and straightening itself out again, so that altogether, for the first minute or two, it was as much as she could do to hold it.
>
> As soon as she had made out the proper way of nursing it, (which was to twist it up into a sort of knot, and then keep tight hold of its right ear and left foot, so as to prevent its undoing itself,) she carried it out into the open air. 'If I don't take this child away with me,' thought Alice, 'they're sure to kill it in a day or two: wouldn't it be murder to leave it behind?' She said the last words out loud, and the little thing grunted in reply (it had left off sneezing by this time). 'Don't grunt,' said Alice; 'that's not at all a proper way of expressing yourself.'
>
> The baby grunted again, and Alice looked very anxiously into its face to see what was the matter with it. There could be no doubt that it had a *very* turn-up nose, much more like

a snout than a real nose; also its eyes were getting extremely small for a baby: altogether Alice did not like the look of the thing at all. 'But perhaps it was only sobbing,' she thought, and looked into its eyes again, to see if there were any tears.

No, there were no tears. 'If you're going to turn into a pig, my dear,' said Alice, seriously, 'I'll have nothing more to do with you. Mind now!' The poor little thing sobbed again (or grunted, it was impossible to say which), and they went on for some while in silence.

Alice was just beginning to think to herself, 'Now, what am I to do with this creature when I get it home?' when it grunted again, so violently, that she looked down into its face in some alarm. This time there could be *no* mistake about it: it was neither more nor less than a pig, and she felt that it would be quite absurd for her to carry it further.

So she set the little creature down, and felt quite relieved to see it trot away quietly into the wood.

We expect babies to grow up, with all the slow physical alterations this process involves. What we don't expect is that they will become creatures from a different species, as if Carroll had decided to use his pen like a wand that could magically transform one thing into another. But here the baby isn't the only thing that is changing: Carroll's words also keep sliding around in their meaning. Even the simple word 'it' – which in Chapter 4 we saw being used for much smuttier reasons – at some point stops referring to the baby and starts referring to the pig, but without giving us enough information to know exactly when this tipping point has been reached.

As we saw in the earlier discussion of *Nineteen Eighty-Four*, usually repetition provides us with a backbone of continuity in a narrative, reassuring us that the same word remains the best fit for whatever is being described from one moment to the next. By contrast, here repeated words reveal what has changed: 'little creature . . . little creature' is an endearment that shows its latent potential to reveal something rather different; the baby's 'turn-up nose' gives us a clue about its physical transformation that will later be confirmed when the same word returns in the phrase 'turn into a pig'. Meanwhile, comparisons with starfish, steam engines and knots remind us that one creature becoming another is only a literal version of what we do in language whenever we affectionately refer to a baby as a pumpkin or a little dumpling: we transform it through metaphor.

In Tenniel's accompanying illustration, Alice is instantly recognisable as the pert little girl with a crisp white pinafore and long blonde hair, just as Sherlock Holmes can be identified by his deerstalker and cape thanks to Sidney Paget's influential illustrations for Conan Doyle's stories when they were originally published in the *Strand Magazine* in the 1890s. This sense of familiarity is encouraged by Carroll's narrative voice, which frequently places us inside Alice's head and asks us to see things through her eyes. For example, when she checks on the baby-pig to see if it is crying, the narrator's comment 'No, there were no tears' seems to be coloured by Alice's relief, and perhaps also her puzzlement. But none of this alters the fact that when we look at Tenniel's illustration we are primarily seeing someone else's interpretation of the story. Possibly this is why so many later artists have chosen to offer their own Alices as visual rivals to Tenniel's version, a whole family of Alice-alikes that stretches from the rosy-cheeked innocent drawn by Mabel Lucie Attwell in 1911 to the snub-nosed coquettes of modern Japanese manga. The sheer range of such images reminds us that when we read a book we are always illustrating it in our own heads, and even if we are looking at exactly the same raw material for inspiration as millions of other readers, we will never all picture it in exactly the same way.

This can also happen in a more limited fashion if we read a book at one stage of our lives and then return to it months or years later. When we reopen it we may feel that it is the same book and not the same, rather as we too are the same and not the same. That's because a book comes alive only when we pick it up and enter into a relationship with it, and just as our relationships with other people can change over time, so they can with books.

This uncanny feeling that the object we are now holding is both familiar and strange can be true of any book we own. I recognise it whenever I open the copy of *Hamlet* that I bought as a teenager and see the earnest marginal notes I scrawled in it at the time: 'flower imagery', 'incestuous desire', 'soliloquy [*sic*]'. The books we first encounter as children can be even more significant. The novelist Francis Spufford has suggested one of the great pleasures of reading stories in childhood which begin in the real world and then take you somewhere else is that 'once opened, the door would never entirely shut behind you'. For many readers the door into Wonderland works rather like that. Wonderland may exist only in Alice's head, but once we have visited it in her company it exists in our heads too.

My own childhood copy of *Alice's Adventures in Wonderland* is now yellow and blotchy, and a few pages even have wrinkles from the time I accidentally spilled a glass of wine on them, but the most interesting changes are not visible to the naked eye. They are the endlessly moving images of the story's characters and incidents I carry around inside me. That is another reason why book illustrations are worth pausing over whenever we come across them. If they allow us to share what someone else once pictured in their imagination, they also remind us that we are free to conjure up a slightly different set of pictures for ourselves every time we open the book and start to read.

Chapter 6

Eat Me

THE MOMENT IN *Alice's Adventures in Wonderland* when Alice realises that she is no longer holding a baby is also a reminder about what happens when we read any story that can be imagined in so many different ways. We grip its pages, we try to hold on to it as something that is fixed and solid, but ultimately it squirms from our grasp and trots off into the wood. *Alice's Adventures in Wonderland* is elusive in other ways too. Despite being a relatively short book, it seems much longer when anyone tries to explain what it's about. A story that is punctuated by puzzles and brimming with unanswerable questions, it continues to expand in our minds long after we have read the final page.

A few years ago I tried to write a joint biography of Lewis Carroll and Alice Liddell, the real little girl for whom he originally invented the story, and quickly discovered that my attempts to explain Wonderland also kept expanding. Long after I had finished a first draft the book continued to increase in size: the chapters became swollen with extra details; individual sentences generated fussy footnotes and nitpicking subclauses. It felt as if I wasn't only writing *about* Alice in Wonderland; I was writing *like* Alice in Wonderland, particularly the moment near the start

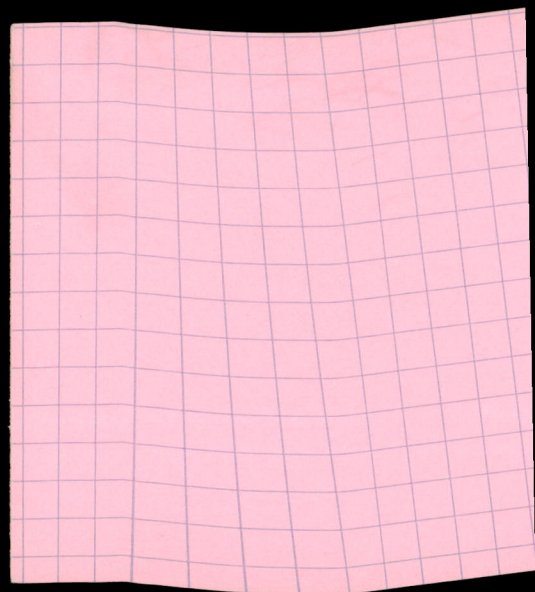

of the story when she nibbles on a cake with 'EAT ME' neatly picked out in currants and discovers that she is 'opening out like the largest telescope that ever was'.

Alice stops growing when her head bumps against the ceiling, and my book only stopped growing when I hit the deadline set by my publishers. I felt guilty sending them such a bulky manuscript to work through, so at the same time I arranged for a giant cupcake to be delivered to their office with 'EAT ME' piped onto it in Barbie-pink icing. It seemed like an innocent-enough gesture at the time: a thank-you note they could enjoy with their morning coffee. Then I came across Patience Agbabi's poem 'Eat Me', published a few years earlier, and started to feel more awkward about what I had done:

> When I hit thirty, he brought me a cake,
> three layers of icing, home-made,
> a candle for each stone in weight.
>
> The icing was white but the letters were pink,
> they said, *EAT ME*. And I ate, did
> what I was told. Didn't even taste it.
>
> Then he asked me to get up and walk
> round the bed so he could watch my broad
> belly wobble, hips judder like a juggernaut.
>
> *The bigger the better*, he'd say, *I like*
> *big girls, soft girls, girls I can burrow inside*
> *with multiple chins, masses of cellulite.*
>
> I was his Jacuzzi. But he was my cook,
> my only pleasure the rush of fast food,
> his pleasure, to watch me swell like forbidden fruit.

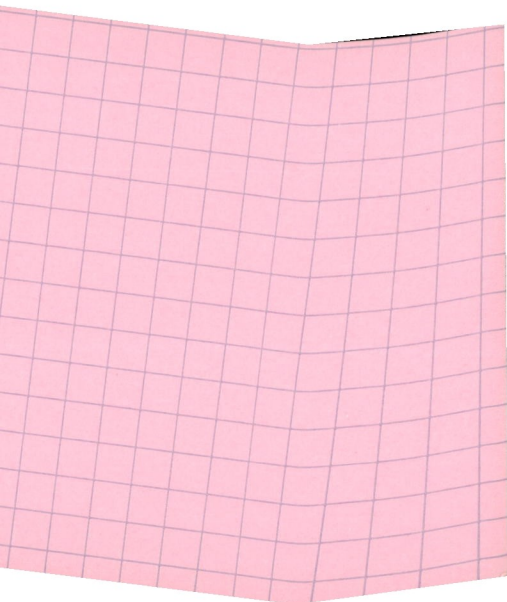

His breadfruit. His desert island after shipwreck.
Or a beached whale on a king-size bed
craving a wave. I was a tidal wave of flesh

too fat to leave, too fat to buy a pint of full-fat milk,
too fat to use fat as an emotional shield,
too fat to be called chubby, cuddly, big-built.

The day I hit thirty-nine, I allowed him to stroke
my globe of a cheek. His flesh, my flesh flowed.
He said, *Open wide*, poured olive oil down my throat.

Soon you'll be forty . . . he whispered, and how
could I not roll over on top. I rolled and he drowned
in my flesh. I drowned his dying sentence out.

I left him there for six hours that felt like a week.
His mouth slightly open, his eyes bulging with greed.
There was nothing else left in the house to eat.

Unlike Alice, the speaker of this poem isn't living in a storybook world, so when she consumes a cake marked 'EAT ME' she doesn't grow any taller. Nor does she appear to grow any older after we realise that the opening lines describe her hitting the milestone of thirty stone rather than thirty years. She just gets heavier, becoming thirty-nine stone in the space of a few stanzas, so that the repetitions of 'fat . . . fat . . . fat . . . fat . . . fat' start to look like the flickering needle on a pair of bathroom scales. And as she continues to eat, so we come to understand that the poem is a twisted variation on the idea that feeding someone is an expression of love, from suckling a baby to making your partner their favourite meal, because here personal choice has been replaced by coercive control.

The speaker's situation is reflected not only in what she says but how she says it. One way of thinking about the shape of any poem is that it reveals how external forces can mould an individual voice, but also how a voice can push back against these forces, creating the sound of a soloist emerging from the chorus. Here, we might notice that traditional couplets have been replaced by off-rhymes ('cake . . . weight', 'walk . . . juggernaut', 'week . . . greed . . . eat') to indicate how ordinary relationships have become kinked and skewed. Similarly, individual words expand ('fat . . . full-fat', 'fruit . . . breadfruit') or overspill their borders ('craving a wave'), while run-on lines suggest physical outlines becoming hazy, edges softening. And underlying everything else, from the first word of the title to the last word of the poem, is repetition. Eat. Eat. Even more obviously than the prose examples we've already looked at, many poems are based on repetition with variation, as we are presented with words falling in and out of a rhythmical pattern or adhering to the verbal snap of rhyme. But here we have a poem that seems to be struggling with a shadowy twin, a non-poem or anti-poem, as if the speaker's situation has started to eat away at her language as well as her sense of self. The more she puts into her mouth, the thinner is what comes out of it – that is, until she crushes her abusive lover to death, at which point her voice playfully sparks back into life. You want rolls of fat? Let me show you what happens when this much fat rolls. You want to feed me? Then I'll tuck into you.

If I'd wanted to send my publishers something other than a cake, there would have been no shortage of Wonderland-based alternatives to choose from: marmalade, licorice comfits, 'Beautiful, beautiful soup'. Indeed, there are times when Carroll's story starts to resemble a shopping list in disguise. Even the mouse she meets splashing about in a pool of Alice's own tears might tempt some readers: early in his career Carroll would probably have come across the Oxford scientist William Buckland, who set himself the goal of munching his way through the entire animal kingdom (mole and bluebottle were especially nasty, he observed), and said that one of his tastiest meals was crispy mice in batter.

This obsession with food probably reflects the fact that *Alice's Adventures in Wonderland* was invented during a picnic for Alice Liddell and her sisters. It certainly reminds us that in a book you aren't restricted to whatever you can find in the nearest supermarket. In Carroll's sequel *Through the Looking-Glass*, we read about 'rough trays of white and brown bread' but also a 'Bread-and-Butterfly' whose wings are thin slices of bread and butter, with a crust for its body and a lump of sugar for its head. Later, Alice meets the White Queen, who responds to Alice's sensible observation that 'one *can't* believe impossible things' by telling her, 'Why, sometimes I've believed as many as six impossible things before breakfast.' Both Alice books take this idea a stage further: creatures like the Bread-and-Butterfly allow us to imagine impossible things *for* breakfast.

But if there's one thing that connects all the items in Carroll's narrative grocery basket, it's that apart from nibbling on the cake and the Caterpillar's mushroom she never gets to eat any of the other foodstuffs she sees or hears about, including goose, eggs, butter, treacle, mustard, whiting, pie and tarts. And of course neither do we. The Hatter's tea party where there isn't any tea turns out to be a perfect model for what it's like to read these stories.

That risks sounding thuddingly obvious. *Of course* it isn't possible to pluck food off the page when we read about it, any more than we can conjure up a new lover simply by reading a few pages of Danielle Steel. But it's interesting how often writers – particularly of children's stories – behave as if it were.

In Roald Dahl's *Charlie and the Chocolate Factory*, Charlie discovers a 50p piece in the gutter and hungrily spends it on a bar of Wonka's Whipple-Scrumptious Fudgemallow Delight, tearing off the wrapper and taking an enormous bite in the shop. 'Then he took another . . . and another . . . and oh, the joy of being able to cram large pieces of something sweet and solid into one's mouth! The sheer blissful joy of being able to fill one's mouth with rich solid food!' Once again verbal repetition captures the steady rhythm of someone chewing and swallowing – 'another . . . and another', 'joy . . . joy', 'sweet and solid . . . rich, solid' – yet while we can imagine Charlie's pleasure, the only things that fill our mouth are words like 'Whipple-Scrumptious Fudgemallow Delight'.

This doesn't stop very young children from sucking and chewing copies of their favourite books, either because they are teething or because one of the ways a child gets to know the world is by sticking small pieces of it into their mouth. Nor is it likely to stop some adults from fantasizing about physically consuming a book, like Mark Strand's poem 'Eating Poetry' ('Ink runs from the corners of my mouth. | There is no happiness like mine. | I have been eating poetry'), or using the same language to explain how we might sample a book rather than consume the whole thing. 'Some books are to be tasted,' writes the seventeenth-century philosopher Francis Bacon – an apt name in the circumstances – in his essay 'Of Studies', 'others to be swallowed, and some few to be chewed and digested; that is, some books are to be read only in parts, others to be read, but not curiously; and some few to be read wholly, and with diligence and attention.' But usually reading involves oral pleasures of a different kind.

Whenever we read something aloud, we bring lines of print to life in our own bodies; we turn a scattering of ink into something that briefly fills our mouth with sound, and for some readers these words can feel almost as substantial as the objects they describe. For example, when Leigh Hunt published an essay on Keats's poem 'The Eve of St Agnes' in 1835, he singled out 'Lucent syrups, tinct with cinnamon' as words that 'make us read the line delicately, and at the tip-end, as it were, of one's tongue'. The twentieth-century critic F. R. Leavis went even further, writing of the line 'To bend with apples the moss'd cottage-trees' from Keats's poem 'To Autumn' that 'It is not fanciful, I think, to find that (the sense being what it is) the pronouncing of "cottage-trees" suggests, too, the crisp bite and the flow of juice as the teeth close in the ripe apple.'

Yet no matter how much reading about apples makes us salivate, it's hard to imagine how saying 'cottage-trees' could fool anyone into thinking that mouth-filling sounds are the same as the crunch and dribble of a real apple. Reading a line like 'To bend with apples the moss'd cottage-trees' is much more likely to remind us that food on the page will always be beyond our physical grasp, just as Tantalus in the classical legend was punished in Hades by being made to stand beneath fruit on a branch that would forever elude him if he reached towards it. When we read about Violet Beauregarde in *Charlie and the Chocolate Factory* eating a three-course meal packed in a single strip of chewing gum ('tomato soup, roast beef, and blueberry pie'), or Alice drinking from the bottle labelled 'DRINK ME' ('it had, in fact, a sort of mixed flavour of cherry-tart, custard, pineapple, roast turkey, toffee, and hot buttered toast'), we all become Tantalus's literary descendants. No matter how far our tongues stretch, they will never be able to turn these foods into more than words.

This might make reading sound like a fairly poor substitute for enjoying a proper snack, but although books cannot satisfy our physical appetites they can satisfy us in a different way. Take William Carlos Williams's poem 'This Is Just to Say':

I have eaten
the plums
that were in
the icebox

and which
you were probably
saving
for breakfast

Forgive me
they were delicious
so sweet
and so cold

At first glance this looks like one of the documents you might find on websites where people can post images of abandoned love letters or anything else that's become unmoored from its original context. Some of the examples I've seen include a Post-it note that reads 'Not Good To Leave This Kind of Thing Lying Around On The Printer', and an American high-school student's apology to his sweetheart that ends with 'Are we still on for prom?', to which she replies 'What the hell do you think?! Asswhole'. (It's a wonderfully felicitous misspelling. Is her boyfriend a bit of an ass? No, he's an ass*whole*.) They are the seeds of lost narratives; they tell us everything and nothing. And we could read 'This Is Just to Say' in a similar way, as the sort of confession someone might make after raiding their flatmate's shelf in a shared fridge. There were some plums and the writer ate them. Sorry-not-sorry.

On the other hand, we might notice what a self-conscious piece of writing this is, as it keeps teasing us with hints of an underlying structure that it refuses to satisfy. There are stanzas that comprise twelve syllables, then another twelve syllables, then – oh – thirteen syllables, and internal echoes such as 'for breakfast . . . Forgive' or 'so sweet . . '. so cold' that never quite settle down into a regular pattern. Even some of the poem's basic grammatical choices are carefully set up and equally carefully smashed up: 'that were . . . which you were'. All of this makes 'This Is Just to Say' sound like another poem that puts us in the position of Tantalus, always reaching after something we will never get, but really it's a poem about the pleasures of reading. After all, if you eat a plum, it's gone for good. Write a poem about plums, on the other hand, and it will produce oral pleasures that can be enjoyed by anyone at any time.

This is an idea that's deeply rooted in both the writing and reading of literature. The contemporary poet Don Paterson has pithily observed that a poem is 'a little machine for remembering itself', and we have already explored some examples of poems such as 'Daffodils' that show how this idea can work in practice, as Wordsworth uses rhyme to make his lines loop back on themselves and help us to remember the events they describe. The notion of a poem as a little memory machine can be especially important when the poet wants to reflect on loss. Most poems that fall into this category are elegies – literary attempts to commemorate the dead. When we read an elegy, we acknowledge the death of the person it was written about, while also appreciating that they have now been transformed into a form of words that is likely to last much longer than frail human flesh. Something similar happens when we read an epic poem like *Paradise Lost*, in which Milton explores the temptation of Adam and Eve (that apple, that snake) and the entrance of death into the world. (Milton's poem is also alluded to in Patience Agbabi's 'Eat Me' when she mentions 'forbidden fruit'.) Here we are introduced to an event that couldn't be set more firmly in the mythical past, but it is written about in such a gripping way that it seems to be happening again as we read about it, right here and now.

'This Is Just to Say' is a far smaller poem than *Paradise Lost* – a mere mouthful – and far less serious in its aims, but it relies on many of the same literary tactics. When we read *Paradise Lost* the apple will always be eaten, but we can repeatedly return to this moment in Milton's poem and try to make better sense of it each time. Similarly, when we read 'This Is Just to Say', the sweet, cold plums will never remain untouched in the fridge, but we can share in the speaker's pleasure long after they have been consumed. Both poems show how a piece of writing can single out particular losses; both remind us that when we start to read, sometimes these losses can be restored.

Chapter 7

CONVERSATIONS

THERE IS A MOMENT AT the beginning of *Alice's Adventures in Wonderland* when Carroll appears to wink at his reader. Sitting on a riverbank and getting increasingly bored, Alice has already peeped into the book her sister is reading and discovered that it doesn't contain any interesting illustrations or dialogue. Her scornful response is to wonder 'what is the use of a book . . . without pictures or conversations?' In what follows, her own book will prove to have plenty of both. We have already considered the importance of pictures in Carroll's story, but it is also full of conversations – not only famous scenes like the Mad Tea Party or Alice's meeting with the Cheshire Cat, but all the other moments when she asks herself questions or scolds herself, which Carroll explains by telling us that 'this curious child was very fond of pretending to be two people'. The joke is that nobody is more fond of pretending to be two (or more) people than an author, because by far the easiest way of creating believable dialogue is to split yourself into different characters and take turns living inside each one's head.

There may also have been a more personal motive behind Carroll's interest in holding conversations on paper. Seated at his desk with a pen in his hand he was a model of eloquence, whereas in person there was always a risk that he might be knocked off course by his stammer. His word for this speech impediment was 'hesitation', and according to witnesses it manifested itself as an occasional blockage that prevented him from making certain sounds. He would open his mouth and language would simply crack apart. This could be socially challenging (in one letter Carroll recalled his 'annoyance' at breaking down in a shop when trying to pronounce a word containing 'a hard "C"') but, worse than that, it was unpredictable. When speaking, and especially when reading aloud, every sentence was a path littered with potential potholes and tripwires, and he had to proceed cautiously, testing the ground as he went.

Writing was a different matter. The blank page released his tongue, because it was an environment where hesitation was just another part of the compositional process, his pen repeating a word for effect or hovering over the page before selecting the next one in the queue. Hesitation could even be made part of a finished text. Carroll's early poem 'Rules and Regulations', written in childhood, includes the advice 'Learn well your grammar, | And never stammer' and 'Eat bread with butter. | Once more, don't stutter'. This sounds like a mocking echo of his parents, but if conversations around the family breakfast table were difficult in person, they were far easier to manage on paper. The line endings of a poem could give the illusion of language breaking down while allowing the reader's eye to roll smoothly on, and Carroll could make a joke out of what might have thwarted him in real life.

Carroll may have been unusually self-conscious about his voice, but he is hardly the only writer to prefer the more controlled conditions of print to the ums and errs of actual speech. As William Hazlitt pointed out in his 1820 essay 'On the Conversation of Authors', 'An author is bound to write – well or ill, wisely or foolishly: it is his trade. But I do not see that he is bound to talk, any more than he is bound to dance, or ride, or

fence better than other people.' There are plenty of examples
to support this claim. When Marcel Proust was introduced to
James Joyce at a black-tie dinner in 1922, the talk of two of the
greatest novelists consisted mostly of the word '*Non*'. As Joyce
later reported to a friend, 'Proust asked me if I knew the duc
de so-and-so. I said, "*Non*." Our hostess asked if he had read
such and such a piece of *Ulysses*. Proust said, "*Non*." And so on.'

Even when authors are less tongue-tied than this, they are
not always adept at the improvised give and take of conversation. Hazlitt reports that when he first met Samuel Taylor
Coleridge, 'I listened for a long time without uttering a word'
and although for the most part he was rapt by the torrent of
eloquence that poured out of the poet (he claims that Coleridge
talked without interruption for a solid two hours), there's more
than open-mouthed admiration in his recollection of walking six miles with his new acquaintance the next day: 'It was a
fine morning in the middle of winter, and he talked the whole
way.' The . . . whole . . . way. The following year John Keats also
met Coleridge, this time when they were both out walking on
Hampstead Heath, and as they went on together for a couple of
miles, according to a letter Keats later wrote to his brother, Coleridge talked about 'a thousand things', including nightingales,
poetry, dreams, nightmares, different kinds of touch, metaphys-
ics, monsters, mermaids and ghost stories. 'I heard his voice as it
came towards me – I heard it as he moved away – I had heard it
all the interval – if it may be called so.'

Yet although Keats describes what it felt like to have a fire
hose of words turned on him, his letter doesn't make a serious
attempt to capture the particular qualities of Coleridge's voice –
all the non-verbal cues, changes in tone and so on, that make
a real conversation (if that is the right word for this one-sided
verbal encounter) so much more than just the words people use.

Writers do have some resources they can dip into if they

want us to hear *how* a character is speaking as well as *what* they are saying. In *Lolita*, for example, when Humbert asks Dolores 'Don't you want to tell me of those little pranks of yours in camp?' and receives the withering response 'You talk like a book, *Dad*', the italics chiselled into *Dad* neatly capture her scorn at the way he keeps mixing up literature and life. (An additional joke is that she is being made to do exactly the same thing herself: nobody talks in italics in real life.) Some writers have emphasised the importance of giving the reader these extra clues. Sir Walter Scott, for example, thought that the novelist 'must not only tell what the characters actually said', but 'must also describe the tone, the look, the gesture, with which their speech was accompanied, – telling, in short, all which, in the drama, it becomes the province of the actor to express'.

On the other hand, there are writers who show how much they can do with very little of this extra information. Sally Rooney's *Normal People* (2018) was her second novel, published a year after her debut *Conversations with Friends*, and in some ways it plays a set of variations on the implications of her previous title. *Normal People* is full of conversations between two Irish teenagers, Marianne and Connell, who cannot work out whether they should be friends, or lovers, or friends who just happen to be in love with each other. At first sight these conversations look like passages of ordinary speech from two perfectly ordinary young people. It is only when we look at them more closely that they turn out to be as carefully staged as a piece of modern theatre.

In the following scene, the pair awkwardly share a car journey with Connell's mother, Lorraine, during one of the 'off' periods of their on-again off-again relationship:

They all get in the car together, Marianne sitting in the back seat, while Connell and Lorraine have a conversation about someone they know who has died, but an elderly person so it's not that sad. Marianne stares out the window.

Well, I'm delighted we bumped into you, says Lorraine. It's great to see you looking so well.

Oh, thank you.

How long are you in town for?

Just the weekend, says Marianne.

Eventually Connell indicates at the entrance to the Foxfield estate and pulls in outside his house. Lorraine gets out . . .

It's a short drive from Connell's house to Marianne's. He takes a left out of the estate, towards the roundabout. Only a few months ago he and Marianne used to stay up all night together talking and having sex. He used to pull the blankets off her in the morning and get on top of her with this little smiling expression like: Oh hey, hello. They were best friends. He told her that, when she asked him who his best friend was. You, he said. Then at the end of May he told her he was moving home for the summer.

How are things, anyway? he says.

Fine, thanks. How are you?

I'm alright, yeah.

He changes gears with a domineering gesture of his hand.

Are you still working in the garage? she asks.

No, no. You mean where I used to work? That place is closed now.

Is it?

Yeah, he says. No, I've been working in the Bistro. Actually your mam was in the other night with her, uh. Her boyfriend or whatever it is.

Marianne nods. They are driving past the football grounds now. A thin veil of rain begins to fall on the windshield, and Connell turns the wipers on, so they scraped out a mechanical rhythm on their voyage from side to side.

While some writers have a good ear for dialogue, Rooney has just as good an ear for the awkward verbal fumbling of people who aren't quite sure how to talk to each other. We have already been told that a few months ago their conversations in bed were so synchronised they felt like figure skaters working in perfect harmony. It was a time when 'talking and having sex' were like two sides of the same coin; that was what they had become used to. Now the phrase 'used to' has taken on a more elegiac air ('He used to pull the blankets off her in the morning . . . You mean where I used to work'), and as a result the things they have to say to each other are more like the jigsaw pieces from two different puzzles. Awkward silences are intercut with conversational gambits that are rippled with erotic tension, and any attempts to deflect attention end up rebounding on the speaker. (Connell's reference to 'Her boyfriend or whatever it is' is especially awkward coming from him as Marianne's former boyfriend or whatever he was.) Their separation is even extended into Rooney's paragraphing. The brief flashback to the time when they were a couple who enjoyed 'talking together' includes some dialogue that squashes their voices together and makes it hard to tell them apart, but now that they have split up their voices are kept separate on the page.

With so little information to go on, we might be tempted to look for metaphors that act as little carnival mirrors of what has become of their relationship, from sharing a bed to merely sharing a car. How much should we read into passing references to an elderly acquaintance who has died, or a garage that has closed? In this atmosphere, even the mechanical rhythm of the windscreen wipers starts to sound like a mocking echo of the passionate nights they once spent together: now it's only the wipers Connell is turning on.

Sometimes a writer includes adverbs as stage directions for a character's voice: 'he said happily', 'she sighed ruefully', and so on. These are called 'reporting clauses' by language experts, and they link what is going on in a character's head with what is coming out of their mouth. Here these little clues have been stripped away, along with traditional quotation marks, and all we are left with is 'says . . . says . . . says . . . says . . . asks . . . says'. This makes Rooney's dialogue a perfect vehicle for the difficulty her characters have in understanding each other, but it is also a reminder that the better we get to know them, the more confidently we can fill in some of their blanks. (They are like real people in this respect.) And this process is further enhanced by the fact that some of the words Rooney's characters use are perfectly empty in terms of their meaning.

Take the 'Oh' in 'Oh, thank you'. According to the *Oxford English Dictionary*, starting a clause with 'Oh' can express, 'according to intonation', any number of emotions including 'surprise, frustration, discomfort, longing, disappointment, sorrow, relief, etc.' We are not told the tone of voice in which Marianne says 'Oh, thank you', any more than we are told how Connell used to say 'Oh hey, hello.' But because we have got to know them as characters over the past hundred or so pages, we can start to imagine how each 'oh' is said, just as we can supply some of the mixed yearning and embarrassment reverberating in the silences of this encounter – the realisation that sometimes people fail to speak because they are scared of saying too much rather than too little.

There are earlier models for this sort of fictional dialogue. In a talk he gave for the BBC in 1950, the novelist Henry Green argued that the best way a novelist could communicate with their readers was through printed conversation and, contrary to Sir Walter Scott's advice, their speech shouldn't be hedged around with fussy authorial explanations. Even adverbs ('he said crossly', 'she observed pithily') should be avoided, according to Green, no matter how tempting it might be to treat them as conversational signposts. 'We certainly do not know what other people are thinking and feeling', he claimed. 'How then can the novelist be so sure?' Instead of turning characters inside out to reveal their hidden secrets, Green claimed, the novelist should create 'a gathering web of insinuations' to reveal feelings these characters would never admit out loud, and might not even recognise in the privacy of their own heads. This is what turns the reading of a novel into 'a long intimacy between strangers'. Similarly, although Rooney doesn't tell us what her characters are thinking and feeling, as we continue to read they gradually become less opaque to us, just as they do to each other.

Although Rooney's writing is unusually spare and – to use Green's term – insinuating, it behaves in a similar way to many other literary works. The writer Italo Calvino once suggested that when we read a new story for the first time, it involves 'confronting something and not quite knowing yet what it is'. This could be the substance of an idea, like the importance of freedom that lies at the heart of *Nineteen Eighty-Four*, or it could be the shape of one, like the jagged appearance of lines that gradually resolve themselves into poems like 'Eat Me' or 'This Is Just to Say'. But in a novel like *Normal People*, this 'something' can be as simple – or as complicated – as the human relationships that lie at its heart. And this can make our growing understanding of the novel's characters surprisingly similar to the way we get to know real people.

When we meet someone for the first time, they are usually close to being a blank slate to us; we might be able to guess their favourite colour from what they are wearing, and possibly even their taste in music (a faded denim jacket and studded wristbands: heavy metal? rhinestone cowboy boots and glittery eyeshadow: Taylor Swift?), but we can't know for sure.

Over time we may get to know them much better; in some cases (lovers, best friends, close work colleagues) we may end up knowing them so well we don't only remember what they did and said in the past, but can accurately predict how they might behave in the future.

Our relationships with certain fictional characters can work in a similar way. When we first encounter Dorothea Brooke in George Eliot's *Middlemarch*, she is little more than a name – someone who is highly unlikely to wear either studded wristbands or rhinestone cowboy boots (the novel's first sentence is 'Miss Brooke had that kind of beauty which seems to be thrown into relief by poor dress'), and not that different to any of the other fictional characters who surround her. Yet over the course of the novel things gradually change. Page by page, more layers are added to her personality, and by the end of the novel we feel that we know her well enough to anticipate how she might behave even in situations that Eliot didn't write. Like all of the greatest literary characters, she turns out to be somehow bigger than her story, capable of slipping out from between the covers of Eliot's novel. And as we follow the twists and turns of her adventures, something similar happens to us. In entering the life of this fictional character, we realise that for a few hours we can escape our own lives; when we raise the book to our eyes, we are temporarily lifted out of ourselves.

Eliot herself tried to explain this phenomenon by arguing that 'Art is the nearest thing to life; it is a mode of amplifying experience and extending our contact with our fellow-men beyond the bounds of our personal lot.' And as we've seen in this chapter, fictional dialogue is one of the most important ways in which an author like Sally Rooney can help us to expand the circumference of our selfhood. By pretending to be two people holding a conversation she shows us how we can learn to be more than ourselves.

Chapter 8

Points of View

IMAGINE THIS SCENARIO: somebody's camera captures a young skinhead running along a pavement past some scaffolding towards a well-dressed man, and trying to wrestle his briefcase off him. Clearly the skinhead is a mugger. Now look at the scene again from the viewpoint of a different camera: the scaffolding is part of a building site, and a pile of bricks is about to fall on the man when a brave youth who has spotted the danger rushes up and pushes him out of the way. Clearly the skinhead is a hero.

This scene was shown from both angles in a 1986 TV advert for the *Guardian* newspaper, which ended with the tagline 'It's only when you get the whole picture you can fully understand what's going on': a sensible reminder that it's helpful – often essential – to have more than one perspective on a set of events. The same lesson could usefully be applied to the passage from *Normal People* we considered in the last chapter. If Sally Rooney had attached some straightforward adverbs to this conversation, there's no guarantee that both characters would agree they were the right ones. It's easy to imagine how a seemingly neutral description like 'he said happily' could be twisted into 'he gloated' by a suspicious listener, just as 'she said sadly' could be heard as 'she said theatrically' if Marianne was thought to be the sort of person who exaggerated her feelings for dramatic effect.

Even if Rooney's characters agreed on a form of words that accurately captured their encounter, they might not understand these words in exactly the same way. For example, Connell's 'domineering' driving style looks forward to Marianne's submissiveness in a number of later sexual encounters, and so could be seen as thrilling by her and/or teasingly flirtatious by him: a reminder that two people can experience the same event very differently.

This offers an important refinement to an idea we've already touched on, which is that stories expand our boundaries by allowing us to see the world through someone else's eyes, and enter into a voice, or a set of ideas, or even a form of desire, that may be nothing like our own. After all, it isn't only that everyone's angle of vision is slightly different. As the *Guardian* advert shows, some angles may give us a more accurate view of events than others. 'I'm telling you stories', writes Jeanette Winterson in her 2001 novel *The Passion*. 'Trust me.' In part this is a self-conscious joke about the idea that 'telling stories' is a common euphemism for lying, but it's also an invitation to recognise how individuals can rearrange a set of facts to fit any narrative they choose. And reading about this tendency is likely to do more than encourage us to exercise our powers of sympathy. It can also help us to develop our powers of scrutiny.

The narrator who cannot be trusted to tell the truth is so common in fiction it has its own label: the 'unreliable narrator', a term originally coined in the 1960s by the American critic Wayne C. Booth. Of course, some narrators are more unreliable than others. In Dickens's *David Copperfield* (1849–50), David is mostly believable but tends to put on the narrative equivalent of blinkers whenever he describes his charming but morally questionable friend Steerforth. By contrast, Humbert Humbert appears to be telling us the story of *Lolita* while locked up in an insane asylum, which might encourage us to be suspicious of his trustworthiness as well as his lack of scruples. But what all unreliable narrators share is an ability to reveal the gap that can open up between an event and how it is understood, and so how tempting it can be for someone to distort or evade the truth – and not only when representing it to other people.

This is especially the case when the narrator thinks they are telling one story, but cannot quite suppress another version of events glinting between the cracks of their account. Zoë Heller's 2003 novel *Notes on a Scandal* is told from the perspective of Barbara Covett, a middle-aged schoolteacher whose surname accurately indicates her tendency to desire what those around her seem to enjoy: youth, innocence, sexual attractiveness. From the start she makes us arch a quizzical eyebrow at what she is choosing to tell us, and the extent to which she is taking us into her confidence or merely putting on an act. These questions become even more pronounced after she meets a new female art teacher and sizes her up as a potential staffroom ally, or possibly something more:

> I took Sheba's failure to forge an instantaneous friendship as an encouraging sign. In my experience, newcomers – particularly female ones – are far too eager to pin their colours to the mast of any staffroom coterie that will have them. Jennifer Dodd, who used to be my closest friend at the school, spent her first three weeks at St George's buried in the welcoming bosoms of Mary Horsely and Diane Nebbins. Mary and Diane are two hippies from the Maths Department. They both carry packets of 'women's tea' in their handbags and use jagged lumps of rock crystal in lieu of anti-perspirant. They were entirely ill-suited – temperament-wise, humour-wise, worldview-wise – to be Jennifer's friends. But they happened to get to her first and Jennifer was so grateful for someone being nice to her that she cheerfully undertook to ignore their

soy milk mumbo-jumbo. I dare say she would have plighted her troth to a Moonie during her first week at St George's, if the Moonie had been quick enough off the mark.

Sheba displayed no such new-girl jitters, and for this I admired her. She did not exempt me from her general aloofness. Owing to my seniority at St George's and the fact that I am more formal in manner than most of my colleagues, I am used to being treated with a certain deference. But Sheba seemed to be oblivious of my status. There was little indication, for a long time, that she really *saw* me at all. Yet, in spite of this, I found myself possessed by a strange certainty that we would one day be friends.

Early on, we made a few tentative approaches to one another. Somewhere in her second week, Sheba greeted me in the corridor. (She used 'Hello', I was pleased to note, as opposed to the awful, mid-Atlantic 'Hiya' that so many of the staff favour.) And another time, walking from the arts centre after an assembly, we shared some brief, rueful comments about the choral performance that had just taken place. My feelings of connection to Sheba did not depend upon these minute exchanges, however. The bond that I sensed, even at that stage, went far beyond anything that might have been expressed in quotidian chit-chat. It was an intuited kinship. An unspoken understanding. Does it sound too dramatic to call it spiritual recognition? Owing to our mutual reserve, I understood that it would take time for us to form a friendship. But when we did, I had no doubt that it would prove to be one of uncommon intimacy and trust – a relationship *de chaleur* as the French say.

Later we learn this was a 'gold star day', a teacherly phrase that Barbara uses to mark the days in her life when something special has happened. That makes it sound like an obvious success.

But although she says in passing 'I had no doubt', there is plenty going on here to make us doubt what she is telling us.

Narrating these events in the past tense opens up a gap in time, and therefore the possibility that Barbara is looking back at her actions and trying to make sense of them or justify them, whether to us or to herself. There are several clues in this passage that this is indeed what she is doing. We notice her desire to assert herself as more educated and socially refined than her colleagues, and to separate herself from those she perceives to be ignorant or common: hence her precise, somewhat pedantic diction, so that when she tells us 'I am more formal in manner', she underlines her point by preferring 'I am' to the less formal 'I'm'. Hence also her criticisms of how other people speak.

Yet already there are some cracks opening up in this facade. Although Barbara is a stickler for good grammar, she has a habit of using phrases such as 'quotidian chit-chat' that start off in self-conscious refinement (possibly with a touch of mannered irony at her own expense) before slipping a few rungs down the social ladder. She is equally prone to clichés: 'pin their colours to the mast', 'quick off the mark'. Usually clichés are pieces of social shorthand that allow us to adopt a position on something without getting too personally involved. ('It's Adam and Eve, not Adam and Steve'; 'Brexit means Brexit'.) Giving them a personal spin, as Barbara does here, indicates a tension in her mind between wanting to fit in and hoping to stand out from the crowd.

Meanwhile, tiny details of her encounters with Sheba, such as saying hello in the corridor, are brooded over with the intensity of a lover's tryst. The gradual shift over very few sentences from 'shared' comments to 'an intuited kinship' indicates that she is whipping up a romantic fantasy based on the most ordinary of circumstances, and this is intensified by the little hint of illicit passion that comes across in her use of the French phrase *de chaleur* (literally 'hot') – presumably not the sort of thing she imagines any of her colleagues saying, and therefore another way for her to make herself sound special. A little later in the novel she will describe sex as a constant 'background hum' in a school that is filled with randy teenagers, but already she is using language in a way that makes her own desires a bit more audible than that, even if she tends to deflect them onto other people, with talk of her colleagues' 'welcoming bosoms' and an echo of the marriage service when she says that Sheba would have 'plighted her troth' to a Moonie if he'd been quick enough off the mark. Soon we will also learn that the passing reference to Jennifer Dodd is not accidental. It turns out that she was an earlier target of Barbara's clingy attention, but despite a trip to Paris their friendship ended badly – presumably after Jennifer worked out what was really going on. It is the sort of information that retrospectively adds an extra edge of pathos to this scene, while making Barbara's anticipation of 'uncommon intimacy' with Sheba sound oddly like a threat.

All of this makes the passage out to be extremely serious, like a police report about stalking or an entry in a psychiatric textbook. Actually it's very funny, as Barbara's waspish sense of humour turns her colleagues into caricatures who clutch rock crystal anti-perspirants and offer up 'soy milk mumbo-jumbo'. Yet while this entertains us, and to some extent encourages our complicity, it also serves as a warning that Barbara may be doing the same thing to events, by flattening them out and twisting them into new shapes that more closely match her view of the world. She may have 'no doubt' about her ability to forge a friendship of great 'trust' with Sheba, but already seeds of doubt and distrust are being sown in our minds.

This is a pattern that is duplicated across many other literary works. We have already seen that one of the great satisfactions of reading a novel or poem is that it allows us temporarily to inhabit a world that seems true to life even though we know it doesn't actually exist. These imaginary worlds are places where we can negotiate with reality. When we read about Peter Rabbit wearing a blue jacket with brass buttons, or a clock striking thirteen, we take our knowledge of how the world really works and enjoy the sight of an alternative sliding up against it and even temporarily taking charge. Indeed, we might think that this is one of the biggest pleasures of reading. Whereas in our daily lives certain facts are impossible to avoid – we ruin our new coat by spilling coffee on it; we sleep through our alarm and miss an important meeting – literature introduces us to a dimension where *is* and *as* can be hard to distinguish. But of course there's a danger in not being able to tell the difference between what is true and what we would like to be true, and by pinning this state of moral confusion onto its central character a novel like *Notes on a Scandal* shows us what its consequences might be.

There are also some more general conclusions we might draw from this example. I suggested earlier that literary works can raise quite complicated questions, but that most of these can be boiled down to the three very simple questions of *what, how* and *why*. What are we being told? How is it being done? Why is it being done like this and not in another way? The answers to these questions will tell us a good deal about an author's priorities and blind spots, but when a work is written in the voice of a character the same answers will also tell us something about the slanted view any individual is likely to have about their place in the world. Even a character like Barbara, who claims to value 'uncommon intimacy and trust', may be hiding her real feelings with rhetorical smoke and mirrors, although that may not be something she is consciously aware of. Indeed, if her narrative teaches us anything, it's that our most important secrets may be those we are trying to keep from ourselves.

How to Meet New People

Chapter 9

THE NEAREST THING TO LIFE

SOME OF THE FUNNIEST PASSAGES in *Notes on a Scandal* are the waspish sketches that Barbara gives of her teaching colleagues. In the opening pages, we are introduced to a Chemistry teacher who sits 'with his legs aggressively akimbo, offering a clearer silhouette of his untidy crotch than is strictly necessary', a deputy headteacher who bellows an introduction to Sheba 'with his customary, chilling good spirits', and several other staff members who gossip about the new pottery teacher like 'eager little fishwives'. Not once does Barbara consider the possibility that these people are just as interesting and complicated as herself. Instead she views the school where they work as the location of a crude morality play in which she is the heroine and they are merely flimsy cardboard villains. Although she is sensitive to details of colour when it comes to Sheba – the first time she glimpses her new colleague cycling through the school gates she notices her purple shoes, and much later she recalls Sheba's faded blue dressing gown being draped over a sofa or left in a heap on the floor – in other respects she sees the world in straightforward black and white.

It's worth observing that Barbara refers to the 'notes' she has assembled as a 'history', suggesting an accurate record of events, but also as a 'story'. Perhaps her notes are supposed to be a trial run of the novel we are reading, because treating people like cartoons is a common tactic in fictional narratives. Borrowing the famous distinction made by E. M. Forster in his 1927 book *Aspects of the Novel*, while a writer may try to make their characters as 'round' as possible, giving us the illusion that – like Dorothea in *Middlemarch* – they could step off the page and enter our world at any moment, the same writer may equally choose to populate their pages with 'flat' characters who are little more than human sketches, the sort of individuals who would be as out of place in real life as Bugs Bunny in a wildlife documentary.

It's tempting to treat this distinction as a sign of literary quality. If we read a piece of fiction expecting it to be 'the nearest thing to life', as George Eliot once claimed, we might assume that its characters should also be as close to real people (i.e., as complex) as possible. In fact, what makes Barbara's withering descriptions of her colleagues so believable is that cutting other people down to the size of a postage stamp isn't restricted to fiction. When I first read *Notes on a Scandal*, it was accompanied by an awkward flush of recognition, because a few years previously I had spent some time teaching English in a school where every day I turned the staffroom into a mental theatre where my colleagues became the characters in an equally crude melodrama, complete with private nicknames ('Oh God, here comes Pubehead') and routine bits of stage business. Even now when I sit in university meetings I have to resist the urge to reduce my colleagues – people whom I genuinely like and admire – into stick-thin caricatures in my mind.

This is another area of life where fiction can help. As we saw in Chapter 7, the most interesting literary characters produce the illusion of possessing an inner world that is far richer than the glimpses of it that can be put into words. This is what makes a character seem as alive as you or me. Such a statement risks sounding overblown or queasily romantic, because by definition literary characters are not actual people; and yet anyone who enjoys reading knows that they can occupy as much space in our heads as if they were. D. H. Lawrence was alert to this powerful trick of the imagination. 'Every tiny bit of my hands is alive, every little freckle and hair and fold of skin', he wrote in his 1936 essay 'Why the Novel Matters', and although the words printed in a novel are made out of paper and ink rather than flesh and bone, they are the emanations of a real human being and will take on a new sense of reality whenever they enter a reader's mind, 'like a chameleon creeping from a brown rock onto a green leaf'. On the page they exist in a limbo state, just waiting to be reanimated by a reader, and when this happens 'the characters can do nothing but *live*'.

The most interesting stories do both things at once. They remind us how inviting it is to turn other people into two-dimensional heroes or villains, while all the time the author is working hard to recover their true complexity.

Nobody performs this psychological balancing act better than Jane Austen, particularly in a novel like *Emma* (1815), which revolves around someone who has long treated other people as characters she can shuffle into stories of her own devising. Yet gradually Emma Woodhouse finds herself involved in a romance plot with the attractive and wealthy Mr Knightley that is far harder to control. The climactic scene is a marriage proposal that is not to her friend Harriet, as Harriet had fondly hoped, but to Emma herself, as Mr Knightley tells her that 'you understand my feelings—and will return them if you can'. While he is speaking, we are told that 'Emma's mind was most busy, and, with all the wonderful velocity of thought, had been able—and yet without losing a word—to catch and comprehend the exact truth of the whole'. And at the heart of her whirling thoughts, 'The dread of being awakened from the happiest dream, was perhaps the most prominent feeling':

She felt for Harriet, with pain and with contrition; but no flight of generosity run mad, opposing all that could be probable or reasonable, entered her brain. She had led her friend astray, and it would be a reproach to her for ever; but her judgment was as strong as her feelings, and as strong as it had ever been before, in reprobating any such alliance for him, as most unequal and degrading. Her way was clear, though not quite smooth.—She spoke then, on being so entreated.—What did she say?—Just what she ought, of course. A lady always does.—She said enough to shew there need not be despair— and to invite him to say more himself. He *had* despaired at one period; he had received such an injunction to caution and silence, as for the time crushed every hope;—she had begun by refusing to hear him.—The change had perhaps been somewhat sudden;—her proposal of taking another turn, her renewing the conversation which she had just put an end to, might be a little extraordinary!—She felt its inconsistency; but Mr Knightley was so obliging as to put up with it, and seek no farther explanation.

Seldom, very seldom, does complete truth belong to any human disclosure; seldom can it happen that something is not a little disguised, or a little mistaken; but where, as in this case, though the conduct is mistaken, the feelings are not, it may not be very material.—Mr Knightley could not impute to Emma a more relenting heart than she possessed, or a heart more disposed to accept of his.

This may be the most psychologically realistic proposal scene ever written. Finally Emma realises that she loves Mr Knightley just as much as he loves her – a discovery that is beautifully captured in the way she picks up his word 'feelings' and finds it reappearing in her own thoughts, rather as a couple who have been together for a long time might find themselves echoing each other's favourite expressions. Yet alongside this happy reciprocity there is also the admission that even at such moments some things will inevitably be 'mistaken'. Just as Mr Knightley's proposal is the climax of their slow-burning romance, so Austen's use of 'mistaken' draws attention to how often her characters misread each other, and how this gradually helps us to become better readers both of them and of the sorts of situation in which they find themselves.

It isn't just the number of times that the words 'mistake' or 'mistaken' appear in *Emma* (more than three dozen altogether), or that fact that they sit alongside many other examples of things being misunderstood, or misapplied, or simply missed. (At times it's tempting to read the whole novel as an elaborate pun on the name of the character who is repeatedly referred to as 'Miss Woodhouse', given how often she misses opportunities or just misses the point.) As we read, we too are encouraged to make mistakes in how we interpret events, while simultaneously tuning into a narrative voice that observes and judges these mistakes.

This tuning in and out of a particular perspective is usually referred to as 'free indirect style', although that is a suspiciously neat critical label to apply to Austen's skill at juggling the emotional lives of her characters with her own dry commentary. In this scene, for example, 'The dread of being awakened from the happiest dream, was perhaps the most prominent feeling' captures Emma's joy while also briskly putting it into perspective. Similarly, the earlier deadpan description of Mr Knightley's voice as he makes his marriage proposal, with a 'tone of such sincere, decided, intelligible tenderness as was tolerably convincing', could be Austen observing her characters with the detachment of a theatre critic, or Emma showing that she still retains her habit of evaluating others even in the middle of a life-changing moment.

We are told that Emma's 'busy' mind is whirring away while Mr Knightley is speaking, which presumably is why she can process so many thoughts in a matter of seconds. Her speed of uptake reflects the narrative convention that time can be slowed down or speeded up on the page to suit the writer's needs, giving readers an opportunity to pause over important events and examine them from many different angles. Here it is mostly achieved by following the path of Emma's thoughts, as she looks back on the events that have brought her and Mr Knightley to this point and imagines how they might continue into the future. But Austen also deploys an extra resource to help her achieve this sort of psychological realism: punctuation.

Punctuation might sound like one of the least glamorous pieces of the novelist's toolkit, involving the very smallest nuts and bolts that make up a piece of writing. But it matters. Get it wrong and a sentence can turn into a boomerang, disappearing off in a completely different direction to the one originally intended, as was the case a few years ago when a newspaper used the headline 'Students get first hand job experience', which implied something rather different to the reporter's intention. So did a sign someone came across in the American countryside that announced:

HUNTERS
PLEASE USE CAUTION
WHEN HUNTING
PEDESTRIANS
USING
WALK TRAILS

– where the lack of a punctuation mark between 'HUNTING' and 'PEDESTRIANS' made a request for hunters to treat pedestrians considerately look more like a threat.

Even a punctuation mark that is as simple as a dash can signal many possible links between two parts of a sentence, from a connection that is as solid as a plug in a socket, to one that is as uncertain as a tightrope. Like other punctuation marks, a dash can fulfil a purely grammatical function, or it can perform in a way that is more mimetic or metaphorical, as when Emily Dickinson's poems use dashes to suggest distant horizons or ties of friendship, or indeed when the famously gloomy philosopher Søren Kierkegaard writes in an 1836 diary entry that he has just returned from a party where 'witty banter flowed from my lips, everyone laughed and admired me – but I came away', before adding 'that dash should be as long as the radii of the earth's orbit —————————— wanting to shoot myself'. A set of dashes can equally indicate how tightly a piece of writing is stitched together, or hint at the cracks of logic or confidence that are opening up in its surface.

Most importantly, in a novel like *Emma* they can capture the way that a character thinks and speaks, like a whole series of hidden stage directions built into the narrative, and can therefore make a scene like Mr Knightley's proposal come even closer to the psychological complexity of such encounters in real life. The pell-mell rush of dashes in his speech reveal a gasping passion not otherwise described, and they are matched by Emma's own fragmentary thoughts, suggesting that this will be a marriage of both hearts and minds. At the same time, these dashes show Austen's own cool manipulation of the scene as she stages it, and thereby give us a practical demonstration of how passion can be balanced with reason. Like a wedding photograph, the passage captures a moment of genuine emotion while also keeping it carefully under control.

In Chapter 7, I suggested that one of the benefits of reading a novel is that it allows us to become more intimately acquainted with characters who may not themselves be larger than life, but do enlarge our sense of life's possibilities. I also suggested that the most successful literary characters are those who appear ready to step off the page and enter the world of their readers. One measure of this success might be a character's ability to surprise us, by doing or saying something that makes us realise that we didn't know them nearly as well as we thought. Mr Knightley's proposal will fall into this category for some readers. But an even greater measure of a successful novel might be its inclusion of characters who are capable of surprising themselves. Emma is just such a character. As Mr Knightley speaks, her tumble of conflicting thoughts is beautifully captured in Austen's choppy sentences. But then she has to reply, and she does so in a way that shows her pulling herself together and taking charge of the situation:

> She spoke then, on being so entreated.—What did she say?— Just what she ought, of course. A lady always does.

The joke is that she has spent much of the novel saying things she ought not to have said, so if 'A lady always does' adds a touch of free indirect style to show Emma reassuring herself that she is a suitable wife for her wealthy suitor, it also offers Austen an opportunity to give her heroine a last gentle poke in the ribs.

Emma is a novel that is particularly loved by its readers, and that may partly be because at its heart it is a celebration of reading. After all, Emma herself is a champion mis-reader, as we have already seen, albeit one who gradually learns how to look and listen more attentively. It is as if she starts the novel assuming that she is in one kind of story, namely a drawing room comedy full of crudely drawn caricatures, and slowly discovers that she is in a far more interesting one – a romance in which she will unexpectedly take on the role of a three-dimensional heroine. This is what fleshes her out in our heads until we start to think of her as 'the nearest thing to life' rather than just a figment of Austen's imagination. And as we follow her on this stumbling journey of self-discovery, it is the playfulness of Austen's narrative voice that allows *Emma* to keep surprising us, just as Emma continues to surprise herself.

Chapter 10

What's in a Name?

AUSTEN WAS GOOD AT COMING UP with titles that offered a neat summary of what readers could expect from the pages that followed. Before *Emma*, in 1811 came *Sense and Sensibility*, which carefully unpicked these twin personality traits and showed how to achieve a sensible (i.e., both rational and emotional) balance between them, followed in 1813 by *Pride and Prejudice*, which turned out to be a thesaurus entry on the possible variations of such feelings that was spread out across a whole novel. In this context, the title of *Emma* might seem far less willing to offer clues about the kind of story we are about to read, but it too gives us a distilled version of the novel as a whole, which begins with the name of the heroine ('Emma Woodhouse, handsome, clever, and rich . . . ') and ends with a sentence confirming 'the perfect happiness of the union'. From the heroine being single (Emma Woodhouse) to her being married (Emma Knightley) is a narrative arc every bit as elegant as the one that spans Proust's enormous work *À la recherche du temps perdu* (*In Search of Lost Time*), published in seven volumes between 1913 and 1927, which opens with the word 'Longtemps' ('For a long time') and more than 4,000 pages later ends with 'Temps' ('Time'), like a giant piece of elastic stretching out before returning to something close to its original shape.

A character's name might seem pretty inconsequential compared to the big questions some literary works ask, such as 'What do we live for, if it is not to make life less difficult to each other?' (Eliot's *Middlemarch*), or 'Do we indeed desire the dead | Should still be near us at our side? (Tennyson's *In Memoriam*), but they can provide us with significant clues about their lives, and even about the kind of fictional world we find ourselves in when we read.

The most obvious examples are 'cratylic' names, a term that comes from Plato's dialogue *Cratylus* in which he considers the existence of words that seem to capture the essence of something or someone. We have already encountered an example of this in the form of Barbara Covett, the narrator of *Notes on a Scandal*, whose surname accurately indicates how much envy and yearning is stored up behind her tightly buttoned exterior. She is part of a rich tradition that stretches from the 'comedy of humours' popularised at the end of the sixteenth century by playwrights like Ben Jonson and George Chapman, in which characters seem destined to act out a set of variations on a single personality trait, through to tragic figures like Miss Flite in Dickens's *Bleak House* (1852–53), who is waiting for the legal judgement that will set her free but meanwhile remains as trapped as her caged birds. There are even hints of this tendency in more complex characters like Pip in *Great Expectations* (1860–61), who longs to escape from his old life and blossom elsewhere, but at the end of the novel finds himself back where he started, just as his name inescapably loops back on itself: P-I-P.

The names of characters we pass over without a great deal of thought can still carry a latent cratylic charge. One of the reasons Thackeray chose the surname Sharp for his heroine

Rebecca in *Vanity Fair* (1847–48) seems to have been that she is admirably clever (the sense of 'sharp' as quick-witted can be traced back as far as Old English), but as dangerous as a razor for those who come into contact with her. Similarly, 'Harry Potter' brings together suggestions of noble leadership (in Shakespeare's *Henry V* the young king refers to himself as 'Harry' rather than 'Henry') and of escapology, always somehow managing to extricate himself from dangerous situations (Harry Houdini), while also raising the question of what this 'Potter' will make of himself. The name is, suggestively, at once noble and ordinary; it singles him out, while simultaneously inviting any reader to put themselves in his position and work out how far his heroism is something they can share.

So names in a story are always chosen, always meaningful, even if what they capture is a nothing-to-see-here ordinariness. Yet life is usually far harder to predict than a cratylic name suggests. While knowing someone's name in a book can give us their personality in a nutshell, real people tend not to carry around this information in such an easily accessible form. That is why there is such a special pleasure in discovering that the chief financial officer appointed by the footwear retailer Shoe Zone in 2021 was a man named Terry Boot (the story was improved even further by the news that he was taking over from Peter Foot), or that the senior official sent by the Lord Chamberlain's office after the Second World War to inspect shows at London's Windmill Theatre that featured scantily clad female performers was named George Titman. We enjoy these coincidences between someone's name and what they do or what they look like precisely because they are so unlikely. They are the linguistic equivalent of winning the lottery.

Some of the most interesting names in literature play with these ideas rather than simply taking them for granted. The narrator of Anita Loos's 1925 novel *Gentlemen Prefer Blondes* is a wide-eyed flapper, Lorelei Lee, whose first name means 'The Temptress' or 'The Enchantress', after the legendary siren who dwelt on the banks of the Rhine and lured sailors to their deaths. The novel follows Lorelei as she travels across Europe with her friend Dorothy, always heeding the advice of her American sugar daddy Gus Eisman to 'take advantage of everybody we meet'. He means it in the sense of learning from experience, but they have a much more mercenary understanding of how to 'take advantage of' the wealthy men they encounter. (The joke is that this is usually a sexual euphemism applied to what men do to girls, not the other way round.) When they reach Paris, Lorelei's diary bubbles over with the famous hotels and brand names she associates with luxurious living:

> So we came to the Ritz Hotel and the Ritz Hotel is devine. Because when a girl can sit in a delightful bar and have delicious champagne cocktails and look at all the important French people in Paris, I think it is devine. I mean when a girl can sit there and look at the Dolly sisters and Pearl White and Maybelle Gilman Corey, and Mrs Nash, it is beyond worlds. Because when a girl looks at Mrs Nash and realizes what Mrs Nash has got out of gentlemen, it really makes a girl hold her breath.
>
> And when a girl walks around and reads all of the signs with all of the famous historical names it really makes you hold your breath. Because when Dorothy and I went on a walk, we only walked a few blocks but in only a few blocks we read all of the famous historical names, like Coty and Cartier and I knew we were seeing something educational at last and our whole trip was not a failure. I mean I really try to make Dorothy get educated and have reverance. So when we stood at the corner of a place called the Place Vandome, if you turn your back on a monument they have in the middle and

look up, you can see none other than Coty's sign. So I said to Dorothy, does it not really give you a thrill to realize that that is the historical spot where Mr Coty makes all the perfume? So then Dorothy said that she supposed Mr Coty came to Paris and he smelled Paris and he realized that something had to be done. So Dorothy will really never have any reverance.

So then we saw a jewelry store and we saw some jewelry in the window and it really seemed to be a very very great bargain but the price marks all had francs on them and Dorothy and I do not seem to be mathematical enough to tell how much francs is in money. So we went in and asked and it seems it was only 20 dollars and it seems it is not diamonds but it is a thing called 'paste' which is the name of a word which means imitations. So Dorothy said 'paste' is the name of the word a girl ought to do to a gentleman that handed her one. I mean I would really be embarrassed, but the gentleman did not seem to understand Dorothy's english.

Names are important to Lorelei, starting with a roll call of some earlier American women who had used their sex appeal to achieve an impressive degree of financial independence: the Dolly sisters, who toured the theatres and dance halls of Europe and were courted by numerous wealthy men and royalty including Carol II of Romania, Christian X of Denmark, and Alfonso XIII of Spain; Pearl White, a Hollywood actress who made a fortune by the time she retired in 1924, which she invested in a Paris nightclub, a Biarritz casino, and a string of racehorses; Maybelle Gilman Corey, a Broadway star who married the president of United States Steel and received as wedding presents from him a French chateau, some valuable jewels and a million dollars in cash; and Mrs Jean Nash, the celebrity socialite popularly known as 'The World's Best-Dressed Woman', who divorced her fourth husband, an Egyptian prince, in 1925 after only being married to him for a month, and would later marry the French drinks tycoon Paul Dubonnet.

All of these people are real. By contrast, not only is Lorelei a fictional character, we learn in the novel that her name was given to her by a judge who 'said a girl ought to have a name that ought to express her personality' after she shot one of her admirers. A number of the other people she encounters have equally slippery identities. In London she learns that rich and powerful men have 'generally some quite cute name like Coocoo whose real name is Lord Cooksleigh', while she also meets here a 'delightful gentleman' named Mr Ginzburg who later changes his name to Mr Mountginz 'which he really thinks is more aristocratic'. Lorelei is similarly fond of giving her admirers new nicknames: Gus Eisman becomes 'Daddy'; Sir Francis Beekman becomes 'Piggie'. Perhaps this is why she gravitates to places with equally unstable identities. In this passage, the 'Place Vandome' (i.e., Vendôme) is a square in Paris that has rich historical associations, but it has often been renamed, just as the monument she turns her back on has a long history of being torn down and rebuilt. By contrast, names like Coty and Cartier seem to Lorelei far more reliable, representing values that are as enduring as diamonds – just so long as you check that they aren't made out of paste.

It's tempting to read the passage through Lorelei's eyes and concentrate only on these names. Actually, as is often the case in a literary work, and as we've already seen in earlier chapters, the really important words turn out to be the far less glamorous ones that are doing much of the heavy lifting behind the scenes. For example, many sentences begin with the conjunction 'So', which is both a careless speech tic from Lorelei and a carefully weighted clue from Anita Loos about the kind of story we are in. It is a comedy in which every event is helping to move the main characters towards a happy ending, and a fictional world in which not only 'everything always turns out for the best', as

Lorelei tells us, but 'the best' also turns out to mean 'the most lucrative' – hence her realisation, while anticipating her marriage to an American millionaire at the end of the novel, that 'American gentlemen are the best after all'.

Why does *Gentlemen Prefer Blondes* have this structure? From one angle Lorelei is a 'Professional Lady', as she is described in the subtitle to the novel: a sexual predator who charms men like a modern mermaid. Yet from another she is a wide-eyed innocent moving through the moral confusion of the modern world: a figure with simple (though expensive) tastes whose buoyancy of mood guarantees that in any situation she will find herself bobbing to the surface. (The fact that she is accompanied by a character called Dorothy supports this idea, because although her friend's taste for waspish one-liners is reminiscent of Dorothy Parker, whose wit was already starting to make her famous at the time this novel was published, her name also calls to mind the heroine of *The Wizard of Oz*.) Put another way, she is a female equivalent of contemporary entertainers like Charlie Chaplin, whose film *The Gold Rush* was released in the same year as *Gentlemen Prefer Blondes* and depicted a very similar mood. In one scene Chaplin's tramp character finds himself with nothing to eat but a boiled leather shoe, yet still manages to turn this moment of adversity into one of improvised comedy, as he fillets the shoe like a fish, then twirls the laces onto his fork like spaghetti, and finally sucks a nail clean before trying to crack it like a wishbone. It is a magnificent demonstration of what the philosopher Hegel had earlier described as the comedian's 'absolute freedom of spirit' that allows him to move through life magically untouched by disaster. Lorelei too seems to be possessed by this 'comic spirit', which according to Hegel 'declares that the objective world is really nothing but the subjective world we create for ourselves'. She may be a siren, but she is also a clown.

This is why her mistaking of 'worlds' for 'words' when she gazes at rich women drinking in the Ritz bar ('it is beyond worlds') is so significant. For although Lorelei sees some things as fixed and certain – champagne cocktails, expensive perfumes, diamonds – others are endlessly capable of being reshaped, and this is a type of behaviour that is especially characteristic of comedy.

In its simplest form we see it in cartoons where Wile E. Coyote paints a tunnel entrance onto the side of a mountain before Road Runner dashes through it with a triumphant 'meep meep'. More complicated examples include Shakespeare's comedies such as *Twelfth Night* or *As You Like It*, where many different forms of desire are explored and the scripts are so full of puns and gags that for the duration of the play language itself appears to have gone on holiday. At the end of these comedies most of their characters have to return to the real world, and so do we, but for a few hours we enter an alternative world where language creates reality and it seems that anything is possible.

Something similar happens when we open a novel like *Gentlemen Prefer Blondes* and find ourselves in a fictional setting where names sometimes refer to what already exists, like a Cartier watch or a bottle of Coty perfume, but just as often reflect Lorelei's ability to reinvent her surroundings – just as she has reinvented herself – through the words she uses. Later we understand that we will have to go back to a world where attractive young women do not always achieve a siren-like hold over wealthy older men, and if they do it should not necessarily be thought of as a happy ending. But for a couple of hours we can enjoy the spectacle of Lorelei visiting places like the 'Eyefull Tower' (the Eiffel Tower: quite an eyeful) or 'Versigh' (the Palace of Versailles: beautiful enough to make anyone sigh), as she bends both language and the world until they fit the shape of her desires.

Chapter 11

My Family and Other Animals

WHEN LORELEI AND DOROTHY return to the Ritz to unpack their luggage, they meet a 'delightful waiter who brought us up some delicious luncheons and who is called Leon'. He swiftly becomes 'our friend', Lorelei reports, reminding us of all the other waiters, shopkeepers and assorted background figures in *Gentlemen Prefer Blondes* who aren't even given the dignity of a name. Such anonymous characters draw our attention to the people we encounter all the time without us trying to imagine their hidden inner worlds. In my own life I could assemble a cast list most days that includes taxi drivers, shop assistants, students I only know on smiling terms, and anyone who kindly gives me a bit of extra room on the pavement as I shuffle towards them with my walking stick. And of course I am of no greater personal interest to them than they are to me. Regardless of how complicated or 'round' I consider my own character to be – and most of us think of ourselves as so round we are practically spherical – as far as most other people are concerned I am as flat as a pancake.

Yet one of the greatest things a literary work can do is show individuals emerging from the crowd. Dickens's novel *Little Dorrit* (1855–57) begins with an indiscriminate wide-angle view of London ('Nothing to see but streets, streets, streets') before zooming in to notice a figure named Arthur Clennam sitting quietly in a coffee house. Eventually, in the final sentence of the novel, the narrative zooms out again as Clennam and his new wife rejoin the world of their readers: 'They went quietly down into the roaring streets, inseparable and blessed; and as they passed along in sunshine and shade, the noisy and the eager, and the arrogant and the froward and the vain, fretted and chafed, and made their usual uproar.' In a brilliantly staged narrative dissolve, Dickens's characters sink back into their surroundings, like two swimmers disappearing beneath the busy waves, but only after he has reminded us that it is possible to create lasting and meaningful human relationships even in the anonymous swirl of the city. Usually books divide up the world for us into more and less important people. What novels like *Little Dorrit* do is ask us to think again about such crude distinctions, and to realise that we are also bound up with all the people we haven't met. Such stories expand our sense of social relevance.

Other writers go even further, by reminding us that it's not only people who can be literary characters. The same is true of animals, although getting inside an animal's head is more of a challenge than creating a fictional human being. One of the most frequently cited articles on the subject, by the American philosopher Thomas Nagel, 'What is it Like to Be a Bat?', concludes that although it is possible to imagine what it would be like to fly, navigate by sonar, hang upside down and eat insects, that is not the same as having a bat's perspective on life, because our human consciousness is not capable of inhabiting such an alien form of experience. But although we cannot be sure what it is like to be an animal, that does not prevent us from imagining it, once again replacing the *is* of empirical knowledge with the *as* of fictional understanding.

Most literary animals are seen only in passing, like the dog Laska that goes hunting with its owner Levin in Leo Tolstoy's *Anna Karenina* (1875–77), briefly allowing us into its thought processes as it obeys a command to go and fetch a snipe, although as it hasn't yet spotted its prey it doubtfully wonders why: ' "But I can't go," thought Laska. "Where will I go? I can smell them from here, but if I move forward I won't have any idea where or who they are . . . Well, if he wants it so badly, I'll do it, but I'm not responsible for myself now anymore." ' Alternatively, animals may be used as a rich source of metaphors: the critic William Empson once pointed out that 'dog' has been used to represent many ideas that aren't directly linked to being an animal with four paws and a tail, including as a way of describing human beings as sycophants, underdogs and so on, and it is therefore a word of 'very mixed feelings'. Not least, animals may be written about as animals, with the central aim of imagining how the world might be perceived through physical senses that are far more sensitive than those of the author or their readers.

By the time Virginia Woolf published *Flush* in 1933, there had already been several attempts to assess the human world from a dog's perspective, including Francis Coventry's *The History of Pompey the Little* (1751), which followed the adventures of a Georgian lapdog, turning him into an unblinking witness to the riotous and ridiculous antics of the social world he pads through. This history of fictional dogs may be one reason for the literary self-consciousness of Woolf's novel. *Flush* begins with an allusion to *Pride and Prejudice* ('It is universally admitted . . . ', she writes, echoing 'It is a truth universally acknowledged . . . ') and then takes Austen's use of free indirect style a stage further, by putting the main narrative consciousness inside the mind of a spaniel.

Let's look more closely at how she does this. On a first reading, *Flush* seems to be as simple as a story written for a child, or possibly even a story written by one. Flush has been bought for the reclusive Victorian poet Elizabeth Barrett, and after spending

part of the summer cooped up in his owner's bedroom, one day
he is finally taken for a walk:

The carriage was ordered; Miss Barrett rose from her sofa;
veiled and muffled, she descended the stairs. Flush of course
went with her. He leapt into the carriage by her side. Couched
on her lap, the whole pomp of London at its most splen-
did burst on his astonished eyes. They drove along Oxford
Street. He saw houses made almost entirely of glass. He saw
windows laced across with glittering streamers; heaped with
gleaming mounds of pink, purple, yellow, rose. The carriage
stopped. He entered mysterious arcades filmed with clouds
and webs of tinted gauze. A million airs from China, from
Arabia, wafted their frail incense into the remotest fibres of
his senses. Swiftly over the counters flashed yards of gleaming
silk; more darkly, more slowly rolled the ponderous bomba-
zine. Scissors snipped; coins sparkled. Paper was folded; string
tied. What with nodding plumes, waving streamers, tossing
horses, yellow liveries, passing faces, leaping, dancing up,
down, Flush, satiated with the multiplicity of his sensations,
slept, drowsed, dreamt and knew no more until he was lifted
out of the carriage and the door of Wimpole Street shut on
him again.

And next day, as the fine weather continued, Miss Barrett
ventured upon an even more daring exploit—she had herself
drawn up Wimpole Street in a bath-chair. Again Flush went
with her. For the first time he heard his nails click upon the
hard paving-stones of London. For the first time the whole
battery of a London street on a hot summer's day assaulted his
nostrils. He smelt the swooning smells that lie in the gutters;
the bitter smells that corrode iron railings; the fuming, heady
smells that rise from basements—smells more complex, corrupt, violently contrasted and compounded than any he had

smelt in the fields near Reading; smells that lay far beyond the range of the human nose; so that while the chair went on, he stopped, amazed; defining, savouring, until a jerk at his collar dragged him on. And also, as he trotted up Wimpole Street behind Miss Barrett's chair he was dazed by the passage of human bodies. Petticoats swished at his head; trousers brushed his flanks; sometimes a wheel whizzed an inch from his nose; the wind of destruction roared in his ears and fanned the feathers of his paws as a van passed.

If the specificity of this description draws our attention to Woolf's pouncing eye for detail, it also reflects her more general fascination with animals. When she was growing up, her family enjoyed giving each other animal nicknames, with Virginia herself being Billy, or Goat, or Ape, and as an adult she frequently compared the people she met to animals, writing that Freud had 'a monkey's light eyes', W. H. Auden was a 'small rough haired terrier man', and Aldous Huxley a 'gigantic grasshopper'. When *Flush* was reviewed positively in the *New Statesman* she wrote to thank the critic responsible, signing herself 'Your affectionate old English springer spaniel Virginia'. Indeed, her nephew Quentin Bell commented that '*Flush* is not so much a book by a dog lover as a book by someone who would love to be a dog', as if the author of the novel secretly aspired to be Virginia Woof rather than Virginia Woolf, or possibly a Woolfhound.

Her pleasure in giving a delicately doggy perspective on life is evident throughout this passage. Here we are presented with the world we know, but in a way that makes it almost unrecognisable. Viewed from a point just a few inches above the ground, people are reduced to little more than petticoats and trousers, and the tumbling syntax of that final quoted sentence captures Flush's bewilderment at plunging into the city streets and not knowing what to look at next. But the emphasis here is not on

seeing but on smelling, because the 'swooning smells' of gutters, 'bitter smells' of corroded iron railings, and 'fuming, heady
smells' rising from basements are only tiny parts of what the
novel will later describe as 'the world of smell' in which Flush
lives.

This is very different to the way most human beings experience the world, which is why we are likely to be shocked when we
read in other contexts about characters whose nostrils similarly
twitch at every passing scent. For example, some of the creepiest
scenes in Thomas Harris's thriller *The Silence of the Lambs* (1988)
involve serial killer Hannibal 'the cannibal' Lecter undressing
FBI agent Clarice Starling not with his eyes but with his nose.
'You use Evyan skin cream, and sometimes you wear L'air du
Temps, but not today,' he tells her on their first encounter in
prison, and later he sniffs out a fresh Band-Aid hidden under her
trousers like a shark scenting a drop of blood in the ocean.

These moments when Starling realises that 'He could smell
everything' are disturbing, because Lecter's sensitive nose warns
the reader that it is possible to incorporate bits of other people
without eating them. Smells remind us that we cannot help
releasing small parts of ourselves into other people's bodies.
Wherever the air touches us, some part of us is airborne, so we
are forever leaving invisible vapour trails in our wake, ready to
be accidentally stumbled upon – or in Lecter's case, deliberately
snuffed up – by any nose that happens to be passing.

Perhaps understandably, this idea has provoked responses
that range from delight to disgust. They include Proust's childhood memories of lime-flower tea and warm bread, 'smells lazy
and punctual as a village clock', Swift's uneasily jocular description of 'the smell of young Men's Toes', Flaubert's erotic account
of inhaling the fragrance of his lover's slippers and mittens, and
Baudelaire's plunges into a world of smell until 'his soul soars
upon perfume as the souls of other men soar upon music'. All

this, despite the fact that writers might be tempted to shy away from a sense that is unusually resistant to language. Where our eyes might notice a flower as 'purple' or 'mauve' or 'indigo', its scent is far more likely to be described in relation to how it makes us feel: 'intoxicating', for example, or 'sickly'. For this reason, the repetitions in Woolf's writing of 'smells' and 'smelt' show how pervasive this sense is for Flush, but also how comparatively limited a vocabulary we have to capture it. If these smells lie 'far beyond the range of the human nose', they also seem to be largely beyond the range of human speech. We might further notice how adjectives are repurposed in descriptions like 'swooning' or 'fuming', and how other words start to edge into each other in sentences like the one that tries to capture 'smells more complex, corrupt, violently contrasted and compounded', as if trying to echo the rich brew of scents by forming a kind of linguistic melting pot.

Like the puns discussed in Chapter 4, the world of smell mixes up categories that human society usually tries to keep separate. Later in the novel, Flush is stolen and taken to the violent squalor of Whitechapel before Elizabeth Barrett pays a ransom and brings her dog back to her cosy bedroom in Wimpole Street. Later still they travel together to Italy alongside Elizabeth's new husband Robert Browning, and Elizabeth explores the world of spiritualism, convinced that there is an invisible realm where the dead live just as in the East End she 'had discovered a world that she had never dreamt of within half an hour's drive from Wimpole Street'. She is excited by the idea that there may be many other worlds hidden in the one we share. But for most readers this is something they will already have worked out with the help of Flush's nose. The smells that spread from the slums 'not a stone's throw from Wimpole Street' remind us that however hard a middle-class family might try to separate itself from the dirt and disease of the poor, the air they share is no respecter of social boundaries.

There is a comic echo of this idea in Craig Raine's poem 'A Martian Sends a Postcard Home', which describes an alien visitor viewing even the most humdrum aspects of life on earth with all the wonder of Adam casting his eyes on Eden for the first time:

> Only the young are allowed to suffer
> openly. Adults go to a punishment room
>
> with water but nothing to eat.
> They lock the door and suffer the noises
>
> alone. No one is exempt
> and everyone's pain has a different smell.

It takes us a minute to realise that what the Martian is describing here isn't a prison cell or a fully equipped dungeon, but a toilet. Ordinary domestic habits are made to seem as unusual as living in a zoo. What Woolf's writing shows us is that the same trick can be done by imagining life from the perspective of characters who are already inside our homes.

We have already seen that one of the most important things a literary work can do is help its reader step into a life or a voice that is different to their own. A novel like *Flush* takes this idea even further. We might compare it with some of the other ways we behave towards our pets, from dressing them up to putting them in *New Yorker* cartoons like the one that shows a dog as a psychiatrist telling his patient 'Well, *I* think you're wonderful.' Such actions treat animals as if they were small furry people rather than animals. By contrast, in *Flush* Woolf tries to see things from their point of view – although because we cannot know how a dog really thinks, any more than we can know what is going through a bat's mind when it is snapping up insects in mid-air, ultimately this is a novel that uses its narrative consciousness to offer a fresh perspective on the human world just as much as the non-human one. Indeed, although Woolf's novel is unusual in many ways, in this respect it is typical of several literary works we have considered so far.

In 1917, sixteen years before the publication of *Flush*, the Russian critic Viktor Shklovsky wrote an essay, 'Art as Technique' (sometimes translated as 'Art as Device'), that argued for many of the literary tactics Woolf would later put into practice. Most of the time we don't think too deeply about our experiences, Shklovsky points out, and the words we use are equally superficial. Often they group themselves into formulas that we draw on almost automatically, like feeding a coin into a machine. When we choose these words, we do so out of habit rather than because they perfectly match our intentions. Literature is different. Its aim 'is to impart the sensation of things as they are perceived and not as they are known', Shklovsky claims, and the main technique he suggests to achieve this aim is to write in such a way that common objects and experiences are made 'unfamiliar' and we can dwell on the materials – words, sentences, paragraphs – we usually try to turn into something else. Anyone can do this, but when a poet or a novelist describes the world they are more likely than most people to present it in an unusual way. (One of Shklovsky's examples is a short story by Tolstoy that is told from the perspective of a horse.) The result is a form of *defamiliarisation*, in Russian остранение or *ostranenie*, that encourages us to look at ordinary experiences as unexpectedly fresh and raw.

In previous chapters we have considered a number of passages that use the resources of writing to defamiliarise what they are describing – a technique that may not perfectly succeed in capturing these subjects, but does at least make the holes of the net slightly smaller. Woolf's novel offers an even clearer example of the same imaginative impulse. Like many of the literary examples we've encountered so far, it works its way beneath the surface of everyday life and discovers something new. And if the result is interesting to us, that may be because it helps to make us more interesting to ourselves.

How to Be Surprised

Chapter 12

KEEPING IT REAL

CHILDREN ARE PROBABLY MORE familiar than most adults with books that blend a human and an animal perspective. Classic works such as Kenneth Grahame's *The Wind in the Willows* (1908) and A. A. Milne's *Winnie-the-Pooh* (1926) rely on the fact that their animal characters not only talk but have acquired many of the other traits we think of as distinctly human, such as displays of swaggering boastfulness (Toad) or crushing depression (Eeyore), in addition to the possession of comfortable homes with armchairs and fireplaces. Sometimes this blending happens in a more extreme way, as is the case in American comic books where the main character has extraordinary natural powers (Spider-Man) or carefully honed skills (Batman) that reveal them to be an eye-catching hybrid of the human and non-human.

This isn't the only way such characters manage to blend two different identities in one body. Assembled between the ages of roughly eight and ten, the brightly coloured piles of Marvel and DC comic books in my bedroom testified to my fascination with the idea that the same people could be extraordinary in some ways yet wholly unremarkable in others, just as the thickly muscled Superman apparently only needed to cover up the scarlet

S on his chest and don a pair of thick-framed glasses in order to resume his identity as mild-mannered newspaper reporter Clark Kent.

What made these comics even more exciting were the promises given by their breathlessly written advertisements that some of a superhero's special powers were available to anyone with a bit of pocket money to spare. If I sent a few dollars to the manufacturers of 'X-Ray Specs', one advertisement claimed, I would be able to hold up my hand and see the bones hidden within, or even spy on the bodies of strangers underneath their clothes. ('Loads of laughs and fun at parties.') Send a few dollars more to the representatives of a flexing Charles Atlas, and in theory I would soon possess the sort of muscular physique that would make me a 'Real Man' and a 'HERO OF THE BEACH' – an especially tempting offer for someone whose experience of beach holidays so far had mostly consisted of making crumbly sandcastles and wearing a floppy sunhat.

The best advertisement of all appeared to take the ingredients of a modern science experiment and shake them together with those of a traditional fairy tale. For just $1.25 I was promised that I could 'Enter the WONDERFUL WORLD OF AMAZING LIVE SEA-MONKEYS', which were sold as 'the most adorable pets ever to bring smiles, laughter and fun into your home'. Next to a drawing of a wholesome all-American family clustered around a fish bowl, a close-up view of some sea-monkeys showed what I could expect: another family with bright pink skin and toothy grins, with only some spiny tails and a hint of scales to distinguish them from their owners. 'Because they are so full of tricks, you'll never tire of watching them', promised the advertisement, adding that sea-monkeys could be trained 'to obey your commands like a pack of friendly seals'.

When a school friend swallowed the advertiser's bait and sent off his postal order, he was disappointed a few weeks later to receive a packet of eggs that hatched into common brine shrimp rather than the humanoid fun-lovers he had been led to expect, but he probably shouldn't have been surprised. If he had read Charles Kingsley's *The Water-Babies* (1862–63), where young chimney sweep Tom is transformed into a darting underwater creature, he would already have been prepared for what can happen when reality and fantasy merge:

> Then sometimes he came to a deep still reach; and there he saw the water-forests. They would have looked to you only little weeds: but Tom, you must remember, was so little that everything looked a hundred times as big to him as it does to you, just as things do to a minnow, who sees and catches the little water-creatures which you can only see in a microscope.
>
> And in the water forest he saw the water-monkeys and water-squirrels (they all had six legs, though; everything almost has six legs in the water, except efts and water-babies); and nimbly enough they ran among the branches. There were water-flowers there too, in thousands; and Tom tried to pick them: but as soon as he touched them, they drew themselves in and turned into knots of jelly; and then Tom saw that they were all alive – bells, and stars, and wheels, and flowers, of all beautiful shapes and colours; and all alive and busy, just as Tom was. So now he found that there was a great deal more in the world than he had fancied at first sight.

That last sentence does more than tell us what Tom is starting to learn about his new underwater world. It also reminds us of one of the reasons many people continue to read as adults. Books too show us how much more there is in the world than we had fancied at first sight. Novels in particular have often been celebrated for helping us to understand the difference between what we see and what we notice, as we are encouraged by the writer to scrutinise small fragments of the world we might previously have taken for granted. Such works seize on the idea that nothing is beneath our attention if it is examined with a truly open mind; they celebrate what John Updike once described as the writer's task 'to give the mundane its beautiful due'.

Of course, it isn't possible for a writer to pay equally careful attention to everything. As I've already pointed out, any act of writing involves grasping some details and letting others go; selection requires rejection. What a writer like George Eliot does is to combine these details in two different ways. She recreates the ordinary textures of life as they are gradually revealed to us, and at the same time she uses her narratives to rearrange them into meaningful patterns. This technique is usually described as realism, and few writers are as clear-sighted as Eliot in showing us how it works – and also why it matters.

Eliot was far from radical in her political opinions, believing that human development came about through slow and gradual change rather than armed struggle. Although she had been fired up by the European revolutions of 1848, within a few years she had become politically much more cautious, writing in one letter that 'the bent of my mind is conservative rather than destructive'. She was even worried about giving urban working-class men the vote, fearing that without a decent moral education they might degenerate into a lawless mob like the one she had witnessed as a girl during the 1832 general election, when she had watched from her school window in Nuneaton as Tories and Radicals fought in the streets. Yet however complicated her feelings were about political reform, she was undoubtedly a democrat when it came to her writing. And that's because she found everything potentially interesting.

In a celebrated passage in her first novel *Adam Bede* (1859) she breaks off the narrative to offer what is in effect a manifesto for a new kind of realism, as she praises artists who do not restrict themselves to drawing angels or other ideal forms:

All honour and reverence to the divine beauty of form! Let us cultivate it to the utmost in men, women, and children – in our gardens and in our houses. But let us love that other beauty too, which lies in no secret of proportion, but in the secret of deep human sympathy. Paint us an angel, if you can, with a floating violet robe, and a face paled by the celestial light; paint us yet oftener a Madonna, turning her mild face upward and opening her arms to welcome the divine glory; but do not impose on us any aesthetic rules which shall banish from the region of Art those old women scraping carrots with their work-worn hands, those heavy clowns taking holiday in a dingy pot-house, those rounded backs and stupid weather-beaten faces that have bent over the spade and done the rough work of the world – those homes with their tin pans, their brown pitchers, their rough curs, and their clusters of onions. In this world there are so many of these common coarse people, who have no picturesque sentimental wretchedness! It is so needful we should remember their existence, else we may happen to leave them quite out of our religion and philosophy and frame lofty theories which only fit a world of extremes. Therefore, let Art always remind us of them; therefore let us always have men ready to give the loving pains of a life to the faithful representing of commonplace things – men who see beauty in these commonplace things, and delight in showing how kindly the light of heaven falls on them. There are few prophets in the world; few sublimely beautiful women; few heroes. I can't afford to give all my love and reverence to such rarities: I want a great deal of those feelings for my every-day fellow-men, especially for the few in the foreground of the great multitude, whose faces I know, whose hands I touch, for whom I have to make way with kindly courtesy.

Eliot goes on to apply this moral to one of her minor characters, a rector who is good but far from faultless: 'And so I come back to Mr Irwine, with whom I desire you to be in perfect charity, far as he may be from satisfying your demands on the clerical character.' Her conclusion is that we should be as sensitive to the lives of ordinary people as we are to the regular surfaces of life, and we should remind ourselves that such categories are the result of our attitudes towards the world rather than unavoidably built into it.

The figures Eliot describes here who shouldn't be banished from art are taken from the sort of seventeenth-century Dutch paintings that attempted to depict life as it was, complete with gnarled peasants and knobbly vegetables, rather than life as we might wish it to be. And her ambition that writing should perform a similar role is more than theoretical. Throughout this passage, her narrator takes us by the hand and gives us a practical lesson in how to achieve the sort of sensitivity and patience she recommends. In particular, she describes 'commonplace things' in a way that might seem to glance over their surfaces, but situates them within a narrative structure that asks us to think about their wider importance.

For example, the mention of 'clusters of onions' provides the sort of detail we could easily ignore, but it is quietly significant given that there are two other references to onions in the novel. Earlier we have listened to Dinah preaching to a group of villagers and asking ' "how do we know [God] cares for us any more than we care for the worms and things in the garden, so as we rear our carrots and onions?" '; later we will read how Old Martin opens the farm gate when he sees his family approaching on their way to church, as 'he liked to feel that he was still useful – that there was a better crop of onions in the garden because he was by at the sowing'. It's easy to miss such narrative echoes, as we saw earlier when looking at the repetition of ordinary phrases such as 'it was' in Orwell's *Nineteen Eighty-Four*, but that's precisely the point Eliot is trying to make. Just as onions have layers hidden under their papery skins, so even a detail as seemingly insignificant as this can reverberate in a way that gives it extra richness and depth if examined closely.

Eliot models this idea for us through her use of repetition. In previous chapters we have seen some of the reasons an author may have for repeating themselves. Here the return to particular words and images works to catch our attention and encourage us to think again about what we have just read, as we are told about the faithful representation of 'commonplace things', and the hidden beauty of these 'commonplace things', and then discover that earlier we went past a reference to 'common coarse people' without a pause. On rereading the whole passage, we might respond by acknowledging that 'common' can be a form of praise as well as abuse (common sense, common courtesy, the common good), just as a 'stupid' face may be one that is exhausted or numbed by overwork rather than simply foolish. And because terms like 'coarse' can be evaluative as well as neutrally descriptive, they are likely to reveal just as much about our own attitudes as they do about the people themselves. In this way, if we read the passage carefully, we start to realise that for a writer like Eliot the ordinary things in life are far more than just matter. They really matter.

Naturally this is rather different to how most of us get through an average day. Usually we divide the world up into more and less significant elements and attempt to respond to each with an appropriate level of attention, which is why we might scan through a long email from the office in a matter of seconds but spend much longer poring over a brief phone message from a lover. We also invest the material world with private meanings that are invisible to anyone else, from the engagement ring that was given to us at a favourite restaurant, to the mangy toy dinosaur with a missing eye that our son or daughter insists on sleeping with every night. For most people a cluster of onions wouldn't fall into this special category of objects.

Yet what a novel like *Adam Bede* does is to remind us that the same level of attention can be given to almost anything, and just as the objects themselves don't have to be remarkable, so the way we write about them doesn't have to involve an unusual narrative perspective like Virginia Woolf's Flush nosing around London. All it requires is the sort of care and patience that Eliot demonstrates in her fine-fingered prose. 'To do something very common, in my own way' writes Adrienne Rich in her 1970 poem 'A Valediction Forbidding Mourning'. Much the same is true of the way that a novelist like George Eliot writes about the material world. She adds an element of surprise to it by doing something very common, but in her own way.

Chapter 13

Making It New

GEORGE ELIOT'S SKILL AT singling out and scrutinising ordinary fragments of the world – even objects as unglamorous as onions – demonstrates something I have been suggesting is a central value of imaginative literature: its ability to make us look more closely at aspects of reality we might otherwise take for granted. As a result, we can add to our stock of experience while simultaneously recovering a form of lost innocence in the way we regard our surroundings. Reading becomes a way of rinsing our senses clean.

Although in earlier chapters we have seen this unusual degree of attentiveness being demonstrated by novelists such as Woolf and Eliot, for many years it was more often associated with poetry. Coleridge explained that his aim in *Lyrical Ballads*, the volume of poems he co-authored with Wordsworth in 1798, was to awaken 'the mind's attention from the lethargy of custom', and a few years later Shelley echoed the same language in arguing that poetry 'strips the veil of familiarity from the world' after it has been 'blunted by reiteration' and so 'creates anew the universe'.

If poetry can work to sharpen and deepen our vision of life, it can also invite us to pay just as careful attention to its own way of going about things. In a good poem, even the most commonplace words can be rotated on the page so that unexpected facets of them catch the light. This is partly a result of the fact that most literary works don't make use of any special materials. Exactly the same words can be found in the greatest literature as in the most ordinary conversations. Think of famous fictional opening sentences like Ford Madox Ford's 'This is the saddest story I have ever heard' (*The Good Soldier*) or Herman Melville's 'Call me Ishmael' (*Moby-Dick*). In one case we are presented with something that sounds like a piece of gossip, and in the other a snatch of conversation we might overhear in a bar. Neither is particularly 'literary' in the sense of writing that is aesthetically rich or intellectually challenging. Yet in each case the author turns a simple sentence into the first piece in a complex narrative puzzle that will be slotted together over the pages that follow, and so rescues it from the inconsequential chatter of daily life. Ordinary language is transformed into something rich and strange.

Ezra Pound famously urged writers to break with tradition: 'Make it New', he trumpeted in a collection of essays he published in 1934. Although his slogan is usually viewed as a call for innovation, it could equally remind us of how much writing depends on renovation – on adding a little extra friction to details that our eyes usually slide over. For example, in Chapter 10, I suggested that in many pieces of writing there are bits of grammatical scaffolding, such as conjunctions ('So . . . '), that we tend to ignore, particularly if our eyes are distracted by a writer's formal innovations or flashy metaphors. In a poem like Wendy Cope's 'The Orange', such unglamorous elements of style quietly and unobtrusively edge their way into the spotlight:

> At lunchtime I bought a huge orange –
> The size of it made us all laugh.

I peeled it and shared it with Robert and Dave –
They got quarters and I had a half.

And that orange, it made me so happy,
As ordinary things often do
Just lately. The shopping. A walk in the park.
This is peace and contentment. It's new.

The rest of the day was quite easy.
I did all the jobs on my list
And enjoyed them and had some time over.
I love you. I'm glad I exist.

Like many of Cope's earlier poems, which include a set of lim-
ericks based on T. S. Eliot's *The Waste Land* and a parody of
Ted Hughes's mythopoeic masterpiece *Crow* that ends ' "Who's
a pretty boy then?" Budgie cried', this starts off as a joke about
poetry. In particular, it draws on the claim that's often made
about there being no perfect rhyme for 'orange', so that although
the first line of the poem ends with 'orange', the word we might
expect to match up with it in line three turns out to be a comic
non sequitur: 'Dave'. This establishes a pattern for what follows,
as the second stanza again fails to land a rhyme between the first
and third lines, and even the second-and-fourth-line rhymes we
are given ('laugh'/'half', 'do'/'new') appear slightly wonky on the
page. Often rhymes rely on connections that are already established in our minds, such as the opposition of life and death that
we hear in 'womb'/'tomb' or 'breath'/'death', and then deepen
these grooves in the language with each new iteration. Cope's
rhymes here work rather differently, by offering us incomplete
verbal links to match the sort of activities she is describing: sharing an orange, going shopping and so on, which are sociable but
only up to a point. In fact, for most of the poem Cope's sentences

and stanzas work rather like the sections of an orange, capable of being teased apart while also working together as one. But then we arrive at 'list' and 'exist', the only full rhyme in all three stanzas, and at this point we finally realise what we've been reading.

It's a love poem.

This isn't just because in the final line the speaker explicitly says 'I love you', but because when we look back at the previous lines we understand that the same sentiment is written into the way she talks about everything else. For example, the earlier rhymes show how two things can be joined together in a way that makes each of them look slightly different, as if the speaker is gradually realising that being in love can feel a bit like finding a rhyme for yourself in the world. We also notice how she singles out perfectly ordinary events for special attention, like someone applying a highlighter pen to her diary and not knowing where to stop. But perhaps the most interesting way she turns her observations into a love poem is by focusing her attention not only on 'ordinary things' like shopping or a walk in the park, but also on ordinary words – the sort of language that in other circumstances would risk being rubbed smooth from overuse.

To take just one example, few words are as easy to skim over as 'and': William Empson once described it as 'perhaps the flattest, most general, and least coloured in the English language'. Grammatically you can use it to join anything to anything else, which is why it is such a powerful tool in nonsense poems such as Lewis Carroll's 'The Hunting of the Snark', where the Baker advises the other sailors on how to search for the elusive creature: 'You may hunt it with forks and hope . . . You may charm it with smiles and soap'. There is no logical connection between forks and hope, or smiles and soap, but in the hands of a nonsense poet like Carroll each 'and' briefly opens up a window into a world where such connections would be no more unusual than the friendship in Edward Lear's famous poem between an owl and a pussycat.

Wendy Cope also uses the word in a way that might make us think a bit more closely about the different fragments of experience she is describing. It is at the heart of the social connections of 'I peeled it and shared it' and the joke of 'They got quarters and I got a half'. It acts as a form of grammatical glue sticking together the values of 'peace and contentment', love of others and satisfaction with one's own lot. (This couldn't be more different to the sort of culinary bullying I discussed in Chapter 6.) Finally, it captures the bubbling enthusiasm of the speaker's 'And enjoyed them and had some time over', as if she has suddenly realised that being in love can feel like a permanent state of 'and', of one thing endlessly being added to another.

In a way all poems are love poems, because they are in love with the possibilities of language itself. But a poem like 'The Orange' goes a stage further. We have already seen that the Russian critic Viktor Shklovsky thought the key to writing a successful work of literature was to choose unusual language ('difficult, roughened, impeded') in order to make life 'unfamiliar' to the reader, as if they were encountering it for the first time. Many of the best poems extend this principle, by using ordinary language in unexpected ways. We see this in the work of poets like John Donne, who specialises in making outlandish comparisons that are gradually revealed to be intellectually plausible, if head-spinningly strange. (In 'The Flea' his speaker links a fleabite with the mingling of bodily fluids during sex; in 'A Valediction: Forbidding Mourning' he compares the souls of himself and his lover to a pair of compasses that are permanently joined together.) We also see it in 'The Orange'. In the previous chapter, we noticed how Eliot singles out ordinary objects such as onions for special attention, but here we might conclude that Cope does much the same thing with language. A poem like 'The Orange' uses perfectly ordinary words, but as we get closer to them they demand our full, careful consideration. And as a result we do more than share in the speaker's happiness. For a few moments we can imagine what it might be like to see everything in the world with a lover's greedy eyes.

Chapter 14

Foreground and Background

[Cheese grater. Playing cards. Banana. Sequins. Bottle of red nail polish. Paracetamol. Dark glasses. Feather. Ping pong ball. Packet of chewing gum. Pencil sharpener. Condom. Twix.]

SOMETIMES OBSTACLES TO THE SORT of ecstatic vision that were described in the last chapter are deliberately thrown in our way. In his quietly devastating short story 'Un coeur simple' ('A Simple Heart'), first published in 1877 in his collection *Trois contes* (*Three Tales*), Flaubert describes the stray knick-knacks collected by an elderly female servant named Félicité who has remained with the same family for decades. Her room has 'the simultaneous air of a chapel and a bazaar', Flaubert writes, and as he starts to list its contents – a box of shells from her nephew, one of her master's old coats, a little plush hat that used to be worn by the family's now dead daughter, artificial flowers, a picture discarded by her mistress – he encourages us to see it as both a reliquary of cherished memories and a lumber room full of junk. The same list also includes items such as a watering can, a balloon, a pair of shoes and a piece of blue soap in a broken saucer that are more mysterious. It's possible these objects carry around histories that are equally significant to their owner, but it's also possible they are included simply to add to the impression of narrative clutter, as Flaubert swells his sentences until a reader has the sensation of being inside Félicité's room – or even inside her head – and unsure what to look at next. It's a good example of what the critic Roland Barthes once described as literature's 'reality effect': the inclusion in a story of circumstantial details that are not necessary for the plot but are there to make the narrative seem more believable.

Usually print doesn't distinguish between more and less important details, for example by using different-sized fonts to show what looms largest in our understanding and what constitutes life's small print. However, it can reproduce the way we perceive the world, by focussing on what is central to our vision and relegating the rest to a sort of peripheral vagueness.

For example, towards the end of Virginia Woolf's 1928 novel *Orlando*, the sex-swapping hero(ine) decides to go for a drive. As the streets of London flash past, Orlando's attention is repeatedly grabbed by glimpses of the world outside their car. And as these mental snapshots start to accumulate, framed by the windscreen like a camera lens, Woolf's narrative tries to keep pace in sentences that have a suitably reduced attention span: 'Butchers stood at the door. Women almost had their heels sliced off. Amor Vin – that was over a porch . . . Applejohn and Applebed, Undert—. Nothing could be seen whole or read from start to finish.' Nothing apart from Woolf's sentences, we notice, which provide us with both the thrill of life breaking up into fragments and the reassurance of someone piecing it back together again.

Yet although a story is printed evenly across the page, some parts of it are still likely to be more important than others. Occasionally this is flagged in titles like *The Moonstone* or *The Picture of Dorian Gray*. But stories can also draw attention to key details by showing us how easily they can be missed. In Chapter 2 we saw that our attention as readers can be seized by individual words and phrases, and how easy it is to ignore such tiny elements in the narrative. That's why other stories some-times include a model reader in the work itself.

The most popular example of this figure is the literary detect-ive. This is someone who knows where and how to look; he or she understands what is worth our attention and what we can safely ignore. Perhaps most importantly, the literary detective shows us how a confusing world can be put into some kind of order. Regardless of how shapeless and uncertain life is, he or she seems reassuringly capable of tidying up even the messiest corners of it. There are countless examples to choose from: Her-cule Poirot, Miss Marple, Philip Marlowe, Jane Tennison, John Rebus, Jake Jackson . . . But no modern literary detective has ever captured the public imagination as successfully as Sher-lock Holmes, who featured in dozens of short stories written by Arthur Conan Doyle before the detective's fictional death in 'The Final Problem' (1893) and again after his literary resurrec-tion in 'The Adventure of the Empty House' (1903).

We might expect an author to write a story in roughly the same order in which we read it: first the beginning, then the middle, and finally the end. But according to a profile that a journalist published in the *Strand Magazine* in August 1892, Conan Doyle preferred to work in reverse: 'Dr Doyle invariably conceives the end of his story first, and writes up to it. He gets the climax and his art lies in the ingenious way in which he con-ceals it from his readers.' As a result, his stories are like crossword puzzles in which most of the clues have been blanked out. And when we read each of these stories, Holmes is the figure who helps us to discover what has been hiding from us all along.

'The Boscombe Valley Mystery' (1891) provides a helpful step-by-step guide to his sleuthing methods. Near the start of the story, which as usual is narrated by his loyal sidekick and inter-locuter Dr Watson, we learn that Australian expatriate Charles McCarthy was found dead near a pool in Hertfordshire where he was due to meet someone, and his son James has been accused of his murder. Having visited the scene and closely inspected a set of footprints, Holmes quickly deduces that James McCarthy is innocent. It is a conclusion 'founded upon the observance of trifles', he explains, and Watson wants to know more:

'His height I know that you might roughly judge from the length of his stride. His boots, too, might be told from their traces.'

'Yes, they were peculiar boots.'

'But his lameness?'

'The impression of his right foot was always less distinct than his left. He put less weight upon it. Why? Because he limped – he was lame.'

'But his left-handedness.'

'You were yourself struck by the nature of the injury as recorded by the surgeon at the inquest. The blow was struck from immediately behind, and yet was upon the left side. Now, how can that be unless it were by a left-handed man? He had stood behind that tree during the interview between the father and son. He had even smoked there. I found the ash of a cigar, which my special knowledge of tobacco ashes enabled me to pronounce as an Indian cigar. I have, as you know, devoted some attention to this, and written a little monograph on the ashes of 140 different varieties of pipe, cigar, and cigarette tobacco. Having found the ash, I then looked round and discovered the stump among the moss where he had tossed it. It was an Indian cigar, of the variety which are rolled in Rotterdam.'

'And the cigar-holder?'

'I could see that the end had not been in his mouth. Therefore he used a holder. The tip had been cut off, not bitten off, but the cut was not a clean one, so I deduced a blunt pen-knife.'

'Holmes,' I said, 'you have drawn a net round this man from which he cannot escape, and you have saved an innocent human life as truly as if you had cut the cord which was hanging him. I see the direction in which all this points. The culprit is—'

'Mr John Turner,' cried the hotel waiter, opening the door of our sitting-room, and ushering in a visitor.

The man who entered was a strange and impressive figure. His slow, limping step and bowed shoulders gave the appearance of decrepitude, and yet his hard, deep-lined, craggy features, and his enormous limbs showed that he was possessed of unusual strength of body and of character. His tangled beard, grizzled hair, and outstanding, drooping eyebrows combined to give an air of dignity and power to his appearance, but his face was of an ashen white, while his lips and the corners of his nostrils were tinged with a shade of blue. It was clear to me at a glance that he was in the grip of some deadly and chronic disease.

In 'A Case of Identity', another Sherlock Holmes story published the previous month, Holmes tells Watson what he noticed about a client who has just left his Baker Street lodgings. 'You appeared to read a great deal upon her which was quite invisible to me', Watson sighs, and receives the cool reply 'Not invisible but unnoticed, Watson. You did not know where to look, and so you missed all that was important. I can never bring you to realise the importance of sleeves, the suggestiveness of thumbnails, or the great issues that may hang from a boot-lace.' Watson's inability to read people and events with Holmes's forensic skill reveals his main function in the story. He is there to act as our surrogate.

When we read a story like 'A Case of Identity', we too are encouraged to reconsider narrative details we hadn't previously paid enough attention to – not invisible but unnoticed – and assemble them into a coherent narrative. And as a result we too are shown how to look at the world more closely and selectively, turning ourselves into a whole army of Watsons in training.

So if we read 'The Boscombe Valley Mystery' like him, what do we observe? One striking feature of this passage is the number of references it contains to sight ('examination . . . observance . . . I could see . . . clear to me at a glance'), and this might encourage us to look again at Holmes's use of 'you see' slightly earlier in the story, as he explains that he had already rejected a number of possible suspects, telling Watson 'you see, I had narrowed the field down considerably'. When we first read this phrase we are likely to treat it as merely a piece of conversational filler, but in some ways it goes to the heart of detective fiction as a genre. Joseph Conrad once tried to explain what he was trying to achieve in his own novels by claiming that it was 'by the power of the written word, to make you hear, to make you feel – it is, before all, to make you *see*'. What detective fiction does is take this idea and put it at the heart of the reading experience. A character like Sherlock Holmes makes us see in the sense of using our eyes more carefully, and then he makes us see in the sense of acquiring a greater understanding of what we have just been reading. ('Oh, I *see*!') And here too Watson proves to be our representative in the story when he tells Holmes 'I see the direction in which all this points.' He has been shown how to see, and as a result he has learned how to *see*. Other words connected with this idea also start to fall into place ('trifling details . . . observance of trifles'), and the overall effect is to make it seem as if the world itself is slightly out of focus, requiring someone like Holmes to pull it back into line. Even the waiter appears to be in on the act, announcing John Turner's arrival at precisely the moment he is about to be revealed as the murderer. It all adds up.

Watson is certainly a good student. In his sketch of the 'strange and impressive' figure who now enters the room, he notices many of the physical traits Holmes had primed him to look out for, such as the man's limp and evidence of the strength required to smash in somebody's head with a rock. But he also quietly starts to make his own connections, such as one between a 'cut' cigar end and the fact that solving this puzzle has effectively 'cut the cord' of the hangman's noose, or the fact that a man who left 'ash' lying around also has an 'ashen' face, which for a medically trained observer like him produces the diagnosis of a 'deadly and chronic disease' – one that is 'clear to me at a glance'. Even after he has been given a tutorial in which of the suspected murderer's physical attributes are most significant – his lameness and left-handedness – Watson continues to add more of his own, such as the 'bowed shoulders', 'tangled beard', 'grizzled hair' and 'drooping eyebrows' he notices when the man arrives. He is now looking with keener eyes, noticing more. Or, put slightly differently, he is becoming a better reader.

'In a way – nobody sees a flower – really – it is so small,' Georgia O'Keeffe once pointed out, 'we haven't time – and to see takes time, like to have a friend takes time'. One of the pleasures of reading might be that it helps us learn how to take our time, not least by showing us how to switch between a wide-angle and a close-up lens when we use our own eyes. And no form of writing does this better than detective fiction.

You may have noticed a list at the start of this chapter, a bit like the game in which a tray containing various objects is shown to you for a few seconds and then taken away or covered with a tea towel, leaving you to attempt to list all the objects you can. How many do you remember?

If you're like most people, the answer is probably 'not many' unless you have just flicked back a few pages to check. You probably also didn't ask yourself what connection there was between them. (The answer to this question could be anything from 'A shopping list' to 'The ingredients of a good night out.') And of course that is precisely the luxury detective fiction provides us with. On an average day we are likely to find ourselves being overwhelmed by information, deluged by the non-stop data produced by everything from our own senses to the churn of social media, whereas a story like 'The Boscombe Valley Mystery' encourages us to sift life for significance. Occasionally, like Holmes's reminder about attaching importance to 'the observance of trifles', it might even contain some helpful advice on the best way to read it. In common with many of the other stories and poems we have considered so far, if we look closely we sometimes discover that the instructions come in the box.

Chapter 15

ATMOSPHERE

AS WE'VE ALREADY SEEN WHEN examining several different literary works, deciding which parts *are* significant isn't always a straightforward matter. Sometimes even the most anonymous background elements can help to establish a story's mood or generate crucial details of its plot. For example, in the original Sherlock Holmes tales, fog is a companion that is almost as reliable as trusty Dr Watson. There is the 'dense drizzly fog' of 'The Sign of the Four', the 'thick fog that rolled down between the lines of dun-coloured houses' of 'The Adventure of the Copper Beeches', the 'dim, fog-draped streets' of 'The Adventure of the Bruce-Partington Plans', and many other moments when Conan Doyle sets a scene by reaching into the gloom.

Today such descriptions conjure up a nostalgic vision of Victorian London that involves pale grey fingers wrapping themselves around lamp posts, and the muffled clop of horses' hooves on cobblestones. Yet for many years the reality of a London fog was far less romantic. It clogged your lungs and made your eyes smart; it turned the air into a murky kaleidoscope of colours (yellow, green, grey, blue) that appeared to be on the verge of turning into a solid. In a detective story it could also become a metaphor, forming a convenient piece of shorthand for a difficulty in seeing clearly that only a figure like Sherlock Holmes can correct. Sometimes this connection is made explicit: near the beginning of Conan Doyle's 'The Disappearance of Lady Frances Carfax', as details of the latest case are revealed, Watson tells us that 'the mystery began to define itself, as figures grow clearer with the lifting of a fog'.

By the 1960s, legislation such as the 1956 Clean Air Act meant that London's fogs were far more likely to be encountered in a piece of fiction than in the city itself. They could even be turned into a joke, like the can of 'Fresh London Fog' that was advertised in one American newspaper accompanied by a testimonial from 'a charming gentleman called Sir Foggy-Fogget'. Not foggy-forget, though, because even if fog had mostly disappeared from the city's skies it continued to linger in the cultural imagination. Today no film about Jack the Ripper would be complete without a swirl of sour London fog, even though most of the real Ripper's murders took place on clear nights. It's equally common in classic horror films like *The Wolf Man* (1941) or *Night of the Demon* (1957), where its presence not only conceals the threat that is about to be unleashed on an unsuspecting victim, but also reflects the viewer's sense of creeping dread.

Not all writers have approved of this use of the weather to generate a different type of atmosphere, whether this is the intellectual uncertainty of a detective story or the moral muddle of a thriller. In Volume 3 of his influential work of art criticism *Modern Painters* (1856), John Ruskin influentially coined the term 'pathetic fallacy' to describe the projection of human emotions onto the natural world, like Wordsworth's claim that the daffodils he saw 'Outdid the sparkling waves in glee' rather than him simply telling us that he felt gleeful when he observed them bobbing around in the breeze. Ruskin saw such descriptions as examples of 'emotional falseness', because they were the result of our perceptions being coloured by strong feelings, and were therefore not true to the physical facts. If a wind appears to sigh when we are unhappy, Ruskin argued, or an overcast sky strikes us as a projection of our darker feelings, this is 'the difference between the ordinary, proper, and true appearances of things to us; and the extraordinary, or false appearances, when we are under the influence of emotion, or contemplative fancy'. But he was fighting against one of the basic impulses of literature, which is that it is unusually hospitable to our moods. Even if it reminds us that we live in a world that is full of vast, incomprehensible forces, it works hard to make them meaningful in human terms.

Shakespeare was particularly keen on this idea, possibly because when his plays were performed at London's open-air Globe Theatre it wouldn't have been enough to hope that the real weather would match the action happening on stage. Instead it had to be created by hand, using stage machinery that included a thunder machine (a cannonball that was rolled from one end to the other of a wooden box balanced like a seesaw) and a swevel (a wire that was fixed from the roof to the floor of the stage so that a lit firecracker could be shot from the top to the bottom, creating sparks to imitate a flash of lightning). Such special effects turned the weather into a good metaphor for possible connections between a character's inner and outer worlds. When King Lear asks 'What is the cause of thunder?', for example, it is because he is starting to understand that the answer is more complicated than a purely meteorological one. He has just torn off his clothes on the heath, and as his understanding of the world breaks apart, so the external storm he is caught up in starts to mirror what he refers to as 'The tempest in my mind'. To Lear's increasingly mad eyes, the external weather and his own internal mood are becoming hard to tell apart.

This sort of overlap between our private feelings and the world we share with other people doesn't often happen in real life, so when it does it tends to feel significant. In Chapter 3 I mentioned the thunderstorm that drenched me and my nearly new boyfriend in Paris, and pointed out that it is firmly lodged in my memory as well as being captured in a photograph. Luckily neither of us attempted a toe-curling line like 'Is it raining? I hadn't noticed' from the 1994 film *Four Weddings and a Funeral*, which had been released a few years earlier, and not only because we couldn't help noticing. (A shirt that becomes see-through when wet is a lot less sexy when you're the one wearing it.) The weather really did seem to be doing its best to match our mood, as if it somehow knew that we were caught up in something much larger than ourselves.

However, such connections are far more common in literature, and not only in works by Edward 'It was a dark and stormy night' Bulwer-Lytton. The writings of the Brontë sisters are particularly soaked with references to rain clouds and storms, possibly because such natural phenomena didn't require much more than an observant eye to be conjured up on the page. The parsonage where they lived is situated at the top of the main street in Howarth, West Yorkshire, where it is surrounded on three sides by moorland and often exposed to severe winds and heavy rain. That makes it a dreamily romantic tourist destination to visit, although it could be a far more challenging place to live: a letter written by Charlotte Brontë to her friend Ellen Nussey in December 1846 tells her that 'the wind is as keen as a two-edged blade' and the whole family had suffered 'severe colds and coughs in consequence'. Yet the Brontë sisters also took considerable delight in wild, windy weather, and often it sparks some of their most powerful writing.

One of the narrative climaxes of Emily Brontë's novel *Wuthering Heights* (1847) occurs when a passionate Heathcliff rushes out onto the moors and a thunderstorm starts to rumble ominously overhead:

It *was* a very dark evening for summer: the clouds appeared inclined to thunder, and I said we had better all sit down;

the approaching rain would be certain to bring him home without further trouble. However, Catherine would not be persuaded into tranquillity. She kept wandering to and fro, from the gate to the door, in a state of agitation which permitted no repose, and at length took up a permanent situation on one side of the wall, near the road; where, heedless of my expostulations and the growling thunder, and the great drops that began to plash around her, she remained, calling at intervals, and then listening, and then crying outright. She beat Hareton, or any child, at a good, passionate fit of crying.

About midnight, while we still sat up, the storm came rattling over the Heights in full fury. There was a violent wind, as well as thunder, and either one or the other split a tree off at the corner of the building; a huge bough fell across the roof, and knocked down a portion of the east chimney-stack, sending a clatter of stones and soot into the kitchen fire. We thought a bolt had fallen in the middle of us; and Joseph swung onto his knees, beseeching the Lord to remember the patriarchs Noah and Lot; and, as in former times, spare the righteous, though He smote the ungodly. I felt some sentiment that it must be a judgement on us also. The Jonah, in my mind, was Mr Earnshaw; and I shook the handle of his den that I might ascertain if he were yet living. He replied audibly enough, in a fashion which made my companion vociferate, more clamorously than before, that a wide distinction might be drawn between saints like himself and sinners like his master. But, the uproar passed away in twenty minutes, leaving us all unharmed, excepting Cathy, who got thoroughly drenched for her obstinacy in refusing to take shelter, and standing bonnetless and shawlless to catch as much water as she could with her hair and clothes. She came in and lay down on the settle, all soaked as she was, turning her face to the back, and putting her hands before it.

'Well, Miss!' I exclaimed, touching her shoulder. 'You are not bent on getting your death, are you?[']

It's a reasonable question given how many other characters in this novel mysteriously sicken and die. Later we read that Heathcliff hears of Cathy's demise while his gaze is 'bent on the ground', as if he is already starting to think about being buried with her, and Cathy's refusal to come indoors is further evidence that she and Heathcliff remain bound to one another even when they are physically separated. But what most clearly links all the characters together in this passage is the weather.

This isn't very surprising in a novel that is, from its title onwards, as weather-obsessed as *Wuthering Heights*. Heathcliff in particular is often associated with bad weather, from the rain that 'began to drive through the moaning branches of the trees' soon after an early encounter with Cathy, to 'the rain driving straight in' his bedroom on the morning he is found dead. 'Wuthering Heights' is the name of Heathcliff's house, and we learn that 'Wuthering' is a provincial adjective that is 'descriptive of the atmospheric tumult to which its station is exposed in stormy weather'. (It is an especially well-chosen home for a character like Heathcliff, whose own name makes it sound as if he has grown directly out of the landscape.) What makes Brontë's fascination with the weather especially significant in her narrative is that it isn't always clear when storms or sunshine are being provided as realistic details, and when they seem to be part of a more symbolic environment. On the evening when Mr Earnshaw dies quietly in his fireside chair, we are told that 'A high wind blustered round the house, and roared in the chimney.' Similarly, the day after Cathy's funeral the weather appears to change so abruptly that 'the primroses and the crocuses were hidden under wintry drifts: the larks were silent, and the young leaves of the early trees smitten and blackened – And dreary, and chill, and dismal that morrow did creep over!' In each case it's hard to tell if we are being presented with realistic pieces of natural description or a suggestion that the non-human world has gone into mourning.

This pattern is especially concentrated in the passage that follows Heathcliff's exit. 'Storms' is a word that is applied equally to the weather and people's moods in *Wuthering Heights*, and the same is true of several other metaphors. At various points in the novel, Cathy's heart is 'clouded . . . in double darkness', Hareton grows 'black as a thunder-cloud', and Earnshaw is said to have 'blackened and scowled like a thunder-cloud', while Heathcliff often 'thunders' in speech. Even the 'great drops' that 'plash' around Cathy in this scene could be her tears as well as the rain, like a strange premonition of the moment in *Alice's Adventures in Wonderland* where Alice sheds 'gallons of tears' after she finishes off the cake labelled 'EAT ME'.

We don't know if Ruskin read *Wuthering Heights*, but if he did he is unlikely to have approved of a novel in which the pathetic fallacy is far more than just a stylistic tic. Instead it reflects a set of assumptions concerning the relationship of people to the natural world on which everything else rests. This is something Virginia Woolf noted in her essay on the Brontë sisters, where she pointed out that despite their love of nature neither Emily nor Charlotte were particularly accurate observers of it. 'They seized those aspects of the earth which were most akin to what they themselves felt or imputed to their characters,' Woolf writes, 'and so their storms, their moors, their lovely spaces of summer weather are not ornaments applied to decorate a dull page or display the writer's powers of observation – they carry on the emotion and light up the meaning of the book.' This is how they free life from its usual dependence on facts, Woolf concludes, by creating a style that merely by speaking of the moors can 'make the wind blow and the thunder roar'.

What Woolf doesn't say is that in passages like the one about Cathy getting drenched, the person speaking is supposed to be Brontë's narrator: the chatty, superstitious, not-perfectly-reliable housekeeper Nelly Dean. That partly accounts for the weight of attention she gives to powerful winds and torrential rain, because we know from elsewhere in the novel how obsessed Nelly is with the weather, including references to the 'fine summer morning' when Mr Earnshaw sets out on his sixty-mile walk to Liverpool, or 'the lovely afternoon that breathed as soft as summer' shortly before Linton discovers Heathcliff in his wife's bedroom. On both occasions the outcome is far from sunny – Mr Earnshaw returns with young Heathcliff as a 'dirty, ragged, black-haired child' bundled up in his coat; Cathy faints away after shrieking that she will die if Heathcliff leaves her again – allowing Nelly to use the weather as an ironic context for what is about to happen. Her recollection of Heathcliff's departure in the storm scene is more straightforward, as an emotional crisis with long-lasting aftershocks that is reflected in gathering clouds, but it too indicates that in a novel like *Wuthering Heights* we cannot simply treat the weather as a set of objective facts. This is a world where sunshine and rain involve more than literal warmth and wetness, and events in the outside world are not always separable from what is happening inside the characters.

In the previous chapter we saw that the literary detective lives in a world where everything is connected, and a novel like *Wuthering Heights* takes this idea a stage further. Here even the weather is linked to human experience, as emotions that are usually far harder to detect are projected onto the atmosphere – sighs and tears become storms and tempests – and made to appear as large as they feel. That can make it an unusually involving novel to read, because when we open *Wuthering Heights* we are not just encountering a fictional world that is sealed off like a glass snow globe. Rather we are conjuring up the windswept Yorkshire moors in our heads, and so bringing to life a place that exists both outside us and inside us.

The passage we've been looking at demonstrates how this aspect of reading can work in practice. Outside the house a storm is raging, while inside it the passions of the human characters are revealing themselves to be equally tempestuous. Throughout it all the narrator is doing her best to keep everything under control. But as we've already seen with a number of other literary examples, the more closely we look at this sort of writing, the leakier the boundary turns out to be between the real world and its fictional double.

How to Find Your
Way Around

Chapter 16

WANDERING AND WONDERING

I FIRST READ *WUTHERING HEIGHTS* as a restless nineteen-year old during a hot, sticky summer spent working in a Soho bookshop. It was an old-fashioned place that specialised in European literature, although every day I walked past many shops catering to less highbrow tastes. They weren't hard to spot, with their red neon signs promising 'SEX SEX SEX' and plastic strip curtains through which drifted the mingled scents of cheap aftershave and bleach. There was an even greater contrast between the events I was reading about in Brontë's novel and my own situation that summer, as I sat in the staff tearoom distractedly eating cheese and pickle sandwiches while on the page violent thunderstorms crackled and howled. On reflection, that was probably why *Wuthering Heights* appealed to me so strongly at the time. A shy and gawky teenager, I was certainly no Heathcliff, but it made for a nice holiday from work – and I suppose also from myself – to take on his personality for an hour or so each day, treating every page I read as a trapdoor that led directly from modern London onto the nineteenth-century Yorkshire moors.

Many readers experience something similar when they open a favourite story, because books can transport us in time and space. Some of these journeys are possible (such as the sprawling

American road trip that Humbert Humbert undertakes with Lolita), some are impossible (such as Edward Lear's nonsense poem about the Jumblies going to sea in a sieve), and many more occupy a hazy middle ground between the two (such as *The Hitchhiker's Guide to the Galaxy*, the title of which makes interstellar travel sound as straightforward as thumbing a lift to Brighton). What links these examples together is the fact that, as I pointed out in the Prologue, reading allows us to travel great distances in the company of other people with just a few tiny movements of our eyes across the page.

First published in 2002, Jan Morris's *Trieste and the Meaning of Nowhere* weaves a haunting set of reflections on this idea. Tucked away at the top right-hand corner of the Adriatic Sea, Trieste is an Italian port that is largely unknown to those who haven't been there, and it remains fairly mysterious even to those who have. Morris begins by admitting that it lacks many of the attractions we might expect from a great city. Why should anyone want to visit Trieste? 'It offers no unforgettable landmark, no universally familiar melody, no unmistakable cuisine, hardly a single native name that everyone knows.' Yet every year it attracts thousands of tourists who want to follow in the footsteps of famous authors like James Joyce, who scratched out a living here as an English teacher while writing *A Portrait of the Artist as a Young Man*, *Exiles* and most of *Dubliners*, or the distinguished Victorian orientalist Richard Burton, who completed his landmark translation of the *Thousand and One Nights* in a large apartment near the railway station, while also assembling an impressive collection of erotica and less easily categorisable works such as *A History of Farting*. (Joyce would probably have appreciated the last of these books; when he attended the Trieste opera he reported that he sat among the 'sour reek of armpits' and 'phosphorescent farts' in the cheap seats of the upper balcony.) Now Morris invites us to accompany her on a different kind of tour:

The outskirts of the city are shabby, drab and colourless, the downtown centre is sombre. Statues, fountains and frescos are everywhere, but in the gathering dusk all seems monochrome. Heavy arcaded streets lurch in parallel past our windows, with pompous palaces of plutocracy one after the other, a Gothically steepled church here, a stately railway station there. The General Post Office is enormous. The Banca d'Italia is immense. The Palace of Justice is foreboding. Steep stone staircases link one street with another. A tunnel inexplicably disappears into a hillside. What looks like a prison is only an old dock warehouse. What is surely the Prefect's Palace is a branch office of an insurance company. Paul Theroux, recording his impressions of Trieste in 1995, employed the adjectives serious, gloomy, dull, solemn and lugubrious. To me Trieste on an evening of the fall suggests the work of those English Victorian painters who specialized in seaports at the end of the day, with pale gaslight shining on wet twilight pavements and pub windows dimly illuminated. Also at such twilight moments I find it easy to imagine a Trieste handed over to the authority of some now defunct People's Republic, as it so nearly was in 1945, to be recreated swart, suspicious and smelling of sausages.

That final sentence confirms Trieste's identity as 'a city of the world' by deploying a suitably cosmopolitan vocabulary, bringing together words from Old English ('swart'), Latin ('suspicious'), Old German ('smelling'), and one ('sausages') that appears in closely related forms in French, Italian, Portuguese and Spanish, like the linguistic equivalent of a sausage's own mysterious innards. Yet although the rest of Morris's book provides us with plenty of equally vivid details, this passage goes far beyond a regular guidebook sketch.

Choosing to examine Trieste in twilight suggests the desire

to capture a mood as well as a time of day, which is appropriate for a book that involves the author returning in old age to a place she first visited as James Morris nearly fifty years earlier, before becoming one of the first people to undergo gender reassignment surgery. Ever since her original visit, she acknowledges, 'this city has curiously haunted me', which is probably an appropriate reaction to a place that seems so haunted by its own past.

If twilight has a dominant mood it is elegiac: that mysterious period between day and night when shadows start to lengthen and the past appears to be on the prowl. This makes it an especially suitable time to wander through the streets of Trieste, once a glittering cosmopolitan seaport in the days of the Austro-Hungarian Empire, and now a place that lives chiefly on the memories of its former glory, like a bankrupt businessman in a shabby suit. Twilight is also traditionally viewed as a time of uncertainty, and that is carried over into Morris's stuttering syntax in this passage, as she tries to list some of the architectural highlights of the city but repeatedly runs into narrative cul-de-sacs: 'Steep stone staircases link one street with another. A tunnel inexplicably disappears into a hillside.' A few paragraphs later she will point out that the city is built on a grid pattern, and here she also draws our attention to Trieste's 'parallel' streets, but her own mind likes to make more unusual connections. She has already warned us earlier in the chapter that 'you can *drift* through this place, thinking about something else, as easily as anywhere in Europe' (her emphasis), and her writing responds by producing its own form of syntactic drift – easily distracted and repeatedly letting its focus slide from one thing to another.

This elusiveness is reflected in the tiniest details of Morris's writing. In the chosen passage, we notice how she mostly sticks to straightforward declarative sentences involving a noun and a defining adjective ('the X is Y') that organise the city into neat categories: 'The General Post Office is enormous', and so on. But this grammatical pattern quickly starts to break down, and instead the same formula is used to draw our attention to odd architectural disguises: 'What looks like a prison is only an old dock warehouse. What is surely the Prefect's Palace is a branch office of an insurance company.' Even her adjectives aren't altogether straightforward, as they tangle together simple facts about the city's buildings ('The Banca d'Italia is immense') with reflections on how these places make her feel ('The Palace of Justice is foreboding').

Occasionally Morris uses other tricks of narrative to suggest unexpected patterns in the city, such as the alliterative rattle of 'Pompous palaces of plutocracy'. But all the time her own presence as an observer is unavoidable. As she tries to make sense of a place that her book begins by describing as 'half-real, half-imagined', the result is a curious narrative hybrid: a guidebook that seems to have become mixed up with a writer's diary, a neutral overview of Trieste that can't quite be separated from one visitor's personal experience of it.

There may be something about a city – any city – that encourages this sort of narrative reshaping. In his 1974 book *Soft City*, the travel writer Jonathan Raban argues that 'Cities, unlike villages and small towns, are plastic by nature' and tend to be moulded in our own image. We do this not only in the buildings we choose to erect, such as church spires that point hopefully towards the sky, or terraces that are full of democratically identical houses, but also in our own minds. 'The city as we imagine it, the soft city of illusion, myth, aspiration, nightmare,' Raban concludes, 'is as real, maybe more real, than the hard city one can locate on maps in statistics, in monographs on urban sociology and demography and architecture.' It is why, in the passage we have been looking at, fellow travel writer Paul Theroux's adjectives – 'serious, gloomy, dull, solemn and lugubrious' – are all different from those chosen by Morris, further evidence that a city is forever being remade even in the eyes of its visitors.

Trieste isn't the only place that readers might come to think of as 'half-real, half-imagined'. Other writers have described many cities in similarly hybrid terms. Joyce's *Ulysses* (1922) is full of people who never existed and events that never happened, yet the novel is also studded with references to genuine shops, pubs, libraries, schools, churches, museums, Turkish baths, cemeteries and bookshops that are as accurately laid out as a map. (Joyce told Frank Budgen that he wanted his picture of Dublin to be so complete that 'if the city one day suddenly disappeared from the earth it could be reconstructed out of my book'.) Virginia Woolf, similarly, includes some memorable descriptions of London's landmarks in her fiction, such as Big Ben in *Mrs Dalloway* (1925) striking out on the half-hour 'as if a young man, strong, indifferent, inconsiderate, were swinging dumb-bells this way and that', yet in a 1905 essay on 'Literary Geography' she acknowledged that 'a writer's country is a territory within his own brain; and we run the risk of disillusionment if we try to turn such phantom cities into tangible brick and mortar'. Like Housman's Shropshire, which we visited briefly in Chapter 5, such fictional cities occupy a sort of borderland that exists somewhere between the real world and that of the writer's imagination.

We might think of this borderland as the peculiar province of literature. Usually we find ourselves limited to a single location: we are sitting in this living room, or that café, and nowhere else. Reading a travel book like *Trieste and the Meaning of Nowhere*, on the other hand, or a novel like *Ulysses* or *Mrs Dalloway*, allows us to be in two places at once. We are living in Oxford, or Liverpool, or Glasgow, and simultaneously in Morris's Trieste, or Joyce's Dublin, or Woolf's London. Our reading also performs an additional task. By introducing us to a place that is 'half-real, half-imagined', it makes us realise that although we cannot make our ceiling any higher or the view out of our window any better simply by thinking about it, this is still how we tend to treat our surroundings. Whenever we look at a mark on our living room wall and remember the party when it happened, or cook dinner while dreaming of a gleaming new oven, we are also living in a place that is half-real and half-imagined – another reason why reading may not only distract us from our lives but help to show us how we try to make sense of them every day.

Chapter 17

There's No Place Like Home

EVEN THE MOST WELL-TRAVELLED authors sometimes have a thing about home. Writing from America as his first reading tour drew to a close in 1842, Dickens admitted that he was 'FEVERED with anxiety for home', his letter generating an urgent crescendo of homesickness. 'Oh home – home – home – home – home – home – HOME!!!!!!!!!!!', he wrote, adding eleven exclamation marks like someone letting off a box of emergency flares. His fiction was particularly taken by the idea that human hearts and domestic hearths were intimately connected. Many of his novels involve the central character wandering around or getting lost before they are rewarded with a form of household happiness when they reach the final chapter – Mr Pickwick and Sam Weller comfortably settled in the rural idyll of Dingley Dell, Oliver Twist finally secure by the fireside of Mr Brownlow – where the door closes on them ('THE END') with a gentle thud. It's an equally common idea in quest narratives, from Odysseus's bloody return to Ithaca twenty years after the conclusion of the Trojan War, to Dorothy's happy homecoming at the end of *The Wizard of Oz*, as she clicks the heels of her ruby slippers and chants 'There's no place like home' as if it were a spell.

Going home isn't always as straightforward as it sounds.

When Pip opens a note in *Great Expectations* that tells him 'DON'T GO HOME', it is primarily a warning that his London lodgings are being watched in case the returned convict Magwitch turns up, although it also anticipates what will happen when he travels back to the Kent village where he was born. Too much has changed for it still to feel like the place he knew as a child; although he can return there physically, he will never be able to go home again.

But it isn't necessary to experience a sudden change in fortune like Pip to view one's home in a different light. Many children's stories play around with perfectly ordinary elements of domestic life, such as teatime in Judith Kerr's *The Tiger Who Came to Tea* (1968) or C. S. Lewis's *The Lion, the Witch and the Wardrobe* (1950), where Lucy is invited for tea by the mysterious faun Mr Tumnus, keeping child readers tethered to a familiar domestic routine while writing about it in a way that makes it seem as strange as eating upside down or using a sieve as a spoon.

Even writers who deal with the most humdrum household settings can do so in a way that invites us to look at them in a new way. Take Philip Larkin's poem 'Home Is So Sad':

> Home is so sad. It stays as it was left,
> Shaped to the comfort of the last to go
> As if to win them back. Instead, bereft
> Of anyone to please, it withers so,
> Having no heart to put aside the theft
>
> And turn again to what it started as,
> A joyous shot at how things ought to be,
> Long fallen wide. You can see how it was:
> Look at the pictures and the cutlery.
> The music in the piano stool. That vase.

Larkin's own home life was famously, deliberately dull. While he had fun in 'Poetry of Departures' describing the existence of a happy-go-lucky wanderer who 'chucked up everything | And just cleared off', and claimed that 'We all hate home | And having to be there', all the evidence indicates that he much preferred imagining a life swaggering the nut-strewn roads to doing anything that might bring it about. When he moved to take up a job as head librarian at the University of Hull, he was given temporary lodgings in a flat overlooking Pearson Park, and ended up staying there for eighteen years until the flat was sold and he grudgingly had to buy a home of his own. Interviewed eight years later for the *Paris Review*, he explained that in this ugly 1950s red brick house his life was as simple as he could make it: 'Work all day, cook, eat, wash up, telephone, hack writing, drink, television in the evenings. I almost never go out.' His daily routine hadn't essentially changed since he claimed in an earlier interview that 'I wouldn't mind seeing China if I could come back the same day . . . A novelist needs new scenes, new people, new themes. The Graham Greenes, the Somerset Maughams . . . travelling is necessary for them. I don't think it is for poets. The poet is really engaged in recreating the familiar; he's not committed to introducing the unfamiliar.'

There may have been an element of self-parody in these remarks – Larkin appears to have enjoyed playing the role of a literary Eeyore for interviewers, and there was usually the twitch of a smile hovering around his mouth – although it's certainly true that he spent most of his adult life trying to remain in the same grooves he had carefully worn away for himself over the years. Yet in a poem like 'Home Is So Sad' he takes just as much pleasure in jumping out of these grooves, like an old gramophone needle playing one of his favourite jazz records. To some extent the poem is an elegy for the life that drains out of any home after its residents depart, when all that remains is a handful of monuments to the dreams they once had. And yet, by putting his descriptions of simple objects like 'The music in the piano stool. That vase' into a poem, Larkin also introduces an element of the unfamiliar into the familiar. The line doesn't quite fit a traditional rhythmical template (our voice trips over 'the piano stool' and settles too heavily on 'That vase' for it to be a perfect example of iambic pentameter), just as the rhymes of 'vase', 'was' and 'as' don't quite match up, like the patterns on badly laid wallpaper. In effect, it is a poem that dramatises the gap between 'how things ought to be' and how they are by incorporating this misalignment into its own form.

Fiction can achieve similar effects by describing a character's home in a way that makes it seem both familiar and strange. Marilynne Robinson's 1981 novel *Housekeeping* provides several good examples. The plot centres on two orphan sisters, Ruth and Lucille, who are growing up in the small and isolated town of Fingerbone in the bleak American north-west. Abandoned by a succession of relatives, eventually they find themselves being looked after by their aunt Sylvie, an eccentric drifter who comes to stay in their house. Yet as the weeks and months tick by, it becomes increasingly clear to the sisters that Sylvie's understanding of how to run a home – which she does by hoarding old cans and newspapers, and allowing the dust and cobwebs to grow thickly around them – is very different to that of most adults.

Ruth describes one particular moment when this is revealed to them:

> We sat listening to the rasp of the knife as Sylvie buttered and stacked the toast, bumping our heels with a soft, slow rhythm against the legs of our chairs, staring through the warped and bubbled window at the brighter darkness. Then Lucille began to scratch fiercely at her arms and her knees. 'I must have got into something,' she said, and she stood up and pulled the

chain of the overhead light. The window went black and the cluttered kitchen leapt, so it seemed, into being, as remote from what had gone before as this world from the primal darkness. We saw that we ate from plates that came in detergent boxes and we drank from jelly glasses. (Sylvie had put her mother's china in boxes and stacked them in the corner by the stove – in case, she said, we should ever need it.) Lucille had startled us all, flooding the room so suddenly with light, exposing heaps of pots and dishes, the two cupboard doors which had come unhinged and were propped against the boxes of china. The tables and chairs and cupboards and doors had been painted a rich white, layer on layer, year after year, but now the last layer had ripened to the yellow of turning cream. Everywhere the paint was chipped and marred. A great shadow of soot loomed up the wall and across the ceiling above the stove, and the stove pipe and the cupboard tops were thickly felted with dust. Most dispiriting, perhaps, was the curtain on Lucille's side of the table, which had been half consumed by fire once when a birthday cake had been set too close to it. Sylvie had beaten out the flames with a back issue of *Good Housekeeping*, but she had never replaced the curtain. It had been my birthday, and the cake was a surprise, as were the pink orlon cardigan with the imitation seed pearls in the yoke and the ceramic kangaroo with the air fern in its pouch. Sylvie's pleasure in this event had been intense, and perhaps the curtain reminded her of it.

In the light we were startled and uncomfortable. Lucille yanked the chain again, so hard that the little bell at the end struck the ceiling, and then we sat uncomfortably in an exaggerated darkness.

Here the distinction between the familiar and unfamiliar becomes increasingly fragile, as Ruth's attention switches, under the harsh introduction of an electric light, from orderly stacks of toast to growing heaps of dirty crockery, peeling layers of paint and a thickening fuzz of dust. In this context, words like 'boxes' ('detergent boxes . . . boxes of china') look in two directions at once, because although in a different setting they could indicate an organised household, here they are just another example of Sylvie's hoarding tendencies. (Later on, Ruth explains that Sylvie appears to keep old cans and newspapers that are otherwise without any value because she considers 'accumulation to be the essence of housekeeping'.) Where for most homeowners a house is a place where precious memories can be stored in the form of objects like Larkin's pictures and vase, or the contents of Félicité's room discussed in Chapter 14, it seems that Sylvie's habits are instead a reflection of her life as a transient, where everything must be kept just in case it later proves to be useful.

Central to this passage is a tension between physical clutter and imaginative organisation. When Lucille pulls the chain of the overhead light, disrupting the 'slow, soft rhythm' of their daily routines, it dissolves the 'primal darkness' all around them like God creating a new world out of chaos. (The fact that Lucille's name comes from a Latin word meaning 'Light' makes this moment – an echo of the biblical 'Let there be light' – seem oddly symbolic.) Robinson further develops this idea by making key details both brute facts and metaphors. The overhead light and ringing bell also represent the sisters' sudden awareness of how unusual are their domestic arrangements, while the 'unhinged' cupboard doors offer a sly commentary on their aunt's odd behaviour.

The singed curtain is a particularly rich metaphor. Usually we would expect curtains to suggest the theatre, an artificial world that is more beautiful or impressive than reality, and drawing back the curtain to be a revelation of what has been going on behind the scenes, as when Dorothy's dog Toto pulls aside a green curtain in Oz to reveal that the terrifying Wizard is really just an old man pulling a few levers and barking orders into a microphone. Here the curtain reminds Ruth of her aunt's love of putting on a show, reflected in her choice of birthday presents that are also pretending to be something they're not (imitation pearls and a kangaroo with a fern in its pouch), but in its current burned and tattered state it draws just as much attention to itself.

Most importantly, switching on the overhead light creates a clear division of time into before and after. Before, the sisters were ignorant and perhaps more content; after, like Adam and Eve eating the apple in Eden, they know more and are correspondingly less satisfied. But the narrative voice can't be divided up this neatly, because Ruth, like Jane in the early chapters of *Jane Eyre*, is looking at things from two perspectives at once: from that of the child who experienced these events, and that of the adult who is now looking back at them. When Ruth remembers Sylvie stopping a kitchen fire with a copy of *Good Housekeeping* magazine, for example, she is turning that occasion into a joke, but also looking forward to the moment later in the novel when they will deliberately set fire to the house before escaping. As with some of the other examples of unreliable narration discussed in Chapter 8, a form of double vision is at work that makes us wonder how far the narrative is a straightforward account of what happened, and how far it is being filtered through Ruth's powers of hindsight. She has already warned us earlier in the novel that memories are by their nature as fragmented and arbitrary 'as glimpses one has at night through lighted windows'. The implication here is that they can pile up in our minds in a way that isn't very different to Sylvie's hoarding.

If we wanted a critical model for this sort of narrative effect, a good one can be found in Henry James's preface to his novel *The Portrait of a Lady* (1881), in which he points out that 'the house of fiction' has not one window but a million, each of which offers its own angle on life according to 'the need of the individual vision' and 'the pressure of the individual will'. He is reminding his readers that books give us any number of different homes to live in – homes that we can carry around with us, like a tortoise and its shell – each of which has a slightly different outlook on the world. Some of the novels we've already considered, such as *Emma* and *Adam Bede*, go further still, by inviting the reader to see events from the perspective of a centrally placed narrator but also that of many different characters. Such novels are 'dialogic', to use the term popularised by the Russian critic Mikhail Bakhtin, because they allow us to hear a range of voices bumping up against each other in the narrative, and so allow us to look out of several different windows in turn.

But in a novel like *Housekeeping* we are only given a single window to look through – that provided by the narrator – and for several chapters we are quietly, carefully warned that it may contain glass that is just as warped and bubbled as the one Ruth describes. (This is another example of writing that takes Orwell's claim about good prose being like a windowpane and gives it an unexpected twist.) Only when the electric light is switched on do we realise with a sense of shock that from now on it isn't only the sisters who will see their surroundings differently. Our understanding of what we are reading may also never be quite the same again.

Chapter 18

IMAGINARY WORLDS

SCIENCE FICTION IS A GENRE that works especially hard to make us more attentive to the world around us. In H. G. Wells's *The Time Machine* (1895), the time traveller describes how he journeys far into the future, surrounded by trees whose lives appear like 'puffs of vapour' and huge buildings that rise up and 'pass like dreams' as centuries come and go in seconds. Only when he pulls the lever to stop his machine spinning through time do we realise that it hasn't moved an inch in space. The workshop where it was built has been destroyed and replaced by a neat lawn surrounded by rhododendron bushes, but the time machine itself has remained in exactly the same place the traveller used to call home. It is an early warning from Wells that the future we are about to encounter will seem both familiar and unsettlingly strange.

In some ways *The Time Machine* is a literal version of the pattern we've already seen being repeated in a novel like George Orwell's *Nineteen Eighty-Four* – another literary work that twists the reader's surroundings around, in that case by imagining how current social and political trends might mutate. Such dystopian fantasies offer themselves as fictional thought experiments that Margaret Atwood has described as 'dark shadows cast by the present into the future'. Perhaps this is why so many writers are fascinated by the challenge of imagining the shape of things to come. In her essay 'Writing Utopia', Atwood points out that 'All fictions begin with the question *What if?*'A story represents an investigation into the limits of the possible, a glimpse of the unknown. And dystopian novels offer a nightmarish extension of the same basic principle: they are pieces of imaginary disaster planning.

Of the many possible enemies these stories have taken aim at – freedom of thought, freedom of expression, reproductive rights, and more – books themselves have proven to be an especially popular target. In Jules Verne's *Paris in the Twentieth Century* (1863), they have fallen into almost total cultural neglect, preserved only in the private, carefully concealed collections of those few who do not share the general passion for technological advancement, while in Ray Bradbury's *Fahrenheit 451* (1953) government-appointed 'firemen' burn any books they find, on the grounds that they might add unwelcome complexity and nuance to their owner's thoughts. Aldous Huxley's *Brave New World* (1932) is even more self-conscious in the way it describes one future while making a strong case for an alternative, as we meet a professional writer (or 'Emotional Engineer') who specialises in coming up with catchy slogans and hypnotic rhymes, but cannot quite repress the strange feeling that 'I've got something important to say and the power to say it – only I don't know what it is, and I can't make any use of the power. If there was some different way of writing . . . Or else something else to write about . . . ' A little glimmer of hope can be heard in that 'If' – another example of the *'What if?'* that Atwood sees as central to all fiction – almost as though Huxley was secretly hoping that the reader would conclude there already was such a literary work and its title was *Brave New World*.

Books are equally significant in Atwood's own dystopian fantasy *The Handmaid's Tale* (1985), which is set in a region of the near-future USA that has become a military dictatorship known as the Republic of Gilead. Here the childbearing women, known as 'Handmaids', are treated as property – the narrator's name is 'Offred', signalling the name of the man she originally belonged to – and they are forbidden to read or write, with the risk of having a hand cut off if they are caught breaking the law more than twice. The only official reading material permitted in Offred's room is 'a hard little cushion' with 'FAITH' picked out in needlepoint (tellingly, there is no sign of two more cushions bearing the legends 'HOPE' and 'CHARITY'), and she confesses to spending 'minutes, tens of minutes, running my eyes over the print', like someone being offered a thimbleful of water in a desert. In the house where she is forced to live with her 'Commander' and his wife, even the Bible is locked up, 'the way people once kept tea locked up, so the servants wouldn't steal it'.

When Offred is unexpectedly invited into the Commander's office, her eyes are greedily drawn to the bookcases crowding the walls: 'Books and books and books, right out in plain view, no locks, no boxes . . . It's an oasis of the forbidden.' In the weeks that follow, occasionally she is invited to return at night to play an equally forbidden game of Scrabble, fingering the glossy cardboard letters like a lover who is now permitted to do whatever she likes with the object of her desire. 'The feeling is voluptuous. This is freedom, an eyeblink of it. *Limp*, I spell. *Gorge*. What a luxury.' Then the Commander reaches into his desk and casually brings out a magazine for her to look at, which soon becomes part of a regular routine in which he lends her old copies of *Esquire* or *Reader's Digest*, and even a handful of novels, which she reads 'quickly, voraciously, almost skimming, trying to get as much into my head as possible before the next long starvation'.

During one of these sessions, Offred sees an opportunity to make sense of the only other reading material she has discovered in her room: a mysterious piece of graffiti that is scratched onto the floor of her wardrobe, and has begun to haunt her like a piece of code she cannot crack. The Commander asks her to write it down:

I've never held a pen or pencil, in this room, not even to add up the scores. Women can't add, he said once, jokingly. When I asked him what he meant, he said, For them, one and one and one and one don't make four.

What do they make? I said, expecting five or three.

Just one and one and one and one, he said.

But now he says, 'All right,' and thrusts his roller-tip pen across the desk at me almost defiantly, as if taking a dare. I look around for something to write on, and he hands me the score pad, a desk-top notepad with a little smile-button face printed at the top of the page. They still make those things.

I print the phrase carefully, copying it down from inside my head, from inside my closet. *Nolite te bastardes carborundorum*. Here, in this context, it's neither prayer nor command, but a sad graffiti, scrawled once, abandoned. The pen between my fingers is sensuous, alive almost, I can feel its power, the power of the words it contains. Pen Is Envy, Aunt Lydia would say, quoting another Centre motto, warning us away from such objects. And they were right, it is envy. Just holding it is envy. I envy the Commander his pen. It's one more thing I would like to steal.

The Commander takes the smile-button page from me and looks at it. Then he begins to laugh, and is he blushing? 'That's not real Latin,' he says. 'That's just a joke.'

'It's a joke?' I say, bewildered now. It can't be only a joke. Have I risked this, made a grab at knowledge, for a mere joke? 'What sort of a joke?'

'You know how schoolboys are,' he says. His laughter is nostalgic, I see now, the laughter of indulgence towards his former self. He gets up, crosses to the bookshelves, takes down a book from his trove; not the dictionary though. It's an old book, a textbook it looks like, dog-eared and inky. Before showing it to me he thumbs through it, contemplative, reminiscent; then, 'Here,' he says, laying it open on the desk in front of me.

What I see first is a picture: the Venus de Milo, in a black-and-white photo, with a moustache and a black brassiere and armpit hair drawn clumsily on her. On the opposite page is the Coliseum in Rome, labelled in English, and below a conjugation: *sum es est, sum us estis sunt*. 'There,' he says, pointing, and in the margin I see it, written in the same ink as the hair on the Venus. *Nolite te bastardes carborundorum.*

The final sentence is an example of 'Dog Latin', a hybrid of actual and made-up words (in real life 'carborundum' is another name for the chemical compound silicon carbide, a substance formerly used in coal mining), and its source is the phrase *Illegitimi non carborundum*, or 'Don't let the bastards grind you down'. Other phrases written in Dog Latin, once a popular source of humour in English public schools, include *Caesar adsum iam forte, Brutus aderat. Caesar sic in omnibus, Brutus sic in at* (Caesar had some jam for tea, Brutus had a rat. Caesar sick in omnibus, Brutus sick in hat) and *iti sapis potanda bigone* (it is a piss-pot and a big one). More recent examples include spells in the Harry Potter novels such as *Expelliarmus*, a 'Disarming Charm' that forces whatever an opponent is holding to fly out of their hand, and spoof names in the 1979 film *Monty Python's Life of Brian* such as Naughtius Maximus and Bigus Dickus. However, now that we learn it's a joke the Handmaid who previously occupied Offred's room was shown by the Commander, it's far from clear how we're supposed to read it. Is it a coded warning that the house is a place without secrets? Or evidence that dissent is still possible so long as it's kept hidden?

The other piece of Latin written in the Commander's book also poses awkward questions. The Latin conjugation *sum es est* (I am, you are, he or she is) is based on a straightforward grammatical template, but importantly, whoever wrote it down – presumably the Commander himself when he was younger – got the rest of it wrong. Following *sum es est* it should be *sumus* (we are) not *sum us*. The mistake harks back to the Commander's earlier comment about sums, when he glibly assumes that women can't do basic maths, and it also draws attention to a much bigger ideological fault line in Gilead. It's possible that the Commander's claim about women believing 'one and one and one and one don't make four' is an allusion to the White Queen in Lewis Carroll's *Through the Looking-Glass*, who asks Alice 'What's one and one and one and one and one and one and one and one and one and one', to which Alice sadly replies 'I don't know . . . I lost count.' Equally, it could allude to Winston being tortured into the belief that 2+2=5 in *Nineteen Eighty-Four*. Again, it reminds us that as a dystopia Gilead is not a complete fabrication but an exaggeration of the world that already exists. It's not that women can't count, it's that in this version of the future, where four digits are tattooed on each handmaid's ankle like a human barcode, they don't count – even as they are counted.

This isn't the only word game in the passage. If the Latin joke is one that the Commander recognises but Offred doesn't, 'Pen Is Envy' is a joke that we glimpse in passing (it is a blunted memory of 'penis envy', a notorious stage in Freud's theory of how girls are supposed to develop towards a healthy form of adult sexuality) but nobody else seems to notice. Later, Offred remembers how in the early days of this new political regime, when young women were being imprisoned and bullied into compliance by figures like the ruthless Aunt Lydia, someone scratched 'Aunt Lydia sucks' on a toilet cubicle wall. 'It was like a flag waved

from a hilltop in rebellion,' she explains. 'The mere idea of Aunt
Lydia doing such a thing was in itself heartening.' 'Pen Is Envy'
does something similar in the reader's eyes. It deflates the rulers
of Gilead and adds an element of linguistic play to a world that
is otherwise dominated by misery and terror.

Atwood goes on to describe some more public acts of resistance
carried out by an underground network known as the Mayday
movement, and since its original publication – with the extra cultural impetus provided by a long-running TV adaptation – her
novel has inspired a growing number of real-life protests, carried
out by people who see certain parallels between the authoritar-
ian politics of Gilead and their own situation. In 2020, a group
of women dressed in the Handmaids' blood-red cloaks and
crisp white bonnets, with their heads bowed and hands clasped,
appeared in the streets of Washington during Senate hearings to
confirm the conservative associate justice Amy Coney Barrett
as President Donald J. Trump's pick to fill a vacancy on the US
Supreme Court; by 2023, the same sight had become common
in Israel as part of anti-government demonstrations. But an even
greater act of resistance is already embodied in Atwood's narrative, because a passage like the one about Offred's conversation
with the Commander isn't just another cog in the machinery of
the plot. It's a model of the sanity-preserving values, including a
sense of humour and a sense of proportion (deep down they may
be the same thing), that those who run Gilead violently reject.

This is a more specific version of a literary tendency we identified in Chapter 8: the ability of a piece of writing to blur the line
between what *is* true and what we can imagine *as* true. Sometimes this can be an optimistic process: Seamus Heaney, whose
early poems grappled with the Troubles in Northern Ireland
with a remarkable combination of gravity and grace, has suggested that 'we go to poetry, we go to literature, to be forwarded
within ourselves', allowing us to rehearse a more generous, more

balanced approach to life before having to decide whether or not to embrace it in reality. But in the case of a novel like *The Handmaid's Tale*, when we project ourselves into this imaginary future, optimism is likely to be tempered by fear. Indeed, if a phrase like 'Pen Is Envy' waves a little flag of defiance in the face of Gilead's rulers, we might notice that it isn't surrounded by many other examples of comedy. Perhaps some things are simply too serious to joke about.

Chapter 19

Once Upon a Time

MOST READERS GROW UP with a different kind of story existing at a curious angle to the real world: fairy tales. In a 1956 newspaper article entitled 'Sometimes Fairy Stories May Say Best What's To Be Said', C. S. Lewis borrowed from the German Romantic writer Novalis to define the form of the fairy tale as 'a way of thinking up a way out', and extended it further to argue that 'A *true fairy tale* must also be a *prophetic account of things* – an ideal account – an absolutely necessary account. A true writer of fairy tales sees into the future.' And unlike dystopian stories, which tend to imagine a future that reflects the present rather like a carnival mirror, making some parts bulge out alarmingly while others shrink almost to nothing, this sort of 'prophetic account' allows readers to rehearse possible happy endings (the frog turns into a prince; Beauty marries the Beast) as well as manage various threats.

There may be sound psychological reasons for this sort of reading experience. According to the psychologist Bruno Bettelheim in his influential 1976 book *The Uses of Enchantment*, life can seem bewildering and even overwhelming to children, and if they are to learn how to cope with their feelings they may need a little help. This is where fairy tales come in: stories that deal with fantasies and conflicts that are 'unreal, but not untrue', as Bettelheim puts it. Because many of these stories involve cruel or gruesome events, he argues, they prepare children to cope with adult life by rehearsing danger while keeping it at a safe distance. They also allow children to make sense of their feelings about life's more ordinary challenges. Any child who feels unappreciated can read *Cinderella* and enjoy reassuring fantasies of revenge; if they want to acknowledge their fears about getting lost, they can read a story like *Babes in the Wood* and do so without ever having to leave their bedroom. This is how the child can 'bring his inner house into order', Bettelheim concludes, 'and on that basis be able to create order in his life'.

It's unclear how far this type of psychological adjustment has been modified by modern retellings of fairy tales that deliberately blunt their edges, a bit like the scissors designed for toddlers. For example, in the 1938 Disney cartoon version of *Snow White* the wicked Queen, disguised as a cackling hag, falls off a rocky ledge after it is hit by lightning, and is presumably crushed by the giant boulder she had been trying to roll onto the dwarves and their menagerie of helpful woodland creatures. But her death is never seen on screen; it is merely implied by the fact that the dwarves gaze open-mouthed as two watching vultures lazily start to circle downwards. (The Queen's death is equally invisible in Disney's read-along book, occurring in the turn of a page.) It's all very different to the Brothers Grimm version of the story, which ends with a detailed description of how a pair of iron shoes is put into burning coals, taken out with tongs and placed before the wicked Queen, who is then 'forced to step into the red-hot shoes and dance until she fell down dead'. That is the image that lingers in our minds after we close the book, rather than Snow White's happy ending.

But modern fairy tales can still play a significant role in helping readers – adults as well as children – make sense of their lives, not least by showing us some narrative alternatives to the stories many of us already find ourselves in.

Sometimes this involves giving familiar stories an unfamiliar twist. Angela Carter, whose updated fairy tales take background hints of sex and violence in traditional narratives like *Puss in Boots* and *Little Red Riding Hood* and gleefully thrust them into the foreground, said that she wanted to put new wine in old bottles so that they would explode. It isn't that there was anything intrinsically wrong with the stories everyone knew, but she wanted us to see her new versions as thought experiments that revealed how different life could be. As Carter wrote in a letter to her friend Robert Coover, 'I really do believe that a fiction absolutely self-conscious of itself as a different form of human experience than reality (that is, not a logbook of events) can help to transform reality itself.'

A more recent version of this ambition can be found working its way through Kelly Link's short story 'Prince Hat Underground' from her 2023 collection *White Cat, Black Dog*. Prince Hat is a 'boyishly handsome' fifty-four-year-old with a mysterious past who has lived with his husband Gary for over three decades. Then one day everything changes. While they are eating brunch at a restaurant with the teasing name of Folklore, they meet a young snub-nosed woman named Agnes who asks Gary, 'would you mind if I borrowed your Prince Hat for a little while?' Agnes and Prince Hat walk out of the restaurant and simply disappear. Several empty weeks pass, and eventually Gary decides to go in search of his husband. He visits a bar in Reykjavík, one of Prince Hat's old haunts, where the barman tells him that Prince Hat grew up among the fairies and now has been summoned back to marry the Queen of Hell. A talking snake leads Gary to the shore of a great subterranean lake, where a mangy grey cat is provided as a guide for the next stage of his journey. They walk across the encrusted surface of the lake, and when they reach the centre the crust splinters and Gary and the cat go plummeting down into the darkness, as birds with burning candles in their beaks swoop and soar around them:

> They fall for a long time, more and more of the birds appearing in the air until there is so much light from the candles the darkness is tamed. And then, suddenly, there is a vertiginous moment and Gary is standing beneath a tree on a suburban sidewalk that seems to extend forever. The cat plops down onto his shoulder. Though it is winter in the world above them, here it is the end of a long summer day. The air is velvety, singed, and the grass at his feet is purple and shadowed, the tip of each blade hiding its face.
>
> When Gary looks up, there is no sun in the sky, nor any sign of the subterranean lake. Instead, far above him in the violet dusk are the restless incandescent lines made by the birds and their candles. There are no people on the street. There are cars in the driveways, but Gary doesn't recognise the models or license plates. The trees, too, are strange in a way he cannot precisely identify. He reaches out to touch a leaf, then draws back. The leaf, covered in downy, angled teeth, has drawn a drop of blood. The tree bark, he sees, is semi-translucent, and underneath it rivulets of bright fluid chase upward.
>
> The cat jumps down onto the sidewalk.
>
> 'This is Hell?' Gary says. He sucks the drop of blood from his fingertip.
>
> 'Don't sound so disappointed,' the cat says.

Just as the couple at the heart of the story are a modern American man and someone who comes from the land of once upon a time and far away, so the underworld turns out to be a mixture of the suburban environment many readers will recognise, with its mixture of sidewalks, cars and trees, and more unusual elements such as leaves that can draw blood and semi-translucent tree bark.

At the start of the twentieth century, the German sociologist Max Weber influentially described the 'disenchantment' of modern Western culture, by which he meant the decline of religious belief and magical thinking that accompanied scientific progress. Yet while a short story like 'Prince Hat Underground' is designed primarily to entertain rather than educate us, one of the side benefits of reading it may be to re-enchant our surroundings, and even our sense of the lives available to us.

At a simple grammatical level this is partly down to Link's decision to use the present tense. Unlike the traditional formula 'Once upon a time', which places events in the distant past, here the present tense adds an element of jeopardy to what is being described. There is no narrative safety net, no implicit promise that things are bound to work out for the best. Instead we are presented with something that looks like the script of a film that is unspooling before our eyes.

Another trick Link uses is to take familiar stories, and even standard grammatical conventions, and give them a playful twist. The story 'White Cat, Black Dog' is a reworking of the traditional Norwegian fairy tale 'East of the Sun and West of the Moon', included by Andrew Lang in his landmark collection *The Blue Fairy Book* (1889), but Link's version is also full of echoes of the classical legend of Demeter and Persephone, which revolves around an abduction to the underworld, Lewis Carroll's *Alice's Adventures in Wonderland*, another story where the main character falls into a strange world featuring a talking cat, and perhaps even the creepy parallel universe known as the Upside Down in Netflix's global TV hit *Stranger Things*. (Kelly Link's first collection of stories was published in 2001 as *Stranger Things Happen*.) Alongside these narrative echoes are all the other examples of American Gothic where surface appearances conceal disturbing realities, like the opening sequence of David Lynch's 1986 film *Blue Velvet* in which scenes of idyllic American suburbia (technicolor flowers, white picket fences, bright blue skies) are interrupted by a man having a heart attack as he waters his garden, while the camera slowly sinks down into the grass to reveal a squirming mass of insects living directly under our feet.

Similar effects in Link's writing are achieved through other forms of grammatical manipulation. Like Jan Morris's description of Trieste that we considered in Chapter 16, this passage is full of simple declarative sentences ('There are ... There are') that take the place they are describing for granted, producing a comic friction between what we are being told about this world and what we tend to assume about our own. The number of sentences beginning with a definite article ('The air is velvety ... The trees ... The leaf ... The tree bark') similarly assume a straightforward relationship between words and the world and then give it an unexpected wrench. For example, 'The cat jumps down onto the sidewalk' sounds as obvious as 'The cat sat on the mat' until we remember that this is a sidewalk that obeys the same rules as everything else in the underworld by seeming to go on forever.

Crucially, the fact that this is a same-sex variant of the traditional fairy tale – one that also has parallels with Orpheus's rescue of Eurydice from the classical underworld – is never explicitly remarked upon. In the usual versions of 'East of the Sun and West of the Moon' it is the heroine who undertakes a quest to the ends of the earth in order to find her true love and rescue him from an enchantment that has clouded his mind. A similar narrative line is followed in modern retellings like Edith Pattou's *East* (2003) and Joanna Ruth Meyer's *Echo North* (2019). In each case, the social roles of the main characters are reversed from most other fairy tales, as it is the heroine who must save the hero rather than the other way round, but their sexual identities are never questioned. *She* must save *him*. Not so in 'Prince Hat Underground', where the hero is on a quest to find his husband and restore him to life. *He* must save *him*. A tiny grammatical tweak turns out to involve a major shift in social assumptions.

Changes to some of our other assumptions about how the world works are also sunk into the details of Link's writing. Clichés such as 'it seems to go on forever' are given a new lease of life in a place where the usual rules of time and space don't apply, and things really can go on forever. The up and down movements in the passage ('plops down . . . looks up . . . chase upward . . . jumps down') are echoed in the sudden switches between moments of sublime beauty like the 'restless incandescent lines' made by candle-carrying birds in the violet dusk, and the deliberate bathos of comments like 'Don't sound so disappointed.' This even extends to the name of the hero. Usually we expect a hero to have a suitably muscular name like Achilles or Thor; we don't expect him to be called Gary.

Yet Gary turns out to be every inch the hero. He uses skill and cunning to defeat the wicked queen who had been holding his husband captive, and together they escape from Hell. It seems that, for a while at least, they will be able to build a life together of simple pleasures, as they prepare for these extraordinary events to be replaced by completely ordinary ones like going for walks, petting other people's dogs and eating ice cream. In some ways it's a surprisingly downbeat ending for a fairy tale – there are none of the giant palaces or unimaginable riches of a traditional happy ever after – but it's also perfectly in keeping with the way that Link's writing always keeps one foot in the ordinary world of cats and sidewalks, even as her other foot is sliding ever further into fantasy.

In some ways this develops an aspect of literature I outlined in Chapter 8: the ability of a story to help us negotiate with reality rather than simply accept it without question. Naturally this isn't limited to our experience of reading fiction: something similar happens whenever we dream about meeting a celebrity or scoring the winning goal in a cup final. But what a fairy tale like 'Prince Hat Underground' does is to make a negotiation with reality central to its own workings, as its characters shuttle back and forth between ordinary suburban life and an enchanted underworld. (Couples who have stayed together after a disastrous holiday might be especially sympathetic to the idea that some bonds are so powerful they can even survive a trip to Hell.) In doing this it reminds us that we behave in a very similar way when we read. We too disappear into an imaginary elsewhere before returning to the world of walks and dogs and ice cream. And when we are back in this world, some of us might conclude that the story we have just read has re-enchanted it in a slightly different way, by glossing it with optimism.

How to Keep Your Head

Chapter 20

ACCIDENTS

IF THERE'S ONE THING WORSE than being tongue-tied, like a number of the writers I discussed in Chapter 7, it's being tongue-tangled. Such was the fate of a former university colleague who once tried to explain why he enjoyed teaching a particular female student. 'She's simply the breast in her year,' he told me, before his eyes suddenly widened in panic. If voices could blush, his would have gone a rich shade of scarlet. Mistaking 'breast' for 'best' could be an unfortunate mistake in any context, but here it was especially embarrassing, as intellectual admiration and physical desire, hazy memories of Tina Turner and arguments about the supposed benefits of breastfeeding ('Breast Is Best'), became knotted together in his voice.

Such verbal blunders are popularly known as 'Freudian slips', or what Freud himself described in *The Psychopathology of Everyday Life* (1901) as 'parapraxes'. (That is the term chosen by James Strachey for his English translation; Freud's word was *Fehlleistungen*, meaning 'faulty actions' or 'mistakes'.) According to Freud, slips of the tongue reveal the complex motivations that underlie individual utterances, as we find ourselves confessing the lurking secrets, such as feelings of social aggression or sexual desire, that we usually try to keep hidden. They provide fragmentary evidence of how often we might say one thing but mean ~~our mother~~ another.

To some extent these mistakes can be blamed on language itself. The English language, in particular, is so richly textured that it only takes a tiny alteration to transform what we say into something quite different – hence Margaret Atwood's creation of the Gilead slogan 'Pen Is Envy', which we looked at in Chapter 18, simply by breaking the word 'Penis' in two. But here writing also provides us with some relief, because on the page accidents of speech can be controlled; unintentional self-revelations can be transformed into deliberate displays of how a mind works. For example, when the speaker of Tennyson's long dramatic poem *Maud* (1855) complains that love makes his tongue 'stammer and trip', we are being warned that he may say more than he means to, and in this context his later excitement at listening to Maud sing 'a martial song' is not altogether surprising. Largely ignored by the woman he is obsessed with, it is as if this lonely individual cannot quite admit what he would rather hear: for 'martial', read 'marital'. A single word gives us a keyhole into his secret inner world.

This gap between innocent speaker and knowing reader need not be mournful. It's also one in which comedy can flourish. Indeed, slips of the tongue can work a bit like examples of slapstick. Just as circus clowns are surrounded by objects that appear forever keen to ambush them, from head-cracking ladders to foot-squelching pots of paint, so some speakers inhabit the sort of textual environment in which words appear forever ready to slip them up. And just as the funniest clown is usually the one who seems most confident of avoiding these traps before crashing back down to earth, so the funniest literary banana skins tend to appear at just the moment when a speaker thinks they are securely in control.

Sometimes these accidents are built into the English language: in Chapter 13, for example, I noted how many rhymes work to cement connections that are already present in our minds, such as the one between life (*womb*) and death (*tomb*). Similar effects can also be produced in other languages. Thus, the ability of a character in a tragedy by the seventeenth-century French dramatist Jean Racine to rhyme *loi* (the law) with *roi* (the king) can show rhyme appearing to endorse the history of constitutional monarchy, striking a chord with old ways of thinking and speaking, although the way this chime is approached can show a far broader range of attitudes towards what the words themselves appear to take for granted, from dutiful acceptance, to ironic smirking, to reminiscing over traditional ways of thinking that now seem arch or quaint, like someone humming a tune they can't quite get back.

Of course, rhymes like these are merely coincidental linguistic overlaps, acoustic accidents. There is no logical connection between the sounds of *womb* and *tomb*, or *loi* and *roi*, any more than there was when Robert Browning once accepted a bet to find a rhyme for *hippopotamus* and came up with *toss Eros*. As W. H. Auden pointed out, the traditional rhyme 'Thirty days hath September, | April, June and November' makes sense to us 'because nobody doubts its truth', but if somebody wanted to dispute this claim 'the lines would be powerless to convince him because, formally, it would make no difference if the lines ran: Thirty days hath September, | August, May and December'. That is, the fact that September rhymes with both November and December is a matter of linguistic chance, not calendrical logic, so even as the old saying is assuming some sort of natural pattern in the world it is quietly admitting that there is a good deal we cannot control.

Some writers have gleefully exploited this idea that language can be treated like a giant stage set full of hidden doorways and trick flaps. When Keats in his letters describes a colour as 'purplue' (a mixture of purple and blue), or something ridiculous as 'rediculous' (silly enough to make one blush), his misspellings probably aren't deliberate, but they do suggest there may be some linguistic accidents that are just waiting to happen. Similarly, in his eye-popping experimental novel *Finnegans Wake* (1939), many of Joyce's layered puns ('they were yung and easily freudened', or 'haloed be her eve, her singtime sung, her rill be run, unhemmed as it is uneven') show words sliding in and out of each other in a dazzling display of literary one-upmanship, as he demonstrates the power of the unconscious mind to discover connections between apparently discrete ideas. For both authors, the banana skins of language represent more than threats. They provide extra sources of pleasure.

Many of these ideas come together in a hilarious fictional letter contained in Dickens's *Nicholas Nickleby*, a novel originally published in monthly instalments from 1838 to 1839. So far we have accompanied the idealistic young hero Nicholas as he follows his uncle's recommendation to teach at the Yorkshire boarding school Dotheboys Hall, where the pupils are routinely starved and beaten by the school's gloatingly wicked headmaster Wackford Squeers. After Nicholas witnesses a particularly unfortunate boy named Smike being subjected to a savage flogging, he intervenes, thrashing Squeers with his own cane before escaping from the school with Smike. That just leaves Squeers's coquettish daughter Fanny, who has previously flirted with Nicholas and been firmly rejected, to report to Nicholas's uncle what has happened:

DOTHEBOYS HALL, THURSDAY MORNING.

SIR,

My pa requests me to write to you, the doctors considering it doubtful whether he will ever recuvver the use of his legs which prevents his holding a pen.

We are in a state of mind beyond everything, and my pa is one mask of brooses both blue and green likewise two forms are steepled in his Goar. We were kimpelled to have him carried down into the kitchen where he now lays. You will judge from this that he has been brought very low.

When your nevew that you recommended for a teacher had done this to my pa and jumped upon his body with his feet and also langwedge which I will not pollewt my pen with describing, he assaulted my ma with dreadful violence, dashed her to the earth, and drove her back comb several inches into her head. A very little more and it must have entered her skull. We have a medical certifiket that if it had, the tortershell would have affected the brain.

Me and my brother were then the victims of his feury since which we have suffered very much which leads us to the arrowing belief that we have received some injury in our insides, especially as no marks of violence are visible externally. I am screaming out loud all the time I write and so is my brother which takes off my attention rather, and I hope will excuse mistakes.

The monster having sasiated his thirst for blood ran away, taking with him a boy of desperate caracter that he had excited to rebellyon, and a garnet ring belonging to my ma, and not having been apprehended by the constables is supposed to have been took up by some stage-coach. My pa begs that if he comes to you the ring may be returned, and that you will let the thief and assassin go, as if we prosecuted him he would only be transported, and if he is let go he is sure to be hung before long which will save us trouble, and be much more satisfactory. Hoping to hear from you when convenient

I remain
Yours and cetrer
FANNY SQUEERS.

P.S. I pity his ignorance and despise him.

Fanny ends with a formal postscript that shows her trying to have the last word, but in a way her whole letter is built on the principle of the postscript, of ideas being supplemented and revised. This can be seen in the way her syntax swerves from one idea to the next, playing havoc with logic ('the doctors considering it doubtful whether he will ever recuvver the use of his legs which prevents his holding a pen'), and also in her repeated use of 'and' at the start of new grammatical clauses ('and jumped upon his body with his feet and also langwedge which I will not pollewt my pen with describing') as she tries to bolt on ever more disconnected fragments of thought.

The result is a furious muddle of details, but also of different narrative styles, as she keeps switching between the flatly businesslike ('My pa requests me to write to you') and the loftily overwritten ('a boy of desperate character that he had excited to rebellyon'), with the effect that every attempt to project an impression of tragic dignity soon collapses in ruins: 'We were kimpelled to have him carried down into the kitchen where he now lays. You will judge from this that he has been brought very low.' (The shift in her language from a high to a low register, which matches her father's physical movement from upstairs schoolroom to basement kitchen, is a textbook example of bathos.) And stitching the whole thing together are the clichés of bodice rippers and cheap horror stories ('steepled in his Goar . . . dashed her to the earth . . . sasiated his thirst for blood'), as she reaches for a way of describing what happened, and finds herself becoming a character in the sort of stories she is used to reading rather than the one she is actually in.

We know that Fanny's account is skewed by her own assumptions, because we've already seen the scene she is recalling through the eyes of Dickens's narrator, and over many chapters we have grown to trust the part-sincere, part-tongue-in-cheek filter he places on events. For example, we have learned that the ragged Smike is indeed 'desperate', but not in the way Fanny assumes, because previously we have read about him being the victim of a 'desperate cut' from Squeers's cane shortly before Nicholas intervenes. We have also been provided with a grotesque contrast to Smike in the shape of Fanny herself, who is described as being in 'a desperate flutter' shortly before Nicholas comes to her parlour for tea and is greeted by a vision of ringlets, long gloves and a green gauze scarf that she tosses with measured negligence over one shoulder. In effect, she is being judged out of her own mouth, as every attack she makes on Nicholas and Smike in this letter ultimately rebounds on herself, like a tennis ball that is attached to a piece of elastic and comes back with additional force the harder it is hit.

If we are reading the original version of the novel, we may already have seen the illustration to this scene drawn by Dickens's long-term collaborator Hablot K. Browne ('Phiz'), which depicts Nicholas as a slim, elegant figure raising a cane against the cowering Squeers while the other boys cheer him on. Here we have another witness who treats the events melodramatically, but one who clearly regards Nicholas as a hero rather than a villain. Yet we know that narrators can be unreliable, and illustrations only ever capture one view of events, so why don't we revise our opinion of the scene when we read Fanny's account?

Partly it's because Fanny's misspellings and patchy grammar offer a set of clues that her way of looking at events doesn't align with those of most people. We also get an immediate response after the letter is read aloud, as the 'boy of desperate character' is described sitting 'mute and dispirited, with a most woe-begone and heart-stricken look', which again makes us realise that his desperation is sad rather than dangerous.

Indeed, although some parts of Fanny's letter might make Freud prick up his ears – Nicholas's 'langwedge' has indeed forced itself into a gap in her heart, while accusing Smike of 'rebellyon' darkly hints at the near starvation he has suffered at Dotheboys Hall – for the most part it deals with accidents of a different kind, as her intentions are repeatedly undermined by a narrator who turns every sentence she writes into the literary equivalent of a whoopee cushion.

If this letter tells us something specific about Fanny as a character, it tells us even more about why we enjoy writing that plays around in this way. Here a comparison with another form of writing may be helpful, because the theatricality of her letter reminds us that this is something we especially relish on stage. A modern farce like *The Play That Goes Wrong*, written in 2012 by Henry Lewis, Jonathan Sayer and Henry Shields, in which a group of amateur actors behind earlier (imaginary) shows such as *Two Sisters* and *Cat* tries to put on a 1920s murder mystery similar to the long-running theatrical hit *The Mousetrap*, is based on the idea that we are watching a series of events that appear to be chaotic and unpredictable, but are actually put together like a slickly choreographed dance routine. During the performance, several disasters befall the actors, including doors sticking, floors collapsing, props breaking and a member of the cast being knocked unconscious, and the skill of the performers lies in making us believe that throughout these events they don't know what they're doing, despite us knowing deep down that the *play* can go wrong only if the *performance* goes right.

What Dickens manages to do in *Nicholas Nickleby* is to bring this sort of double awareness to a piece of narrative. When we read Fanny's letter, we know that every mistake she makes has been carefully plotted out in advance by Dickens; every accident is part of a larger narrative design. And at the very moment she thinks she is declaring her independence – 'I pity his ignorance and despise him' – we can enjoy the spectacle of Dickens making her mouth clatter up and down like a ventriloquist's dummy.

Chapter 21

ORDER

THE LETTER WRITTEN BY Fanny Squeers, full of revelations that are both witty (from the author's viewpoint) and unwitting (from her own), is typical of the game that many narratives play. Dickens himself often describes violent riots or seething crowds in a way that shows his narrator remaining coolly in control of matters even as he is describing how other people are losing their heads – literally in the case of *A Tale of Two Cities*. Such writing may appear to embrace chaos, but it does so in a way that successfully puts mess and muddle in their place.

This is a lesson that Dickens had learned from eighteenth-century novelists such as Henry Fielding and Tobias Smollett, and it would later be developed by many other writers, particularly those who sought to capture life in the newly expanding cities, where people's senses were forever being pelted by extra things to notice and unexpected challenges to their understanding. Thus, when Flaubert describes a character wandering through the city streets in *L'éducation sentimentale* (*Sentimental Education*, 1869) he assails us with the fragmentary observations and incomplete reflections produced by modern urban life, so that *reading* about the city is made almost as surprising as *living* in it.

Virginia Woolf was equally interested in the challenge of capturing the experience of life in a modern city. We have already seen in Chapter 16 that one of her responses was to turn a place like London into a 'phantom' that existed primarily in her own head, and many of her later descriptions of this city follow the same pattern, by treating it as an opportunity for her to flex her imaginative muscles rather than describe it with perfect accuracy. 'London is enchanting', she writes in a diary entry from May 1924, 'The nights are amazing, with all the white porticoes & broad silent avenues. And people pop in & out, lightly, divertingly like rabbits; and I look down Southampton Row, wet as a seal's back or red & yellow with sunshine . . . ' With its comparisons to rabbits and seals, such a description tells us little about what the streets actually looked like at the time, but a great deal about how they appeared to someone with Woolf's rapt, visionary way of thinking.

By the time she came to describe a stroll around London's docks in the first of a series of articles she wrote for *Good Housekeeping* magazine between 1931 and 1932, she had learned how to give the reader both an impression of urban clutter and the reassurance of an underlying order:

Now from the dock side we look down into the heart of the ship that has been lured from its voyaging and tethered to the dry land. The passengers and their bags have disappeared; the sailors have gone too. Indefatigable cranes are now at work, dipping and swinging, swinging and dipping. Barrels, sacks, crates are being picked up out of the hold and swung regularly on shore. Rhythmically, dexterously, with an order that has some aesthetic delight in it, barrel is laid by barrel, case by case, cask by cask, one behind another, one on top of another, one beside another in endless array down the aisles and arcades of the immense low-ceiled, entirely plain and unornamented warehouses. Timber, iron, grain, wine, sugar, paper, tallow, fruit – whatever the ship has gathered from the plains, from the forests, from the pastures of the whole world is here lifted from its hold and set in its right place. A thousand ships with a thousand cargoes are being unladen every week. And not only is each package of this vast and varied merchandise picked up and set down accurately, but each is weighed and opened, sampled and recorded, and again stitched up and laid in its place, without haste, or waste, or hurry, or confusion by a very few men in shirt-sleeves, who, working with the utmost organisation in the common interest – for buyers will take their word and abide by their decision – are yet able to pause in their work and say to the casual visitor, 'Would you like to see what sort of thing we sometimes find in sacks of cinnamon? Look at this snake!'

Even looking into the hold of a single ship, the rush of impressions that greets a spectator is potentially overwhelming, and Woolf responds by using her prose to organise the scene like a dockyard supervisor wielding a clipboard. In particular, we observe how she uses lists to tidy up any potential for disorder, not only through the visible containers of 'Barrels, sacks, crates' but also their invisible contents: 'Timber, iron, grain, wine, sugar, paper, tallow, fruit'. Such lists ensure that in her writing, as in the docks themselves, everything is 'set in its right place . . . laid in its place'.

Lists can be an important feature in many kinds of writing, from nonsense rhymes like Lewis Carroll's 'The Walrus and the Carpenter' ('"The time has come," the Walrus said, | "To talk of many things: | Of shoes – and ships – and sealing-wax – | Of cabbages – and kings –"'), where part of the reader's pleasure comes from discovering unexpected connections in sound between items that are usually filed away in different parts of

our brain ('shoes . . . ships', 'cabbages . . . kings'), to satires like
Alexander Pope's *The Rape of the Lock* (1712), where the jumble
of make-up, religious texts and love letters that Belinda keeps
on her dressing table ('Puffs, Powders, Patches, Bibles, Billet-
doux') satirises the idea that she has her ethics mixed up with
her cosmetics. Lists are especially important in texts that seek
to capture the nitty-gritty texture of ordinary life, and they can
provide an equally helpful shortcut in writing that tries to get
inside a character's head and see how they divide up the world.
The lists of desirable consumer objects in a novel like Bret Easton
Ellis's 1991 satire *American Psycho*, for example, invite us to share
the perspective of a psychopath who treats his designer clothes
far more tenderly than he does other people: 'I'm wearing: a
Joseph Abboud suit, tie by Paul Stuart, shoes by J. Crew, a vest
by someone Italian,' he tells us breezily, 'and I'm kneeling on the
floor beside a corpse eating the girl's brain . . . '

Yet because lists tend to be based on a principle of mathematical accumulation rather than formal arrangement (most lists are
heaps of words that could potentially be piled up forever), and
syntactic juxtaposition rather than narrative sequence (in a list
you can put anything next to anything else), they give us only
an illusion of order. The opening sentence of Aracelis Girmay's
poem 'Elegy in Gold' shows how this clenching together of order
and disorder can be used as an imaginative resource:

> Earring, tooth,
> dog breath, shoe,
>
> mango fruit or pocket watch,
> sunlight on my love's
>
> elbow, sunlight
> in the kettle's steam,

> we walk in the rubble
> of the African dream
>
> brushing shipwreck from
> our hair & dresses.

To begin with, the list we are given in this poem appears to be a celebration of everyday clutter, like Félicité's domestic knick-knacks described in Chapter 14, here tidied up and organised into lines of verse like ornaments being displayed on a shelf. Then there is a sudden shift of gear, and the lines 'we walk in the rubble | of the African dream' make us reconsider what we have just read. An unexpected twist to the phrase 'the American dream' reminds us that a good deal of modern America was built on the foundations of slavery, and now those opening lines start to look more like the debris from a shipwreck, perhaps overlaid by memories of 9/11 and fragments of ordinary life – a shoe, a watch – poking out of the rubble. Viewed in this light, Girmay's list is at once a celebration and a commemoration; it shows someone counting their blessings, and with the rhyme of 'steam' and 'dream' (the only full rhyme in the poem) it quietly mourns how vulnerable these things are, how easily they can vanish.

Even without this sort of traumatic context, a list can be an especially useful resource when writers want to capture the jumbled experience of city life, as when Woolf writes in *Mrs Dalloway* (1925) of 'the bellow and the uproar; the carriages, motor cars, omnibuses, vans, sandwich men shuffling and swinging; brass bands; barrel organs' that Clarissa Dalloway encounters as she walks through London one fine morning in June. Here Woolf's syntax seizes on the sudden juxtapositions of the city, as her sentence quickly switches its focus from one clause to the next, but it also uses little dabs of alliteration to suggest that patterns can be glimpsed even within this apparently random scene:

'carriages ... cars', 'sandwich ... swinging', 'bellow ... brass bands; barrel'. Most importantly, her writing shows how lists can be a meeting point between passively registering information and actively organising it, embracing life's unpredictability and showing how even this can be subject to artistic control.

Comedy is especially good at finding this sort of balance between confusion and control. To take an example from the history of cinema, three months before Woolf published 'The Docks of London', Charlie Chaplin met Mahatma Gandhi in a corner of the Royal Docks (it is now the site of the Gandhi Chaplin Memorial Garden) for a conversation about Indian independence and the importance of machinery in the modern world. It's been argued that their encounter may have helped to inspire *Modern Times* (1936), Chaplin's satire on the dehumanising effects of automation, in which he plays a factory worker who is supposed to be tightening nuts on a production line and gradually starts to behave with mechanical single-mindedness, obsessively tightening everything in sight. Yet even here Chaplin's power of improvisation spills over the boundaries of the world in which he finds himself, as he escapes from the factory and pursues a woman down the street, gleefully waving a pair of spanners after spotting the buttons on her chest and deciding that they should be tightened up like anything else.

'The Docks of London' doesn't possess this sort of comic energy, but Woolf seems equally keen to give us an overview of a world we might not have visited in person, and then to make us drill into certain details we might not have noticed without some extra guidance. This stretches from the opening sentence ('we look down into the heart of the ship') to the last ('Look at this snake!'), as Woolf switches from a wide-angle to a close-up lens in the way she writes about the scene. It also reminds us once again that order isn't only something we observe in the world, but can be something we actively seek to make. In the words of cultural theorist Michel Foucault, 'Order is, at one and the same time, that which is given in things as their inner law ... and also that which has no existence except in the grid created by a glance, an examination, a language.'

This imposition of order in Woolf's article about the London docks is largely achieved through her use of syntax. In previous chapters we've already considered a writer's choice of words. Syntax involves the way they are fitted together, like pieces of Lego snapping into place; it's what governs how one word follows another, and so how one idea leads to another, creating another form of 'order that has some aesthetic delight in it' when we read. Here, for example, we might notice how Woolf's syntax arranges itself into a set of rhythms and internal echoes: 'dipping and swinging, swinging and dipping', 'vast and varied', 'without haste, or waste'. Such neatly patterned prose does more than capture the mechanically regular activities of the docks. It shows what these activities look like through a particular person's eyes.

In her experimental novel *The Waves*, published in the same year as 'The Docks of London', Woolf offered another example of how the syntax of a piece of writing might show someone's mind trying to make sense of a tumble of different impressions. Here one of her characters gradually becomes aware of the rhythms of ordinary life in a cheap London restaurant, as he watches the door opening and closing, the hats of passers-by bobbing up and down outside the window, and plates of food coming and going. 'It is like a waltz tune, eddying in and out, round and round', Woolf writes. 'The waitresses, balancing trays, swing in and out, round and round, dealing plates of greens, of apricot and custard, dealing with them at the right time, to the right customers. The average men, including her rhythm in their rhythm ... take their greens, take their apricots and custard ... The circle is unbroken; the harmony complete.'

I remember coming back to this passage in the same year my partner and I bought an apartment in one of the high-rise blocks that had recently been built in the steel and glass forest of London's Docklands. (It was more than a decade after our early romantic adventure in Paris; it was time.) The ships described by Woolf had long since disappeared from the area, and although a sense of bustling energy remained, the reasons for it were very different. Now the only 'vast and varied merchandise' to be found was in the shops of a shiny new arcade, while the people who dedicated themselves to picking things up and setting them down again were far more likely to be Amazon or Deliveroo drivers than crane operators. Yet Woolf's writing still provided a good model to help us understand what we could see from our apartment window most mornings. In the far distance, commuters were trudging across a metal bridge and shoppers were returning with bulging bags of groceries; every few minutes there was the thin metallic flash of a DLR train trundling into the station just below us and trundling off again. At first sight it was chaos, but as we continued to look at these different movements their rhythms gradually started to weave in and out of each other, until it was like watching thousands of dancers taking part in an intricately choreographed waltz.

What a piece of writing like Woolf's article on the London docks does is to capture this process as it is happening. We've seen in previous chapters that writers have many different resources they can draw upon to make us feel we are accompanying them as they move through the world, such as Jan Morris's use of adjectives that shift between neutral description and personal evaluation during her twilight wanderings in Trieste ('The General Post Office is enormous . . . The Palace of Justice is foreboding'), or Woolf's own stress on smells when imagining how a spaniel might map out London in its head.

We've also seen that if we want to understand what a literary device is doing, it can be helpful to see what the same piece of writing looks like when this device is altered or removed.

On this principle, we can imagine how some different writers might try to describe a ship being unloaded. Here is Imaginary Writer A:

> One by one, the barrels, cases, and casks that were on board the ship are removed and assembled in huge warehouses.

Here is the slightly more ambitious Imaginary Writer B:

> The dockyard cranes work tirelessly to lift the various barrels, cases, and casks off the ship and lay them in orderly fashion down the aisles and arcades of the huge, plain warehouses.

Finally, here is Woolf:

> Rhythmically, dexterously, with an order that has some aesthetic delight in it, barrel is laid by barrel, case by case, cask by cask, one behind another, one on top of another, one beside another in endless array down the aisles and arcades of the immense low-ceiled, entirely plain and unornamented warehouses.

Both of our imaginary writers are keen to capture the physical details of *what* they saw, which probably accounts for the humdrum one-thing-after-another quality of their prose, but only Woolf shows us *how* she saw it. And of the many tricks of style she uses to achieve this, one of the most important is her syntax. It's a good example of what the poet Coleridge meant when he described prose as 'words in their best order', as Woolf introduces us to a set of facts while revealing how they have been filtered through her imagination.

Chapter 22

FEELINGS

ENJOYING THE THRILL OF disorder and balancing it against the reassurance of order isn't restricted to reading. Many people experience a similar combination of feelings when they do something as simple as riding a rollercoaster, where their pleasure in losing control as the train loops and plunges ('Aaaaaaaaaaargh!') is underpinned by their knowledge that the source of their feelings is – or at least should be if the rollercoaster has been properly maintained – securely under control. Get this balance wrong and the end of a ride can feel more like exiting a bus than surviving a near-death experience. On the same visit to Paris when we had been caught in a thunderstorm, my nearly new boyfriend and I visited Disneyland, where the gleaming rollercoasters seemed as bored as the staff as they went through the same choreographed routine every few minutes. ('Only you can save the world.' [*Barely suppressed yawn.*] 'Please keep your hands inside the car at all times.') It was all very different to the bone-shaking wooden rollercoaster I had ridden on Coney Island in the early 1990s, which was so ancient (it originally opened in 1927) it made everyone who gingerly clambered on board feel that it would only take one rusty rivet shearing off for the ride to end in disaster. ('Aaaaaaaaaaargh!')

How reading can produce similarly strong feelings is more mysterious, because when we follow characters who are undergoing perilous adventures there's no danger of our own bones being broken. Nor is there any real danger for the characters themselves, given that they only exist as a scattering of ink on paper or pixels on a screen. Indeed, feeling sad when a character dies, or cheerful when they achieve a happy ending, might seem as ludicrous as wondering what our chair is thinking about or developing romantic feelings for a toaster. 'What's Hecuba to him, or he to Hecuba, | That he should weep for her?' Hamlet asks himself after seeing an actor perform a speech about Hecuba's reaction to the murder of her husband Priam during the siege of Troy – a speech that is so moving the actor himself becomes pale and tearful. We might ask ourselves a similar question when we read a passage like the one about Sydney Carton climbing onto the scaffold to sacrifice himself at the end of *A Tale of Two Cities* ('It is a far, far better thing that I do, than I have ever done; it is a far, far better rest that I go to than I have ever known') and discover that we too have tears in our eyes. Who's Sydney Carton to us, or we to Sydney Carton, that we should weep for him?

One theory is that reading taps into our capacity for neurological mirroring, so that the same complex brain cells fire when we see or hear an action being performed by someone else as they do when it is performed by ourselves. Found in several areas of the brain, including the premotor cortex, the posterior parietal lobe, the superior temporal sulcus and the insula, these neurons also fire in response to the chain of intentions that led to this action. So if I enjoy tennis, the same neurons will fire if I serve a tennis ball, watch Andy Murray serve a tennis ball, hear the *thwuck* of his serve on the radio, or even listen to a sports commentator using the word 'serve'. Similarly, if we see someone else who is happy or in distress, mirror neurons in our brain automatically simulate their emotional state; we know how they feel because we literally feel what they are feeling. Crudely put, we seem to be wired for empathy. What reading gives us is a way of fine-tuning this wiring. Even though they only exist in a piece of fiction, seeing Mr Darcy through Elizabeth Bennet's eyes allows us to fall in love with him without having to risk rejection – or indeed without being a remotely plausible match for him. And unlike a real love affair, reading about this invented romance means that we can experience it from both perspectives at once, so that while we are falling in love with Mr Darcy we can also fall in love with Elizabeth Bennet by seeing her through his eyes.

This develops one of the standard explanations for why people write, which is that even before it allows them to share what they think, it helps them to understand what their thoughts are. When E. M. Forster asked 'How do I know what I think till I see what I say?' in *Aspects of the Novel* (1927), he was recognising that we may find it difficult to make sense of our ideas until we have put them into the sense-making structures of language. Reading takes this process a stage further. How do I know what I think until I see what someone else says? How do I know what I *feel* until I have used another person's words to try out those feelings and decide if they are right for me?

This might seem to go against the independence that good readers are supposed to show, as if letting ourselves be guided emotionally by the books we admire somehow robbed us of our own powers of judgement. 'What can it matter to you what Ruskin feels: feel for yourself', Proust imagined someone telling him after he had spent several years painstakingly translating Ruskin's works *Bible of Amiens* and *Sesame and Lilies* into French – a task somewhat complicated by the fact that Proust spoke so little English when he began that, according to his friend Georges de Lauris, he would have had trouble ordering a lamb chop in an English restaurant. Yet drawing such distinctions between himself and Ruskin was a false exercise, Proust concluded, because 'there is no better way of coming to be aware of what one feels oneself than by trying to recreate in oneself what a master has felt'. Temporarily borrowing someone else's heart can help us to understand our own a little better.

Such an expansion of our feelings through reading isn't restricted to literary critics. Every year millions of Valentine's Day cards are sent that contain printed quotations ('I do love nothing in the world so well as you') or catchy slogans ('Roses are red, gender is performative, mass-market romance is heteronormative') based on the assumption that the best way to express our most private feelings may be to project them through someone else's mouth. (Edmond Rostand's 1897 play *Cyrano de Bergerac*, in which the eloquent but large-nosed hero is only able to confess his love for the beautiful Roxane by speaking through handsome, tongue-tied Christian, takes a situation faced by many would-be suitors on Valentine's Day and reworks it as a romantic tragedy.) There are also poems that touch on this idea, sometimes seriously and sometimes more playfully, although they can misfire when it isn't clear who is speaking or what they are trying to say. For example, I once sent someone a sonnet I had written by slicing out lines from fourteen different love poems. (The technical term for a poem made from other poems is a 'cento'.) It was supposed to be a bit of a joke: the opening line was 'How do I love thee? Let me count the ways', which I had borrowed from Elizabeth Barrett Browning's 1850 collection *Sonnets from the Portuguese*, and the answer I expected to receive was 'erm . . . fourteen?' That's not how he read it.

Luckily there are more successful examples, such as Carol Ann Duffy's 'The Love Poem' from her 2005 collection *Rapture*:

> Till love exhausts itself, longs
> for the sleep of words –
>   my mistress' eyes –
> to lie on a white sheet, at rest
> in the language –
>   let me count the ways –
> or shrink to a phrase like an epitaph –
>   come live
> with me –
> or fall from its own high cloud as syllables
> in a pool of verse –
>   one hour with thee.
>
> Till love gives in and speaks
> in the whisper of art –
>   dear heart,
> how like you this? –
> love's lips pursed to quotation marks
> kissing a line –
>   look in thy heart
> and write –
> love's light fading, darkening,
> black as ink on a page –
>   there is a garden
> in her face.
>
> Till love is all in the mind –
>   O my America!
> my new-found land –

or all in the pen
in the writer's hand –

> behold, thou art fair –

not there, except in a poem,
known by heart like a prayer,
both near and far,
near and far –

> the desire of the moth

for the star.

Duffy's poem faces up to a challenge that might be posed by any situation where we find ourselves playing the same social role as countless others before us, from grieving the death of a parent to witnessing the birth of our first child. How can we use a shared language to express feelings that seem so raw and private? But because so much eloquence has already been expended on love, it is likely to pose a particularly acute challenge for anyone who wants to write their own poem. How is it possible to celebrate a unique relationship without falling into language that has already been used so often it has become loose and baggy?

Duffy's response is to set up her poem as a kind of dialogue in which she attempts to reconcile the speaker's unique experience of love with the history of other people sharing similar experiences. The jerky appearance of her lines, full of dashes and blank spaces, initially makes it hard to see what the underlying structure is, but if we look closely we might notice that there are three stanzas each made up of twelve lines. Here it may be worth remembering that the word 'stanza' literally means 'a room', as in Italian phrases like *stanza d'ingresso* (an entrance hall), because at first sight Duffy's stanzas seem to be full of the literary equivalent of old furniture. In addition to Elizabeth Barrett Browning's 'Let me count the ways', 'my mistress' eyes' is from Shakespeare's Sonnet 130, 'come live with me [and be my love]' is from Christopher Marlowe's 'The Passionate Shepherd to His Love' and so on. When we add all the other sources of Duffy's lines, the poem starts to look like a miniature anthology of love poetry, and in this regard it could be read in several different ways. Perhaps these quotations reflect a series of efforts to find a suitable literary model for the speaker's own experience, trying out each poem for a line or two before moving on to the next. Perhaps they are there to remind us that some love affairs survive in writing much longer than they do in real life. Or perhaps they simply show us how hard it is to describe the feeling of being in love, which may be why Duffy has said that all the poems in this collection are concerned with love 'but equally so with language as love's stammering messenger'.

In this context, Duffy's choice of title starts to resonate more ambiguously. In what sense is this 'The Love Poem'? Read through suspicious eyes, it presents itself as a whole series of failures: every time the speaker tries to explain what love means, the definition squirms away or splits apart like someone placing their finger on a blob of mercury. Here Duffy's own autobiographical situation could be relevant. Writing as a gay woman, it's noticeable that almost all the poems she chooses to quote from were written by men, so if her lover is 'near and far' that may partly be explained by the mixture of proximity and distance that is likely to be felt when an earlier author assumes that everyone is heterosexual, or that pronouns like 'he' and 'she' are perfectly stable and straightforward.

Alternatively, the fact that Duffy's lover is 'near and far' may have less to do with her sexuality than it does with feelings that she shares with everyone else who falls in love. This is a love poem not only because it takes love as its subject, but also because it tries to express what being in love *feels like*, as reason is overwhelmed and language starts to seem inadequate for emotions that are too big for words. (Several of the poems referred to in

'The Love Poem' are about earlier struggles to write a love poem.)
For some readers this will be a happy – or unhappy – memory.
For others it will be an opportunity to rehearse situations they
haven't yet encountered, as the relevant neurons in their brain
fizz into life and they mentally prepare themselves for something
they won't be able to stop merely by closing the book. And for a
third group of readers – who won't always be distinct from the
other two – the love affairs they can have via books may be more
emotionally fulfilling, more durable than any they will experience in real life.

The same reasons we might have for choosing to read something like 'The Love Poem' could be applied to many other
literary works. As William Empson once observed in an essay
on teaching literature, we read such works in part so that when
equally powerful emotions arise in us we won't be 'helplessly
surprised by them when they come'. If we have read enough, and
read carefully enough, there is a chance that we will have accumulated sufficient experience to recognise these emotions – not
exactly as old friends, but certainly as acquaintances we have
spent some time getting to know. The sheer number of poems
referred to in 'The Love Poem' might even make us feel that we
are in good company when we come to deal with such situations
in our own lives.

Duffy's final quotation, 'the desire of the moth | for the star',
comes from Shelley's earlier love poem 'To—', and it tugs in two
directions at once. It expresses all the lover's yearning to enjoy an
ideal love, and all the poet's ambition to create a perfect poem,
while recognising that achieving either is about as likely as a
moth reaching a star. Yet still the moth flutters on, and still we
try to make sense out of love by reading other people's sentences
about it.

Chapter 23

ARGUMENTS

BOOKS DON'T ONLY HELP us to understand our feelings; they can also encourage us to follow a line of thought and see where it goes. This can be an even more challenging thing to do when a line of thought develops into a line of argument. Since the rise of social media, many people have become painfully aware of how quickly and easily arguments can become illogical or uncontrolled. One of Monty Python's TV sketches featured a man who attends a clinic to have an argument (£1 for a single argument or £8 for a course of ten) and mistakenly opens the door to an office where someone shouts at him: 'You snotty-faced heap of parrot droppings! Your type makes me puke! You vacuous, toffee-nosed, malodorous pervert!' The customer protests, 'I came in here for an argument!' and the man shouting at him immediately relents. 'Oh! Oh. I'm sorry! This is abuse . . . You want 12a next door.' Many social media spats feel equally absurd. By contrast, one of the benefits of reading a book is that it permits us to entertain arguments without getting too personally involved. I've already suggested that a central value of many literary works lies in how they encourage us to think in new ways, to enter the minds of people whose beliefs are very different from our own. In exploring these differences, one of a writer's aims may be to resolve them, but equally the writer may simply want to revolve them – that is, to see what a belief looks like when viewed from several different angles.

Some works are particularly good at arguing with themselves. As we saw in Chapter 17, a 'dialogic' novel can use its characters to give voice to many rival points of view, while in other chapters we have seen that the compressed form of a poem makes it an especially good vehicle for ambiguity, and hence for offering competing perspectives on a single central idea. Plays can do this sort of thing even more easily. Early in his career, the playwright Tom Stoppard told an interviewer for the *New York Times* that he wrote plays 'because writing dialogue is the only respectable way of contradicting yourself', allowing him to embark on 'a great leapfrog down the great moral issues' as he made one character take up a certain position, then made another character rebut it or refute it, then refuted the rebuttal or rebutted the refutation. 'Forever. Endlessly.'

Sometimes it isn't even necessary to have more than one speaker on stage to present both sides of an argument, and this can occur as much in how something is said as in what we are told. Here is a soliloquy from Shakespeare's *Hamlet* that opens with one of the most famous lines ever written:

> To be, or not to be, that is the question:
> Whether 'tis nobler in the mind to suffer
> The slings and arrows of outrageous fortune,
> Or to take arms against a sea of troubles,
> And by opposing end them: to die, to sleep
> No more; and by a sleep, to say we end
> The heartache, and the thousand natural shocks
> That flesh is heir to? 'Tis a consummation
> Devoutly to be wished. To die to sleep,
> To sleep, perchance to dream; ay, there's the rub,
> For in that sleep of death, what dreams may come,

When we have shuffled off this mortal coil,
Must give us pause. There's the respect
That makes calamity of so long life:
For who would bear the whips and scorns of time,
The oppressor's wrong, the poor man's contumely,
The pangs of despised love, the law's delay,
The insolence of office, and the spurns
That patient merit of the unworthy takes,
When he himself might his quietus make
With a bare bodkin? Who would these fardels bear
To grunt and sweat under a weary life,
But that the dread of something after death,
The undiscovered country, from whose bourn
No traveller returns, puzzles the will,
And makes us rather bear those ills we have,
Than fly to others that we know not of.
Thus conscience does make cowards of us all,
And thus the native hue of resolution
Is sicklied o'er, with the pale cast of thought,
And enterprises of great pith and moment,
With this regard their currents turn away,
And lose the name of action.

Hamlet's speech has become so famous it's hard to read even for the first time without experiencing a strange prickle of recognition. We find echoes of it in other literary works such as T. S. Eliot's poem 'The Love Song of J. Alfred Prufrock' (1917), where the speaker sadly admits 'No, I am not Prince Hamlet, nor was meant to be' – a line that cuts itself off before it can finish 'To be or not to be', and thereby reminds us that an allusion itself involves both sameness and difference, 'to be' and 'not to be', as it borrows a handful of words from an earlier piece of writing and lets the rest go. But we also find Hamlet's speech popping up in far more unlikely places, from films like the 1942 black comedy *To Be Or Not To Be* starring Carole Lombard and Jack Benny, to songs like Mel Brooks's 1983 satire 'To Be Or Not To Be' (also known as 'The Hitler Rap'), all of which show that Hamlet's dreams of escape *in* his speech have in some ways been realised *by* his speech.

So why has a soliloquy about suicide achieved such dizzying levels of fame? Partly it's because Hamlet makes his situation sound so impersonal, despite the fact that his argument is chiefly a response to the events of the play. He has already given a soliloquy that opens with him longing for his 'too solid flesh' (or, as another version has it, 'too sullied flesh') to melt away, while admitting that there is a religious prohibition against 'self-slaughter'. He has also recently encountered the Ghost of his father, who has revealed that he was murdered by Hamlet's uncle, and this adds an unmistakably anxious edge to the claim that most people don't kill themselves because they dread that 'undiscovered country, from whose bourn | No traveller returns'. After all, if the mysterious figure haunting him is indeed his father's Ghost, Hamlet knows at least one traveller who seemingly has passports for both the country of the dead and that of the living. This makes the 'To be or not to be' soliloquy sound highly specific, even idiosyncratic. And yet not once in its lines does Hamlet ever say 'I' or 'me', but always 'we', 'us' and 'our', indicating that although this is a speech made by an individual it is dealing with issues that apply to many other people too.

A related reason for this speech's popularity may be that it works as an introduction to the play as a whole, giving us a rapid summary of ideas that the rest of *Hamlet* explores in far more leisurely detail. For example, asking 'To be or not to be' alerts us to the fact that if this is a play that is full of difficult choices, it is also one that is full of questions: 'Question it, Horatio', 'the question of these wars', 'you question with a wicked tongue' and many more. This is an especially important matter when it comes to death. 'Thou com'st in such a questionable shape | That I will speak to thee. I'll call thee Hamlet', the hero says to his father's Ghost the first time they meet, adding an extra syllable in that final line to the ten we would normally expect from a fragment of blank verse. (The basic metre of blank verse – its underlying pulse – is iambic pentameter, meaning that each line contains five examples of an unstressed syllable followed by a stressed one, *ti-tum, ti-tum, ti-tum, ti-tum, ti-tum*, whereas if you scan 'That I will speak to thee. I'll call thee Hamlet' you get *ti-tum, ti-tum, ti-tum, ti-tum, ti-tum, ti*.) In other words his voice goes beyond the ending we had anticipated, just as the Ghost has done in being dead but also somehow still alive, doomed to spend an unknown period walking the earth in a form of purgatory.

The same pattern resurfaces in the 'To be or not to be' soliloquy, which is also written in lines of blank verse that repeatedly topple over by an extra syllable ('To be or not to be – that is the quest . . . ion') and then start again, like someone peering over the edge of a cliff before drawing back. Not until the word 'end' is reached at the end of the sixth line do Hamlet's speech rhythms coincide with the underlying metre of his soliloquy ('to say we end | The heartache'), as his restless mind reaches a point where he could stop, crosses a tiny bridge in the form of a line ending that is visible on the page but usually inaudible in performance, and carries on. In fact, in the whole speech there is only one metrically regular line that ends with a full stop ('Than fly to others that we know not of'), and even that drags its feet at the end with three stressed syllables in a row, as if trying to put off the full stop for as long as possible.

Perhaps we shouldn't make too much of this. Several different versions of the play were published during Shakespeare's lifetime, and the version quoted here is based on the Folio text that was put together in 1623 after his death. The fact that punctuation was often added by printers rather than the author makes it even more difficult to draw firm conclusions about who was responsible for some of these local effects. Still, Shakespeare's decision to use blank verse *is* significant, not least because it works so closely with what – and how – Hamlet is arguing.

Blank verse is sometimes said to be close to the rhythms of everyday speech, which is why we hear it in ordinary sentences like 'I want to go and make a cup of tea' or 'I love you and I'll never let you go'. It's probably more accurate to say that it was a literary convention Shakespeare's original audience had come to accept for moments in a play when a character gave voice to thoughts that were pitched slightly higher than regular conversation, and therefore made it easier to spot places where the character's speech stumbled or rushed on unchecked. Importantly, there is no natural stopping place for a piece of blank verse; it could in theory carry on forever, as one line of *ti-tum, ti-tum, ti-tum, ti-tum, ti-tum* gives way to another like the steady ticking of a clock. Here, Hamlet describes a 'long life' in sentences that are drawn out across many lines and several subclauses, so that each line ending becomes a little experiment in carrying on through all of life's vicissitudes. Yet something extra is added when we look at his speech on the page (paradoxically, it is a kind of absence), taking the form of a white space at the end of each line.

Poetic line endings often encourage uncertainty about the future, as we reach the final word in a line of verse and wonder what will come next. Indeed, the poet and critic Clive James has described a line ending as a 'phantom comma': an invisible piece of punctuation that asks us to pause on the outer edge of a poem before continuing. But as Hamlet's soliloquy shows, it can also be a way of wondering what will happen when we reach a much larger ending: not just the actual comma that follows a line like 'the dread of something after death', but death itself.

Chekhov once suggested that 'Art doesn't have to solve problems, it only has to formulate them correctly', and we've seen in this chapter that certain kinds of writing are good at formulating some pretty sizeable problems – such as whether or not we should carry on living – without attempting to solve them. Naturally, not everyone enjoys the spectacle of such doubts being acted out in public. One of the funniest scenes in Dickens's *Great Expectations* involves a minor character named Wopsle performing the lead role in a ramshackle London production of *Hamlet*. 'Whenever that undecided Prince had to ask a question or state a doubt, the public helped him out with it,' Pip reports. 'As for example: on the question whether it was nobler in the mind to suffer, some roared yes, and some no, and some inclining to both opinions said "Toss up for it;" and quite a Debating Society arose.' However, for many people the value of a literary work like *Hamlet* partly lies in the fact that a soliloquy like the one Wopsle is attempting already contains a wide range of opinions.

In several previous chapters I've quoted from the critic William Empson, particularly in relation to his idea that one of a creative writer's most important tasks may be to give expression to a number of different points of view, even if they end up coming into conflict with each other. As Empson put it in an introduction he wrote to a selection of Coleridge's verse, 'Large societies need to include a variety of groups with different moral codes or scales of value, and it is part of the business of a writer to act as a go-between; so their differences are liable to become a conflict within himself.' No literary work takes this idea more seriously – or treats it more playfully – than *Hamlet*. While the soliloquy we've been considering in this chapter seems to offer a simple binary choice – live or die? – the Ghost's appearance has already shown us that this might be too crude a distinction. Which category does the Ghost fall into: 'to be' or 'not to be'? Actually he appears to be both, particularly if he is played by a flesh and blood actor on the stage. Elsewhere in the play Hamlet is more explicit about his doubts. He wonders if the Ghost lives 'in sea or fire, in earth or air', and asks himself if this is 'a spirit of health or goblin damned', bringing with it 'airs from heaven or blasts from hell'. And the key word in all these other speeches is also the pivot around which his most famous question revolves: 'or'. To be *or* not to be. It is a little word that sits at the very heart of a play that repeatedly challenges us to see both sides of an argument – and then to wonder if there are more than two sides.

How to Get Involved

Chapter 24

Mind the Gap

WHILE FILMING *SPARTACUS* in 1959, Peter Ustinov once gave another actor pause for thought:

> One of my first scenes with Larry Olivier consisted in my rushing up to his horse as it cavorted among a huge mass of prisoners-of-war, grabbing its bridle, and gazing up at its immaculate rider: 'If I identify Spartacus for you, Divinity, will you give me the women and children?', I said, in the character of the sleazy slave-dealer.
>
> There followed the most enormous pause while Larry let his eyes disappear upwards under his half-open lids, licked his lips, pushing at his cheeks from within with his tongue, let his head drop with a kind of comic irony at the quirks of destiny, hardened once more into the mould of mortal divinity, looked away into the unknown as his profile softened from brutal nobility into subtlety. 'Spartacus!' he suddenly cried, as though slashing the sky with a razor, and then hissed, 'You have found him?'
>
> I was so absolutely staggered at the extent of the pause that I expressed precisely the surprise I felt. Now I gazed over the prisoners with a closed expression, giving nothing away. Then I let a furtive smile play on my lips for a moment at some

private thought, chasing it away, and seemed about to say something, but changed my mind. I ran the gamut of impertinence, of servility, and of insincerity as he had of vanity, power, and menace. At long last, when he least expected it, I let a practically inaudible 'Yes' slip from my mouth.

'Dear boy,' said Larry, in a businesslike voice which ill-concealed a dawning annoyance, 'd'you think you could come in a little quicker with your Yes?'

'No,' I said politely.

We looked at each other straight in the eye, and smiled at the same moment.

Like most good anecdotes, the comedy is in the timing. There are the hypnotic rhythms that describe the workings of Olivier's body until they are suddenly interrupted with 'Spartacus!' There's the sly joke on 'precisely', as Ustinov parodies Olivier's repertoire of actorly tics by dividing them into a series of separate clauses, and then trumps him by devoting a full sentence to each of his own grins and grimaces. Finally, there's the paragraphing, which maps out the lack of contact between the actors by restricting each paragraph to a description of one or the other, until they are finally reconciled in the last sentence with a shared smile.

In real life most people don't leave such gaping holes in their conversation, but they do pause, and an ordinary social encounter is likely to be as much about what wasn't said as what was: embarrassed silences, cautious hesitations, winces of sympathy and all the other ways in which we can express ourselves without saying a word. Writing rarely records these aspects of speech, because while print can construct a voice on the page, it removes the speaker's body – its posture, its facial expressions and all the other clues we usually refer to as body language. However, there is one thing a piece of writing can offer that speech cannot: visible pauses that take the form of blank spaces on the page.

It might sound odd to suggest that readers should pay attention to what isn't written down, but some of the most successful literary works depend as much on what isn't said as on what is. For example, the famous narrative climax of Charlotte Brontë's *Jane Eyre* (1847) involves the narrator telling us 'Reader, I married him', as her slow-burn romance with Mr Rochester finally arrives at the happy ending we have spent many pages cheering on. Yet that sentence comes immediately after a gap between two chapters, as Mr Rochester – now blind and disabled – reaches out his hand to Jane:

> I took that dear hand, held it a moment to my lips, then let it pass round my shoulder: being so much lower of stature than he, I served both for his prop and guide. We entered the wood, and wended homeward.

CHAPTER XXXVIII—CONCLUSION

Reader, I married him.

There are plenty of clues before 'Reader, I married him' that the narrative is heading towards a wedding, such as the way that 'We enter*ed* the *wood*, and wend*ed* home*ward*' is rippled with fond echoes of *Edward* Rochester, but the first time we read *Jane Eyre* we cannot be absolutely sure that this is the ending we will be granted. The 'Conclusion' could just as easily turn out to be a sad parting like that of Pip and Estella at the end of *Great Expectations*, or an even sadder deathbed scene like those found in many other Victorian novels. The blank space between the chapters is one in which we can allow our imaginations to run free and project any number of possible narrative outcomes.

Other gaps are even harder for us to fill, either because we are not given enough information to know what happened, or the writer wants to suggest that in some circumstances even they can be lost for words. In Hilary Mantel's historical novel *Bring Up the Bodies* (2012), one particularly chilling narrative climax is the execution of Anne Boleyn, but the moment of her death isn't described fully: 'The man is behind Anne, she is misdirected, she does not sense him. There is a groan, one single sound from the whole crowd.' At the end of one sentence she is still alive, at the start of the next sentence she is dead, and in the gap between these sentences we are left to imagine the executioner's sword whistling through the air. Similarly, in Thomas Hardy's *Tess of the d'Urbervilles* (1891), the chapter that deals with Alec's rape of Tess ends with the narrator withdrawing into the darkness of the wood where it took place, with a quiet warning about the 'immeasurable social chasm' that will henceforth divide Tess's old self from her new one. But this isn't only something we are told; it is something we see in the gap that opens up on the page between this first section of the novel, which is entitled 'The Maiden', and the second section, 'Maiden No More'. It is a blank space that signals Tess's break with her past because of something that is seemingly beyond the narrator's power – or willingness – to describe, an act that is literally unspeakable.

Poems can do this sort of thing more easily because, as we've already seen with A. E. Housman's flirtatious lines about glancing at a soldier (Chapter 4), and Hamlet's soliloquy that keeps edging towards and then edging away from death (Chapter 23), blank spaces are crucial to how they work. 'Every poem breaks a silence that had to be overcome,' writes Adrienne Rich, suggesting that a poem is a way of saying something that simply had to be said. But every poem is also surrounded by the silence of the page, a kind of muteness that each line of verse must approach before our eyes recoil to the start of the next line and we carry on reading.

Poets have long recognised that line endings are an imaginative resource to be exploited just as much as any other element of print. When Peter Robinson describes his girlfriend taking a bath –

> Seeing as she submerges
> disturbances of the foamy water,
> unnoticed here, I look at her
>
> skin suffused with warmth, the margins
> of her self and I acknowledge
> urges he pressed home, my fears.

– he captures the flick of the speaker's eyes with that sudden shift from 'her' to 'skin', but the blank space between these lines makes it unclear whether the skin being referred to is his girlfriend's, warmed by the bathwater, or his own, flushed with desire, or embarrassment, or possibly even shame given that this poem depicts the aftermath of a sexual assault by another man that Robinson witnessed at gunpoint. (The internal rhyme of 'submerges' and 'urges' is especially striking as a way of acknowledging how trauma can make some thoughts rise to the surface unbidden.) In this way, the gap between the lines is used to imagine more than the couple's physical separation. It demonstrates how people can map out their relationships according to a far more intimate human geography, as someone might feel remote from a colleague who is in the same room and much closer to a friend or lover who is thousands of miles away.

These are all examples of blank spaces that writers can drop into their work for us to negotiate, like someone hopping from one stepping stone to the next. But it's possible for these spaces to be more than marginal presences on the page. Take the short poem 'O Breath' by the American poet Elizabeth Bishop:

> Beneath that loved   and celebrated breast,
> silent, bored really   blindly veined,
> grieves, maybe   lives and lets
> live, passes   bets,
> something moving   but invisibly,
> and with what clamor   why restrained
> I cannot fathom   even a ripple.
> (See the thin flying   of nine black hairs
> four around one   five the other nipple,
> flying almost intolerably   on your own breath.)
> Equivocal, but what we have in common's   bound to be there,
> whatever we must own   equivalents for,
> something that maybe I   could bargain with
> and make a separate peace   beneath
> within   if never with.

This was written in 1950 at a particularly difficult time in Bishop's life. On the verge of turning forty, she was depressed and often drunk; that summer, while living in a writers' retreat at Saratoga Springs, New York, she had also suffered from flu, bronchitis and a bad case of poison ivy. Her relationship with a man named Tom Wanning had broken down, and with it any remaining hopes of leading a traditional heterosexual life. (Her most intense romantic relationships tended to be with other women.) Even more significantly, she was trying to deal with her chronic asthma by giving herself regular injections of adrenalin that left her feeling dizzy and nauseated.

In 'O Breath' she takes that final reference point and makes it central to her verse. Let's examine how she does this. Most lyrical poems pretend to be a stream of private thoughts that just happen to have been made public. This one reveals the thoughts that go through a woman's head as she watches her lover silently lying beside her, self-consciously aware that although they are occupying the same bed there may be some even more intimate things they will never share. Perhaps her lover is silent because she is bored. Or perhaps she is satisfied after sex, or unhappy after an argument, or just unwilling to talk. The speaker simply doesn't know. On the surface, even the smallest details of her lover's body can be seen, such as the individual hairs growing around her nipples that wave around in her breath, but the much larger movements going on inside her head and heart are wholly invisible.

At times Bishop's poem seems equally reluctant to share its speaker's feelings. 'Beneath that loved and celebrated breast' is written in blank verse, and therefore hints at a dramatic speech like Hamlet's soliloquy. When we read this line, we are led to expect another example of a lyric poet voicing their most intimate experiences, as if a poem were really a sort of confessional booth in which absolutely anything could be said. But the printed gap between 'loved' and 'and' warns us that the situation of Bishop's speaker is more complicated than this, and as the poem continues its blank verse quickly stutters and collapses. Instead, a different kind of 'blank' starts to structure the poem: those extra gaps in the middle of each line that present themselves simultaneously as an absence and a literary backbone, keeping each half of the line apart from the other while also joining both halves together.

It's possible to read these blank spaces in several different ways. They could represent the physical space that love is traditionally thought to bypass, like the balcony that Juliet traditionally stands on to talk to Romeo in Shakespeare's play; alternatively, they could represent rifts of understanding, hidden emotions and unspoken desires of many kinds. ('Poetry should have more of the unconscious spots left in,' Bishop wrote in one of her notebooks.) Read with the knowledge of her asthma, the spaces could even represent her struggle for breath – the little gasps that could occur whenever she tried to inhale, here caught within a ribcage of words.

This last possibility starts to involve us too, because when we read 'O Breath' aloud we can synchronise the swell and fall of our own lungs with the rises and dips of Bishop's voice on the page, as we read a phrase like 'and moving' and have to decide how to bridge the gap between it and 'but invisibly', whether with frustration or resignation or simple amazement that even someone who fills your field of vision can still be in some ways invisible to you. Our reading reminds us that even if her lover cannot breathe in sympathy with her struggle, perhaps we can. Through our voice, Bishop's speaker 'lives and lets | live'.

If such poems can be therapeutic to write, they can be equally therapeutic to read. This is an idea worth pausing over, because although some readers might feel embarrassed to acknowledge that they go to literature for more than just a sophisticated game of make-believe, there is a long history of thinking that a good read might actually do us some good.

The term 'bibliotherapy' (or, strictly speaking, 'bibliotherapeutic practice') was originally coined in the story 'A Literary Clinic' published in the *Atlantic Monthly* in 1916. At this stage it still carried a tang of satire: as the story opens, we are told of an advertisement in the local church offering 'Book Treatment by Competent Specialists', and promising 'individual treatment' for 'Tired Business Men's tired wives'. As things develop, however, this 'Bibliopathic Institute' starts to sound like a fairly responsible way of dealing with the background hum of everyday stress, if not the more serious mental problems that psychologists were grappling with at the time. ('A Literary Clinic' was published only a year after the term 'shell shock' first started to appear in medical writings.) 'From my point of view,' explains the main character, 'a book is a literary prescription put up for the benefit of someone who needs it.' Some books are stimulants designed to perk us up, he observes, or irritants to shift us out of complacency. Others fail to work on us because we have become immune to their ideas. In fact the real task of literary criticism, he concludes, should not be to pass judgement on a particular book, but to establish the effect it has on a reader. 'What was his state of mind before reading and after reading? Was he better or worse for his experience?'

However, the idea that books can improve our quality of life goes back much further. According to the ancient Greek historian Diodorus Siculus, the sacred library of Pharoah Rameses II bore the inscription 'Healing-Place of the Soul' over its entrance. More recent authors have been equally convinced that reading can have a therapeutic value. 'Come, and take choice of all my library', Shakespeare's Titus Andronicus tells his daughter, 'And so beguile thy sorrow'. That might seem like a rather tactless suggestion, given that she has just had her hands cut off and is seen turning the leaves of a book with her stumps, but her attempt to find a parallel for her situation in an earlier story, in this case the tragic tale of Philomel in Ovid's *Metamorphoses*, is just one example of how a piece of writing might be used as an inspiration or a source of comfort.

That's certainly been my experience. I first came across 'O Breath' shortly before a failed one-night stand many years ago. There had been an evening of dancing and drinking, although in truth probably more drinking than dancing. What happened next is restricted to a few out of focus snapshots in my head. A first tentative kiss . . . an uninhibited snog . . . a taxi ride home in the early hours . . . some experimental fumbling . . . and then nothing. He lay silently in my bed while I lay next to him. Perhaps he was unable to articulate his emotions, or too embarrassed to express his desires. Perhaps he was simply asleep. Like Bishop's speaker, I too found myself watching someone from a distance of a few inches who might as well have been in another country. And although I could not have expressed myself with anything like her passion or guile, it was reassuring to think that she was keeping me company at a time when otherwise I felt unexpectedly alone.

Chapter 25

Body Matters

ELIZABETH BISHOP'S POEM plays with a paradox, because it describes the impossibility of knowing what someone else is thinking in a way that allows us to overhear the speaker's own thoughts. In previous chapters I have outlined some of the ways in which this sort of activity can involve more than just a temporary escape from selfhood. Indeed, in recent years a number of evolutionary biologists and neuroscientists have argued that an ability to see life through another person's eyes, and hear it through another person's ears, is crucial to the workings of society as a whole. As a group of researchers at Yale University put it in 2016, summarising eleven years of data on the health and reading habits of thousands of men and women over the age of fifty, it isn't just that the longer people spent reading the longer they lived – by an average of two years according to the researchers. The quality of that life was also significantly improved, because the mental effort of reading kept the brains of the research subjects active and developed their 'empathy, social perception, and emotional intelligence'. We will come back to this idea that in building up our powers of empathy we can use a shelf of books as the mental equivalent of a weightlifting bench and a rack of dumbbells. For now, it's worth considering if there are any experiences that might challenge one of the central ideas behind this research, which is that books allow us to slip on someone else's skin and try it for size.

One example is pain. I cannot experience or share your pain, any more than you can experience or share mine. Nor can pain be made visible without undergoing an MRI scan to show the presence of nerve damage or another physiological cause, so that if you claim to be suffering from a headache or heartburn I cannot know how badly you are afflicted or even if you are telling the truth. Pain therefore puts at risk many of the things on which social life is based, such as sympathy and trust. This includes language, because the words we use assume the possibility of shared experience, and the fact that pain is unavoidably private is reflected in the relatively narrow vocabulary we have to describe it. As Virginia Woolf pointed out in her essay 'On Being Ill', 'The merest schoolgirl when she falls in love has Shakespeare or Keats to speak her mind for her, but let a sufferer try to describe a pain in his head to a doctor and language at once runs dry.' It is why, if you search for 'pain' in an English thesaurus, you find words like 'discomfort', 'malaise', 'inconvenience' and 'distress', but soon find yourself scrabbling around for much looser alternatives such as 'thin time' and 'hell'. ('Pleasure', by contrast, is rich with synonyms: 'gratification', 'sensuousness', 'self-indulgence', 'luxuriousness', 'hedonism' and many more.) Pain lives a secret life hidden away in the blanks and gaps of language; it is where nature breaks in and culture breaks down.

However, this is also where some of the other resources of literature can prove helpful, because as I have tried to show in previous chapters when we pick up a book we are encouraged to see things from two perspectives at once: from the outside, as a reader, but also from the inside, as the author or a character. This doubling of our viewpoint means that a piece of writing about someone who is in pain can ask us to put ourselves in their position, while also recognising that pain risks making us strangers to each other – and sometimes even to ourselves.

Let me explain what I mean by looking at a sonnet entitled 'Pain' by the soldier-poet Ivor Gurney, composed in the winter of 1917 as part of a sequence that was intended to be a harder-edged, more realistic alternative to the soft-focus verses written by poets like Rupert Brooke at the start of the war. (Probably Brooke's most famous lines are to be found in 'The Soldier', published posthumously in 1915, a sonnet in which he imagines a soldier proudly declaring 'If I should die, think only this of me: | That there's some corner of a foreign field | That is for ever England.') Gurney had spent the previous few months in France as part of a battalion stationed just behind the front line, where he had primarily been fighting against the sort of cold that froze the cocoa in his mug and against mud that seeped into every pore. 'Pain' goes further still, by trying to imagine what life was like for a soldier in the trenches who found himself being subjected to the same torments hour after hour:

> Pain, pain continual; pain unending;
> Hard even to the roughest, but to those
> Hungry for beauty . . . Not the wisest knows,
> Nor most pitiful-hearted, what the wending
> Of one hour's way meant. Grey monotony lending
> Weight to the grey skies, grey mud where goes
> An army of grey bedrenched scarecrows in rows
> Careless at last of cruellest Fate-sending.
> Seeing the pitiful eyes of men foredone,
> Or horses shot, too tired merely to stir,
> Dying in shell-holes, both, slain by the mud.
> Men broken, shrieking even to hear a gun.—
> Till pain grinds down, or lethargy numbs her,
> The amazed heart cries angrily out on God.

In Chapter 4, I mentioned the fact that *verse* comes from the Latin *vertere*, meaning 'to turn'. Here, we notice that Gurney repeatedly uses his verse to raise the possibility of things changing, before going on to reveal that they don't, as each new line reveals itself to be just another turn of the screw. The result is a poem that offers an accurate assessment of the military stalemate that this form of warfare produced, but also tries to capture the experience of a soldier for whom living in the trenches meant simply surviving from one moment to the next.

The opening words provide a good example. 'Pain, pain continual; pain unending;' – the line is filled with expressions of pain, but not the kind that has an end in sight. There are three repetitions of pain and two semicolons, but no full stop; the rhythm falters but life goes on – although only the kind of life where we know that pain must return at some point, as it does in the penultimate line, where we are told that 'pain grinds down'.

The rest of the poem isn't straightforward to paraphrase: perhaps appropriately, it's hard to understand at times, as if trying to capture a soldier's ground-level confusion in its own style. Indeed, although we usually understand a 'war poem' to be a poem that takes war as its *subject*, there are moments in 'Pain' when Gurney seems to be trying to create a poem out of the *experience* of war. That's one of the reasons why his choice of the sonnet form is so jarring, as his words struggle to fit within this traditional structure like a child with a colouring book who is unable to stay within the lines.

Traditionally, sonnets were written as expressions of love, where the suffering they dealt with was possible heartbreak rather than being mentally 'broken' by constant shellfire or the risk of drowning in mud. This poem adopts many of the conventions of the form, including a rhyme scheme that is familiar from Petrarch's love sonnets, and an iambic metre that thuds away under the words like a rapid heartbeat. Yet this traditional structure is both stretched and squashed in Gurney's hands, indicating that it doesn't altogether fit the shape of a modern soldier's experience. For example, when we read of 'Grey monotony lending | Weight to the grey skies, grey mud where goes | An army of grey bedrenched scarecrows in rows', we realise that in each line the rhythm either undershoots or overspills the ten syllables we would normally expect. It is like watching a traditional sonnet suffering a breakdown, and this isn't restricted to the way its rhythms keep mixing together predictable routines with sudden shocks and spasms. The scarecrows stand in rows; their 'grey' colour blends with the 'grey monotony' of 'grey skies' and 'grey clothes'. In many ways it is a poem that keeps flirting with the opposite of poetry: not eloquence but a kind of verbal grumbling; not elegant variations on a theme but shell-shocked repetition.

Once we realise that repetition is the keynote of Gurney's poem – a feature of writing we have already seen working its way through many other literary works – we might want to return to that opening line, 'Pain, pain continual; pain unending'. Does this imagine different examples of the same experience, or different kinds of experience altogether? Is the pain being suffered by one soldier, three soldiers, or all soldiers? Just as Gurney's repetitions of 'pain' could suggest what the soldiers have in common, or what they cannot share even in the mud of the trenches, so we are reminded that we can never know for sure what it was like to be them, no matter how 'wise' or 'pitiful-hearted' we may be.

If we wanted a contemporary model for the thinking behind this sort of poem, we could turn to Sigmund Freud's essay 'Thoughts for the Times on War and Death'. Written in 1915, when the conflict had already spread across much of Europe, Freud's argument for how this disaster could be approached by readers of literature involves a mixture of optimism and pessimism. On the one hand, he points out that literature gives us a means of seeking compensation for what has been lost in life. If someone dies on the battlefield there is no return, whereas in reading we can die with the hero and yet survive him, ready to die again just as safely with someone else. 'In the realm of fiction,' Freud concludes, 'we find the plurality of lives which we need.' On the other hand, he was convinced that the present war would 'sweep away this conventional treatment of death', because it could no longer be treated as merely a literary conceit. When people really were dying in their thousands every day, enjoying a fictional depiction of death might seem as misjudged as smoking a cigarette while your house was on fire.

This is the world that Gurney's wonderfully unsettling sonnet captures. If the soldiers are described as 'foredone', which can mean anything from 'worn out' to 'destroyed', Gurney's speaker seems similarly exhausted. At the end of the first sentence his voice trails off with a despairing ellipsis: 'Hard even to the roughest, but to those | Hungry for beauty . . . ' Words fail him, just as reading his sonnet reminds us there may be some experiences we cannot avoid keeping at arm's length.

We might think of this as a useful corrective to one of the suggestions I have made in earlier chapters of this book, which is that literature can give us what seems like infinite access into other people's minds. For when we read a poem like Gurney's 'Pain', no matter how hard we try to imagine the 'pitiful eyes' of these soldiers in the trenches, our attempts to be 'pitiful-hearted' will never match up as perfectly as that internal chime of 'pitiful' and 'pitiful'. Even the final rhyme fails to land – 'mud'/'God' – where the lack of a full connection is like an emblem of the way most readers are likely to approach the poem as a whole. Repeatedly, we are invited to experience the trenches alongside Gurney's speaker; repeatedly, we are reminded that there are limits to what we can see with our own pitiful eyes.

Chapter 26

Good and Bad Sex

IT ISN'T ONLY WRITING about pain that poses a challenge to empathy. Writing about pleasure can sometimes be just as difficult. Starting in 1993, the *Literary Review*'s annual Bad Sex in Fiction Award has obligingly highlighted the worst – and therefore in comic terms the best – fictional descriptions of sex published in the previous twelve months. Some highlights, if that's the right word, include nominated passages from Richard E. Grant's 1998 novel *By Design* ('I really have little choice other than to succumb completely, vaguely conscious that should she guide my now throbbing Titanic into her icebergs, I would definitely be sunk'), Jeffrey Eugenides's 2002 *Middlesex* ('I reached under her. I brought her up to me. And then my body, like a cathedral, broke out into ringing. The hunchback in the belfry had jumped and was swinging madly on the rope'), and Rupert Thomson's 2013 *Secrecy* ('I kissed the soft bristles in the hollow of her armpit, then I kissed the smaller hollow of her clavicle. I moved up to her mouth, which smelled of ripe melon. Not the wound-red Tuscan watermelon, but the pale-green variety I had bought in Naples once, and which had grown, so I was told, on the wild coast of Barbaria'), all of which try to build intense narrative excitement but soon collapse into anticlimax.

Earlier writers had tried to tackle this problem in various

ways, including pornographic flourishes, squeamish euphemisms and fading into a discreet silence rather than grappling with the physical realities of sex – the literary equivalent of the old Hollywood convention in which the camera would pan away at steamy moments and politely stare out of the window instead. Other writers attempted to make such scenes signify something far loftier, either by tossing around big abstract nouns like 'bliss' or 'fulfilment', or by using language that seemed to have very little to do with the body at all. We sometimes see this in the novels of D. H. Lawrence, whose attempts to treat sex with a quasi-religious reverence produce metaphors that are so baroque (sacraments, fountains, vibrations, electrical currents), it's not always clear what's happening in terms of the insert-tab-A-into-slot-B side of things. So, when Paul Morel has sex with Clara in *Sons and Lovers* (1913), and we are told that 'It was as if he, and the stars, and the dark herbage, and Clara were licked up in an immense tongue of flame, which tore onwards and upwards', it may take the reader a moment to work out that they are experiencing orgasm together rather than being trapped by a forest fire.

The odd thing is that you might expect sex and writing to have quite a lot in common. Both involve people reaching out to each other to share something that will make them feel less alone; both take something familiar, whether this is words or body parts, and try to create something uniquely memorable from them. Actually, it turns out that writing is much better at capturing the experience of desire or *wanting* than it is at depicting sexual satisfaction. Wanting to tell. Wanting to know. Leaving us wanting more.

There may be an element of evolutionary biology at work here. The neuroscientist Jaak Panksepp has observed that our brains contain a 'seeking' system that originally evolved to help us with activities such as hunting and foraging, and when we are successful in a search our brains give us a temporary chemical hit. Seen from this perspective, our brains work as efficient dopamine delivery systems: they reward us for seeking something by making us want more of the same. Here they can be compared to rats in laboratory experiments who are taught to press a certain lever in order to receive a tasty shot of sugar solution, and continue to press the lever long after the source of their treats has been exhausted. Our brains, similarly, have evolved to want more of what can satisfy us only briefly. That is why, when we repeatedly reach into a box of popcorn, we are not behaving very differently to the laboratory rats; we too have learned that if we perform a certain physical gesture we will be rewarded with a little rush of pleasure, so we move from liking what is in our mouths to wanting more of it, again and again, until either we start to feel sick or the box is empty.

According to the psychologist Norman Holland, this is also how reading works. When we read, we want to know what is coming next, and then we like it when the next line meets or alters our expectations. In this way, our brain switches back and forth between wanting and liking until either we have had enough or we have reached the last page. Satisfaction-seeking of this kind turns any book into what Holland calls 'a self-stimulation system'. Regardless of how complicated the language is or how sophisticated the style, turning its pages is the psychological equivalent of reaching into a big box of popcorn.

This may also be why authors who find sex a challenging subject to write about are far better when it comes to flirtation, or what the psychoanalyst Adam Phillips has described as 'the calculated production of uncertainty'. And few writers are as good at this sort of thing as the eighteenth-century Anglican cleric and novelist Laurence Sterne.

Novelists are sometimes advised to *show* rather than *tell* in their work, as we saw in Chapter 2, so that the reader feels a scene is unfolding without the author's hand nudging it in a particular direction. The brilliance of a story like Sterne's *A Sentimental Journey* (1768) lies in the fact that any obvious distinction between showing and telling is playfully blurred. This was Sterne's final work, as he died of tuberculosis in his London lodgings less than a month after its publication. In the preceding weeks he had been sitting for a portrait by Joshua Reynolds that was left unfinished on his death. Yet in some ways the fact that this portrait remained a work in progress meant that it probably got closer to capturing Sterne's character – frisky, nimble, unpredictable – than the varnished sheen of another portrait of him that Reynolds completed in 1760 and that now hangs in the National Portrait Gallery. *A Sentimental Journey* is similarly elusive.

In terms of the plot, very little happens: the narrator travels to France, meets a handful of people and reflects sententiously on the feelings they arouse in him. And yet, almost every sentence glints with the suggestion that what we are being told is only a fraction of a story that is far too rude to be narrated fully. Indeed, the more we read, the more the narrator's words start to resemble little icebergs poking out of a page that is much better at giving us hints and glimpses than full-scale revelations.

In a chapter entitled 'The Temptation', the narrator returns to his Paris hotel where he learns that a lady's maid is waiting for him in his bedroom. He begins by piously reminding her of a 'lesson of virtue' he gave her when they first met the previous evening, but as he holds her by the hands he soon finds himself trembling at the thought of letting her go:

> The foot of the bed was within a yard and a half of the place where we were standing. – I had still hold of her hands – and how it happened I can give no account; but I neither ask'd her – nor drew her – nor did I think of the bed; – but so it did happen, we both sat down.

I'll just show you, said the fair *fille de chambre*, the little purse I have been making to-day to hold your crown. So she put her hand into her right pocket, which was next me, and felt for it some time – then into the left. —'She had lost it.'— I never bore expectation more quietly; – it was in her right pocket at last; – she pull'd it out; it was of green taffeta, lined with a little bit of white quilted satin, and just big enough to hold the crown: she put it into my hand; – it was pretty; and I held it ten minutes with the back of my hand resting upon her lap – looking sometimes at the purse, sometimes on one side of it.

A stitch or two had broke out in the gathers of my stock; the fair *fille de chambre*, without saying a word, took out her little housewife [i.e. sewing kit], threaded a small needle, and sew'd it up. – I foresaw it would hazard the glory of the day; and, as she pass'd her hand in silence across and across my neck in the manœuvre, I felt the laurels shake which fancy had wreath'd about my head.

A strap had given way in her walk, and the buckle of her shoe was just falling off. – See, said the *fille de chambre*, holding up her foot. —I could not, for my soul but fasten the buckle in return, and putting in the strap, – and lifting up the other foot with it, when I had done, to see both were right, – in doing it too suddenly, it unavoidably threw the fair *fille de chambre* off her centre, – and then—

And then the chapter ends.

What's really going on here? The passage is full of teasing uncertainties. Is the *fille de chambre*'s flourishing of a home-made purse merely proof that she is good at needlework, or is it a saucy piece of symbolism? (Dictionaries of slang note that the use of 'sew' to mean 'have sexual intercourse' is later than this story, dating from the nineteenth century, but 'purse' had been used to mean 'vagina' from as early as the sixteenth century.) Does 'how it happened I can give no account' indicate that they sat down together by chance, or does it imply that he is too embarrassed to tell us what he really did to get her onto the bed? When he informs us that 'doing it too suddenly, it unavoidably threw the fair *fille de chambre* off her centre', is he describing an accidental slip or a carefully rehearsed seduction technique?

One way of trying to make sense of these questions would be to read the passage as an early example of a bedroom farce. Often comedy relies on situations that could be interpreted in more than one way, as we have already seen, and that is especially the case when it comes to farce, where the vicar might drop his trousers for a reason that is perfectly innocent to him but open to gleeful misinterpretation from anyone else. This scene from *A Sentimental Journey* works in a similar way, by offering us a set of events that are completely innocent and smirkingly un-innocent at the same time. The narrator's dashes could suggest panting excitement or simply a measured attempt to recall events as accurately as possible, just as the *fille de chambre*'s promise 'I'll just show you . . . ' opens up a host of lascivious possibilities in our minds before the sentence resumes with '. . . the little purse I have made.' Similarly, the next chapter is entitled 'THE CONQUEST', which could be sexual (the narrator acted on his desires), or moral (he managed to repress his desires), or merely captures his sense of triumph at putting the chambermaid's shoe back on.

One of Sterne's tricks in this passage is to create a chatty style that makes it seem as if we're being taken into the narrator's confidence, when it's really more of a confidence trick that places the responsibility for interpretation squarely on the reader. But we are hardly given a free hand, because it's impossible to read a phrase such as 'nor did I think of the bed' without thinking of beds, just as it's impossible when told 'don't think about an elephant' not to think about elephants. Such now-you-see-it-now-you-don't narrative sleights of hand are repeated in practically every sentence of this passage. Sterne even plays the same game with one of the tiniest words imaginable: 'it'. As we've already seen with seaside postcards, few words are as open to winking innuendo as 'it' ('I beg you, Florence – don't break it off!'), particularly when placed in conjunction with 'doing' – hence the original British version of the TV drama *Queer as Folk*, where fifteen-year old Nathan (Charlie Hunnam) sleeps with the far more sexually experienced Stuart Jones (Aidan Gillen) for the first time, and later boasts to his best friend that 'I'm doing it. I'm really doing it!' Yet in the case of this passage, when we read 'doing it too suddenly' we can entertain dirty thoughts while reminding ourselves that everything might indeed be as innocent as the narrator keeps telling us it is. To the pure all things are pure.

These narrative games haven't always been enjoyed by Sterne's readers. Samuel Richardson wrote of *Tristram Shandy*, Sterne's far longer but equally flirtatious novel, that the author's 'own character as a clergyman seems much impeached by printing such gross and vulgar tales, as no decent mind can endure without extreme disgust!' Even Dickens's contemporary William Makepeace Thackeray, whose own sense of humour could be equally risqué, wrote poker-faced that 'Some of that dreary *double entendre* may be attributed to freer times and manners than ours, but not all. The foul satyr's eyes leer out of the leaves constantly.'

Other readers may wonder if there's something narrowly British about innuendo – after all, the BBC managed to squeeze ten series of the 1970s sitcom *Are You Being Served?* out of little more than jokes about the fact that Mrs Slocombe referred to her pet cat as her 'pussy'. ('Can we get on? I've got to get home. If my pussy isn't attended to by eight o'clock I shall be stroking it for the rest of the evening.') It certainly seems to be the case that a language as pleated with potential ambiguities as English is especially vulnerable to words revealing their unexpectedly rude undersides. (The comedian Kenneth Williams once declared that he couldn't stand innuendo, and 'If I see one in a script I whip it out immediately.') Yet this polysemic richness has allowed innuendo to spread far beyond the shores of Britain: there are even blink-and-you-miss-them examples of it in mainstream US TV shows, such as the fleeting glimpse of a comic in a 2014 episode of *The Simpsons* that depicts Batman lying next to Robin and saying 'TIME FOR BED, DICK'.

What makes *A Sentimental Journey* an especially interesting example of this linguistic phenomenon is that it isn't only sex that Sterne keeps flirting with. He seems equally interested in flirting with narrative itself. The passage is full of words that draw attention to what might be about to happen next ('expectation . . . foresaw . . . and then'), but it is also full of digressions, dead ends and non sequiturs. Like the rest of the book, which starts off as a story about travel but quickly finds itself spending far longer describing the body's emotions than its physical motions, it is a piece of writing that keeps promising revelations and then happily failing to deliver on its promises.

While some readers might find the lack of anything more explicit disappointing, others will recognise that sex is always likely to slip away from any serious attempts to pin it down in words. What we are left with in a novel like *A Sentimental Journey* is something that is in some ways just as intimate, and certainly longer-lasting: the author's measured touch in the form of writing that we in turn touch when we pick up the book and start to read.

A Sentimental Journey isn't as popular with modern readers as Sterne's genre-bending, taboo-tweaking novel *Tristram*

Shandy, which he published in nine volumes between 1759 and 1767 and only stopped writing when its sales started to dip. (*Tristram Shandy* is a perfect example of the claim made by the poet Paul Valéry that a work of art is never truly completed but only abandoned.) But anyone who tries to get to grips with *A Sentimental Journey*'s playful prose is likely to discover that it has far more in common than they might have expected with some of the literary bestsellers we have already considered. Like a detective story (e.g., 'The Boscombe Valley Mystery') or a novel that is centred on romance (e.g., *Emma*), one of the reasons we keep reading *A Sentimental Journey* is that it keeps deferring the outcome we are expecting, and when it comes to fiction a pleasure deferred is usually a pleasure extended. We keep reaching into the box of popcorn, and discover that thankfully there is still enough to keep us going.

In a sense, this question also goes to the heart of what makes a successful novel. Writers of many different genres have to decide what to leave out, whether this is a poet who has to squash their ideas into a fixed number of syllables, or a playwright who can only let a character speak for a certain amount of time before the audience starts to cough and fidget. But the fact that there is no generally agreed-upon limit to the length of a novel, no rim against which it must strike, means that a novelist is likely to be especially sensitive to what George Saunders has described as 'the wisdom of omission'. Saunders's comment comes in the context of a discussion of Tolstoy's richly ambiguous story 'Alyosha the Pot' (1911), where he speculates on why Tolstoy chose not to disclose what his main character was feeling at a key moment in the narrative. 'The secret of boring people,' says Chekhov, 'lies in telling them everything,' and for Saunders what makes 'Alyosha the Pot' so successful is the author's decision to close his eyes at a critical juncture, to swerve away from telling us all we might want to know. Instead he leaves it to us to decide, or to fail to decide, or to ask other people what they have decided.

Sterne does something similar. He seems to have been a writer who realised that when we read a literary work we don't want it to feel like work, and that's probably why reading *A Sentimental Journey* turns out to be quite the opposite. It feels more like a game being played between two people who are both trying to establish the rules as they go along.

Chapter 27

The Attraction of Repulsion

SHORTLY BEFORE STERNE'S narrator and the *fille de chambre* sit down on the bed, they share an even more intimate moment. As the narrator writes a card, he notices that the sunlight is shining through some crimson curtains on the bedroom window, and casting a red glow onto the *fille de chambre*'s face. 'I thought she blush'd', he explains, and 'the idea of it made me blush myself', which then 'superinduced a second blush before the first could get off'. Initially he tries to dismiss this as just a physiological reflex, writing that a 'pleasing half guilty blush' can be caused by the 'impetuous' blood rising from the heart to the face, before adding that a sense of virtue followed and therefore sharpened his original guilt. This is all pretty confusing, and within a sentence he abandons any attempt to make sense of what he was feeling: 'I'll not describe it.' It's an emotional tangle that isn't much helped by the pulsing repetitions of 'blush'd . . . blush . . . blush' in his account, because the more often he uses this word the more fragmented its meaning becomes.

The narrator's flailing attempts to put his blush into words reveal the wide range of emotions that might make someone's face redden, including a prickle of embarrassment, a throb of desire and a tingle of indignation that anyone could imagine their feelings were at all dishonourable. There may even be a quiet nod towards Sterne's tuberculosis, as the progress of this disease was thought to include strong visual contrasts of blooming skin and pallor. Such ambiguity offers even more evidence of something we have already explored in several previous chapters, which is that when we are faced with complex feelings a piece of writing can help us make sense of – or embrace – this complexity. As the critic Christopher Ricks has pointed out in his brilliant book *Keats and Embarrassment* (1974), even something that initially seems as simple as a blush can encourage us to recognise the mixed feelings we might have about the bodies of other people, which can excite a shiver of desire, a shudder of horror, or sometimes a mixture of the two.

This is especially the case when it comes to one of the strongest of all feelings: disgust. From diligently checking what emerges from our noses or bowels, to watching horror films that crawl with maggots and ooze with slime, many of us are drawn towards what would otherwise repel us. To borrow John Forster's description of why his friend Dickens kept returning to the swarming slums of London, this is 'the attraction of repulsion', and it is probably worth spending a few moments exploring how it works in general before investigating why it is particularly important in certain kinds of writing.

As several anthropologists have pointed out, disgust provides us with a means of dividing up the world according to established conceptual schemes, separating the pure from the impure and the safe from the defiling. It works like the body's radar, reminding us which physical substances to use and which to avoid. It also embodies our moral judgements about what is good and what is evil. According to Samuel Johnson, writing in his periodical *The Rambler*, vice 'should always disgust', and it's hard to express a moral judgement without using the lexicon of disgust, from Shakespeare's rich attraction to the language of abomination and loathing, to contemporary phrases like 'that's revolting' or 'you make me want to puke'. Disgust asserts and preserves differences: the difference between me and you, which is why I can pick my nose but not your nose, and much larger differences of class and status, which is why it has been such a powerful political tool in encouraging discrimination, from medieval writings that linked Jews with leprosy and poisoning wells, to Nazi propaganda that linked them with lice and excrement. Above all, disgust patrols the frontier that keeps us distinct from what we are not, especially animals, hence the strong aversion of most people to picking up dog mess with their bare hands or eating from the same bowl as the cat – or even to eating the cat, given how fuzzy the boundary already is between many people and their pets.

At the same time, disgust monitors our personal frontiers, or what the sociologist Erving Goffman has described as the self's 'territorial preserve'. Disgust is especially active around our orifices, where dangerous or contaminating substances can enter or exit. As the psychologist Paul Rozin explains, orifices are the body's checkpoints but also places of transition and magical transformation. Saliva in the mouth, snot in the nose, blood in the veins, faeces in the colon and so on are benign if kept in their proper place, out of sight and mind, but what is safe inside becomes unsafe when it ventures outside. 'Although one is not disgusted by saliva in his or her own mouth, it becomes offensive outside of the body,' Rozin writes, 'so that one is disgusted at drinking from a glass into which he or she has spit'. Much the same is true of chewed food, 'which we accept in our mouths, but refuse to consume once we have spit it out'. The mouth is an especially charged point of transition, not only because something that is in the mouth is in the body but can be expelled from it by spitting it out, but also because the mouth is used to justify disgust by finding separate words to describe the same substance, as we might notice that Rozin's report uses 'saliva' for what is in the mouth and 'spit' for what has left it.

One way of thinking about disgust, then, is that it reflects our need for classification and our anxiety about what threatens the categories we create. The anthropologist Mary Douglas once famously defined dirt as 'matter out of place'. As she writes, 'Shoes are not dirty in themselves, but it is dirty to place them on the dining-table; food is not dirty in itself, but it is dirty to leave cooking utensils in the bedroom, or food bespattered on clothing.' In other words, dirt is not an isolated event but 'the by-product of a systematic ordering and classification of matter, in so far as ordering involves rejecting inappropriate elements'. To this extent, the toddler who proudly brings his full potty into a dinner party to show his mother might make her wince, because here is a sharp example of matter being out of place, but the wince itself helps to restore the adult system of classification that the toddler briefly disturbed: disgust puts things back in their place.

Some pieces of writing do more than merely describe such complex responses. They include models for their readers to adopt. For example, here is a scene from Bram Stoker's 1897 novel *Dracula* in which the earnest, rather dull English solicitor Jonathan Harker describes visiting Dracula's castle in Transylvania and meeting his host for the first time:

> His face was a strong—a very strong—aquiline, with high bridge of the thin nose and peculiarly arched nostrils; with lofty domed forehead, and hair growing scantily round the temples but profusely elsewhere. His eyebrows were very massive, almost meeting over the nose, and with bushy hair that seemed to curl in its own profusion. The mouth, so far as I could see it under the heavy moustache, was fixed and rather cruel-looking, with peculiarly sharp white teeth; these

protruded over the lips, whose remarkable ruddiness showed astonishing vitality in a man of his years. For the rest, his ears were pale, and at the tops extremely pointed; the chin was broad and strong, and the cheeks firm though thin. The general effect was one of extraordinary pallor.

Hitherto I had noticed the backs of his hands as they lay on his knees in the firelight, and they had seemed rather white and fine; but seeing them now close to me, I could not but notice that they were rather coarse—broad, with squat fingers. Strange to say, there were hairs in the centre of the palm. The nails were long and fine, and cut to a sharp point. As the Count leaned over me and his hands touched me, I could not repress a shudder. It may have been that his breath was rank, but a horrible feeling of nausea came over me, which, do what I would, I could not conceal. The Count, evidently noticing it, drew back; and with a grim sort of smile, which showed more than he had yet done his protuberant teeth, sat himself down again on his own side of the fireplace. We were both silent for a while; and as I looked towards the window I saw the first dim streak of the coming dawn. There seemed a strange stillness over everything; but as I listened I heard as if from down below in the valley the howling of many wolves. The Count's eyes gleamed, and he said:—

'Listen to them—the children of the night. What music they make!'

Most film adaptations of the novel show this moment when we first see Count Dracula, although they rarely make it clear that we are supposed to be viewing him through Harker's eyes. Instead, they tend to concentrate on creating a generally chilling atmosphere (looming stone walls, guttering candles, menacing shadows) rather than focusing on the particular details Harker notices, and after a close-up of Dracula's face they usually cut straight to his line about 'the children of the night', which different actors deliver with varying degrees of theatrical relish. Yet although these films pay a good deal of attention to Dracula's appearance, highlighting elements such as his blood-red lips and ink-black clothing (the earlier narrative detail of his 'long white moustache' is usually ignored), it's hard to see how they could capture the awkward paradoxes that Harker brings out in his description.

These include the fact that Dracula is ruddy yet pale, has hair that grows scantily in some places and profusely in others (including on his palms, which is another instance of matter out of place), and displays hands that seem elegant at first sight but upon closer inspection are unexpectedly coarse. That would be a challenging combination for any actor to portray on screen. And we notice that as Harker tries to describe Dracula's ambiguous appearance, his words also start to slip and slide around. So, he draws our attention to Dracula's 'sharp' teeth and 'pointed' ears, but also to the fact that his nails are filed to a 'sharp point'; the hands at first appear to be 'white and fine', suggesting that he is a gentleman, but they have nails that are 'long and fine', forming a visible contrast with hands that are disturbingly paw-like.

Harker's response to someone who muddles together these normal physical distinctions is a feeling of nausea. 'I could not repress a shudder', he tells us, and plainly we are expected to shudder in turn. And yet, his whole description of Dracula also borrows and updates the Renaissance convention of the literary blazon, where a writer (usually male) would lovingly itemise the physical attributes of a body (usually female), dividing it up line by line and phrase by phrase into a set of swelling breasts, shiny tresses, glowing eyes, and so on. This use, or misuse, of the convention adds an extra homoerotic edge to the way Harker looks at Dracula, which is later strengthened by other scenes in the novel where a character shudders in a way that mixes together terror and excitement, as when Van Helsing lifts up the lid of a coffin where a female vampire lies asleep 'so full of life and voluptuous beauty that I shudder as though I have come to do murder', or Harker discovers Dracula after he has killed his latest victim and now rests in his tomb like a bloated leech: 'I shuddered as I bent over to touch him, and every sense in me revolted at the contact'. And, of course, although we may flinch when we first read about Dracula, we want to carry on reading, the attraction of repulsion working like two magnets to force us back and draw us on at the same time.

Ambivalence is also sunk deeply into Harker's narrative voice. Although he tries to stick to a neutral set of facts, describing the 'high bridge' of Dracula's nose and his 'sharp white teeth', this quasi-anthropological approach is mixed up with a far more emotional register: 'rank', 'horrible', 'grim'. Sometimes these vocabularies overlap, as when Harker notices Dracula's 'coarse' hands – a word that relies on the double-jointed properties of adjectives that we have already seen being used in other literary passages, their ability to be both neutrally descriptive and charged with personal judgements. And as a result we are encouraged both to see what Harker sees and to try working out what we feel about it.

When I've taught this novel to my own students, they have usually been fairly unsure how to respond to it. 'Maybe it's about sexual decadence?' one might ask, at which point a second might add 'and postcolonial anxiety. There's a *lot* of postcolonial anxiety here.' Others aren't convinced it's a serious work of literature at all. 'Isn't it all . . . well . . . just a bit kitsch?' a third student might venture, at which point a fourth might revise 'kitsch' to 'camp': 'It's *pure* camp.' Usually my job is to agree with all of them to some extent, and help them to see that even a novel that is as flawed as *Dracula*, with all of its crude melodrama and thudding repetitiveness, may be read in many different ways.

Extending an idea I outlined in Chapter 23, to some extent this reflects the fact that Stoker, like many of the authors we've been considering so far, can be seen as a 'go-between' whose writing embraces a wide range of ideas. It also reflects the fact that he is dealing with feelings that may require a similar kind of negotiation within ourselves.

How to Read Between the Lines

Chapter 28

GHOST HUNTING

ONE OF THE REASONS WE FIND a character like Dracula so scary is that he is cognitively as well as physically threatening. Not only does he mess up categories like the hairy and the hairless, or the flushed and pale, he also blurs the ultimate distinction between the living and the dead.

This is something Bram Stoker describes in lip-smacking detail, and as his narrative develops we might notice how it starts to echo this conceptual uncertainty in its own language. For example, when Jonathan Harker writes that 'I am all in a sea of wonders' shortly after meeting Dracula for the first time (a phrase that collapses together 'all at sea' and 'full of wonder'), or Dr Seward records how Dracula had 'bolted the stable door' to escape his pursuers (a hazy recollection of the traditional advice not to close a stable door after the horse has bolted), we find ourselves in a strange linguistic limbo where clichés – metaphors that have been used so often they have gone dead – are being employed in a way that gives them an unexpected new lease of life. Something similar happens when Stoker borrows from other writers. He often does this, incorporating allusions to Shakespeare's *Hamlet*, *Othello* and *The Merchant of Venice*, Thomas Hood's poem 'The Death-Bed', Byron's *Don Juan*, Coleridge's *The Rime of the Ancient Mariner* and many other literary works, with the result that Dracula's habit of sucking the blood of his victims is strangely echoed in the way that *Dracula* repeatedly draws on the words of other writers to keep itself going. In some respects it is a vampiric novel as well as a novel about vampires.

This process isn't restricted to Gothic narratives. Indeed, we experience something similar in everyday conversation, where we often find ourselves saying things we have read or heard elsewhere, from juicy bits of gossip to other people's opinions we would like to pass off as our own. What many writers do is to extend this habit to a principle of composition, by drawing on (or mimicking, or mocking) earlier pieces of writing. Familiarity breeds content. This can involve the large-scale reimagining of famous literary works, such as Barbara Kingsolver's *Demon Copperhead* (2022) as a crowd-pleasing updating of Dickens's *David Copperfield*, or Michael Cunningham's *The Hours* (1998) as a haunting reprise of Woolf's *Mrs Dalloway*. But it can also involve smaller moments in a book, when we reach a particular phrase or sentence and discover that it is a wormhole leading us into a completely different literary world.

At this point several things can happen. Sometimes the differences between these worlds start to melt away, like strangers entering into conversation with each other and discovering how much they have in common. (We've already seen an example of this in Chapter 22, as Carol Ann Duffy establishes a network of connections with other writers to test the strength of a living human relationship.) Such literary associations can also create stranger, more unexpected points of contact. 'My thighs ache and my clothes are soaked with sweat' writes the gay journalist Oscar Moore of a visit to a disco just a few months before he died of AIDS, reworking the opening lines of Keats's 'Ode to a Nightingale': 'My heart aches, and a drowsy numbness pains | My sense.' Of course it may be that Keats came into his head by accident – writers often find that their memories are as sticky as flypaper when it comes to the books they have read – and it's possible to echo an earlier work without alluding to it. ('Allusion' comes from the same Latin root as 'ludic', and can be thought of as a writer's deliberate attempt to play around with another text, or to bring it into play when we read.) But it's just as likely that Moore wanted to show how some writers seem strangely able to anticipate our most intimate experiences, as he hears a haunting premonition of his own fate, and the fate of so many other young men, in Keats's description of a world 'Where youth grows pale, and spectre-thin, and dies.'

Sometimes allusions are more private than this: like the scaffolding used by builders when constructing a new house, they can form part of the making of a work without thereby forming part of its meaning for anyone outside a very small circle of readers. A good example is provided by Tennyson's long poem *In Memoriam A. H. H.* This began as a tribute to Tennyson's close friend Arthur Henry Hallam, a promising writer who died suddenly in 1833 when he was just twenty-two years old, although by the time the poem was finally completed seventeen years later it mixed together Tennyson's most intimate memories with enough general reflections on death and religion to allow its readers to feel that it spoke for them too. First published in 1850, it quickly became a Victorian bestseller. Queen Victoria herself, whose obsessive mourning of Prince Albert would cast a dark shadow over the second half of her reign, wrote in her journal for 5 January 1862 that 'Only those who have suffered, as I do, can understand these beautiful poems'. She also copied out the whole work (all 2,916 lines of it) in her own hand, keeping it in a special brass container on her desk, and when the Duke of Argyll visited her at Osborne House in February 1861 he observed that, touchingly, she had substituted 'widow' for 'widower' and 'her' for 'his' in one section of the poem.

In some ways these changes matched the inner workings of

In Memoriam itself, because when he was writing it Tennyson often found himself borrowing other people's words and making them his own. Section XCIV comes just before the climax of the poem, and it is full of literary memories:

> How pure at heart and sound in head,
>   With what divine affections bold
>   Should be the man whose thought would hold
> An hour's communion with the dead.
>
> In vain shalt thou, or any, call
>   The spirits from their golden day,
>   Except, like them, thou too canst say,
> My spirit is at peace with all.
>
> They haunt the silence of the breast,
>   Imaginations calm and fair,
>   The memory like a cloudless air,
> The conscience as a sea at rest:
>
> But when the heart is full of din,
>   And doubt beside the portal waits,
>   They can but listen at the gates
> And hear the household jar within.

The surface argument of this section is that only those who are pure-hearted and perfectly calm may be in a fit state to communicate with the dead. Tennyson's language works hard to shift this from a personal anxiety (the idea that, ironically, the sheer strength of his grief may force Hallam further away) to the more general question of how best to mourn the dead, and it does this in particular by playing on a tiny quirk of English grammar: the fact that the definite article can be used both to specify and to generalise. This means that when we read about 'the man', 'the dead', 'the silence of the breast', 'the heart' and so on, we can sympathise with the speaker's plight while also determining how far it applies to ourselves. At the same time, Tennyson's writing continues to keep a wary eye on itself: like many of his best poems, alongside its ostensible subject it seems to be wondering what exactly it is up to, and whether or not it is up to it.

One of the alternative titles Tennyson considered before he settled on *In Memoriam* was *Fragments of an Elegy*, which revealed his fears that the 133 sections he ended up writing wouldn't necessarily add up to a unified poem. (He later tried to justify himself by claiming that 'I did not write them with any view of weaving them into a whole, or for publication, until I found that I had written so many.') Fragmentation of a different kind was to be his poem's fate: the section printed here would later be included in popular anthologies like *Lyrical Poems by Alfred Lord Tennyson*, put together in 1885 by his friend F. T. Palgrave, the man who had earlier been responsible for compiling the bestselling *Golden Treasury of English Songs and Lyrics*. But *In Memoriam* was a patchwork production from the start, as if Tennyson needed the support of other writers before he felt able to express his own feelings. 'They know me not, but mourn with me', he writes in a slightly later section of the poem, as he describes the twittering birds and lowing cattle he can hear in the countryside. That might be an optimistic view of the natural world's capacity for empathy, but it's a good summary of how Tennyson uses many earlier writers in *In Memoriam*. They know him not, but mourn with him.

In this section alone there are echoes of John Webster's play *The Duchess of Malfi*, where the Duchess wonders 'O, that it were possible we might | But hold some two days' conference with the dead!' (a couple of lines that already lay behind another of Tennyson's poetic responses to Hallam's death, the haunting lyric 'Oh! that 'twere possible | After long grief and pain, | To find the arms of my true-love | Round me once again!'), and Edward Young's poem *Night Thoughts* where we read of 'The spirit of the golden day'. The ABBA rhymes of Tennyson's stanzas are also a structural echo of how Shakespeare begins each of his sonnets, which makes each section of *In Memoriam* sound like a series of false starts to a love poem that can never be completed now that their subject is dead. (An extra edge of pathos lies in the fact that the young man in Shakespeare's sonnets never answers back.) Indeed, so many lines of *In Memoriam* hum with fragments of earlier poems that reading it can feel a bit like Tennyson's experience when he once stopped by a telegraph pole to listen to what he described as 'the wail of wires, the souls of dead messages'.

Sometimes this experience is highly personal. Tennyson's son recalled how, on one of the 'sad winter days' that followed news of Hallam's death, the poet 'noted down in his scrap-book some fragmentary lines, which proved to be the germ of *In Memoriam*: "Where is the voice that I have loved? ah where | Is that dear hand that I would press?" ' One answer to these questions would prove to be the writings that Hallam himself had left behind – poems, essays, letters – pieces of which Tennyson lovingly incorporated into his elegy. There's a good example in this section. While 'An hour's communion with the dead' alludes to *The Duchess of Malfi*, it is even more closely related to one of Hallam's poems in which he had described the 'Spirits that but seem | To hold communion with the dead', and Tennyson's own early poem 'On Sublimity' in which he had written 'For thou dost hold communion with the dead.' It's a double allusion that seems partly to be reflecting on the nature of allusion itself, as Tennyson draws together his voice and that of his friend to sustain his hope that death should be no barrier to them remaining closely involved with each other.

Nor does the story stop there, because in his much later poem 'All Catches Alight', Philip Larkin would go on to write about the animals who appear 'Clothed in cloudless air' – a memory of Tennyson's line 'The memory like a cloudless air', and also of various other poets who have deployed the phrase 'cloudless air' in their verse: Percy Shelley, Mary Shelley, Emily Brontë and several more. Here it appears in the context of Larkin's celebration of new life bubbling up all around him in the spring: birds 'crazed with flight', the sprouting of fresh leaves, even a suggestion of sap rising in the usually reliably gloomy Larkin himself. But the fact that 'cloudless air' has been used so often might remind us that some literary echoes may reveal more than one particular influence. They represent something more like a confluence: evidence that a piece of writing may seem as clear and straightforward as a patch of sky, but if looked at closely the vapour trails of earlier users start to become visible as they cross and recross each other.

The fact that two works that are as superficially different as *Dracula* and *In Memoriam* are both full of these literary traces might remind us of just how often a new piece of writing is assembled using materials that have already appeared elsewhere. It is why, the more we read, the more likely we are when opening a new book to have the vertiginous sensation of *reading through* it – not just from left to right and top to bottom, but as if we were sinking into the page and trying to reach something written much longer ago.

Even if we don't recognise all the allusions or echoes in a piece of writing, we can appreciate how many works seem reluctant to keep themselves to themselves. Sometimes these literary overspills and offshoots behave like ghosts, as we saw in Chapter 23, and sometimes they celebrate the ability of a writer to carry on talking long after their own voice has been silenced, as we saw in Chapter 6. They can even set up conversations on the page between authors who could never have met in real life, as we saw in Chapter 22. What links all these examples together is the recognition that, as the philosopher Martin Heidegger once observed, the best works of literature are never 'used up'. They are all fundamentally works in progress.

Chapter 29

Suspense

THE CLIMAX OF *IN MEMORIAM* comes when Tennyson lingers outside on a warm summer's night and decides to read some of Hallam's old letters. Gradually he realises that he is experiencing them not as lifeless pieces of paper, but rather as one hand reaching out to another across the years. 'So word by word, and line by line', Tennyson writes, 'The dead man touched me from the past'.

Before that moment things are far more uncertain. Starting with the opening line of the poem's first section ('I held it truth, with him who sings') words like 'hold' and 'held' are often repeated, as if Tennyson wanted to echo those Victorian gravestones that show two hands clasped together. However, as Hallam's body can no longer be touched, Tennyson almost never uses the words in a straightforward physical sense. The section we looked at in Chapter 28 is fairly typical in this regard. When we read 'the man whose thought would hold', there's a momentary flicker of uncertainty about how physical this 'holding' could be, before we start the next line and discover that all the speaker is holding now is a conversation. The word then returns in a disguised form in the final line as 'household', once again in the context of loneliness. At this stage of the poem it appears that the speaker has lost contact with Hallam forever, so the use of 'hold' followed by a blank space starts to look more like someone reaching for a hand that has unexpectedly been taken away.

For anyone who enjoys old adventure movies, this line might remind them of so-called 'cliffhanger' endings, named after the popularity of black and white serials during the early years of Hollywood in which the plucky hero or heroine would end an episode clinging to the edge of a precipice with no obvious means of escape. (At the start of the next episode they would always be rescued or discover an ingenious means of saving themselves.) So popular was this convention that more playful variations soon began to appear in other films – one of the most famous scenes involving the silent comedian Harold Lloyd saw him hanging off a clock face rather than a cliff face – and decades later it was still being echoed in big-budget spectaculars. One especially memorable scene in *Chitty Chitty Bang Bang* (1968) saw the magical car plunging off a cliff shortly before unfolding its wings and soaring to safety, but when the film was first released in cinemas the intermission, complete with jaunty theme tune, came in the split second between these two events, allowing audiences who didn't know the story to contemplate the prospect of a mangled wreck as they queued for their tubs of ice cream.

However, as is the case with several other film conventions, the novel got there first. (As a side note, the renowned Russian director Sergei Eisenstein claimed in an essay published in 1944 that many of film's most popular devices were anticipated by a writer like Dickens, with his use of vivid descriptive details – the narrative equivalent of a close-up shot – and rapid cutting between different scenes.) The prototype of a cliffhanger ending can be found in Thomas Hardy's novel *A Pair of Blue Eyes*, first published in monthly instalments in *Tinsleys' Magazine* between 1872 and 1873, and it's worth looking at this example in some detail to see what it tells us about narrative suspense more generally.

Hardy's story centres on a love triangle between a young woman named Elfride Swancourt and two rival suitors: the ambitious and boyish Stephen Smith, and the older but still inexperienced Henry Knight. One afternoon Knight and Elfride are walking together along a coastal path when Knight slips on some wet soil and finds himself stranded on a cliff edge, only saving himself from tumbling to his death by desperately clinging onto some patches of greenery that are sprouting out of the sheer rock face. As Elfride scrambles to safety and Knight is left alone with his thoughts, he discovers that her blue eyes have been replaced by something much older and colder: a fossil with eyes that are 'dead and turned to stone' but appear to be staring directly at him.

> Time closed up like a fan before him. He saw himself at one extremity of the years, face to face with the beginning and all the intermediate centuries simultaneously. Fierce men, clothed in the hides of beasts, and carrying, for defence and attack, huge clubs and pointed spears, rose from the rock, like the phantoms before the doomed Macbeth. They lived in hollows, woods, and mud huts—perhaps in caves of the neighbouring rocks. Behind them stood an earlier band. No man was there. Huge elephantine forms, the mastodon, the hippopotamus, the tapir, antelopes of monstrous size, the megatherium, and the myledon—all, for the moment, in juxtaposition. Further back, and overlapped by these, were perched huge-billed birds and swinish creatures as large as horses. Still more shadowy were the sinister crocodilian outlines—alligators and other uncouth shapes, culminating in the colossal lizard, the iguanodon. Folded behind were dragon forms and clouds of flying reptiles: still underneath

were fishy beings of lower development; and so on, till the lifetime scenes of the fossil confronting him were a present and modern condition of things.

These images passed before Knight's inner eye in less than half a minute, and he was again considering the actual present. Was he to die? The mental picture of Elfride in the world, without himself to cherish her, smote his heart like a whip. He had hoped for deliverance, but what could a girl do? He dared not move an inch. Was Death really stretching out his hand? The previous sensation, that it was improbable he would die, was fainter now.

However, Knight still clung to the cliff.

The idea of Death stretching out its hand would have been especially troubling for Hardy. According to the memoir he wrote that was posthumously published between 1928 and 1930 under the name of his second wife, as a boy he did everything he could to avoid being touched by other children, and this 'peculiarity' never left him – 'to the end of his life he hated even the most friendly hand being laid on his arm or his shoulder'. This produces a number of odd moments in his writing, such as a description of some trees in his 1887 novel *The Woodlanders* 'whose mossed rinds made them like hands wearing green gloves', as if even tree branches might be squeamish about reaching out into the world unless suitably protected. By contrast, in this passage from *A Pair of Blue Eyes*, human touch is what Knight longs for, because the alternative is holding onto something that has absolutely no desire to hold him in return. When Hardy describes how 'Knight still clung to the cliff', the repetitions of '*cl*ung . . . *cl*iff' sound like desperate fingers gripping.

Hardy's main source was almost certainly Leslie Stephen's story 'A Bad Five Minutes in the Alps', which appeared in *Fraser's Magazine* in November 1872, just a few months before Hardy published this instalment of his novel. In fact, Stephen wrote to

Hardy that November to request a story for another magazine he was editing at the time, so it's certainly possible that he was in Hardy's head when the novelist sat down to work out what to do with his hero. There are many parallels between the two texts. Stephen's narrator explains how on a walking holiday in Switzerland he takes a short cut across a glacier, slips on a wet rock, slithers down a hill and finds himself grabbing hold of a narrow ledge, with one foot supported by an unknown projection and the other dangling helplessly over what he believes to be a deep chasm. Just as Knight is a geologist, so Stephen's narrator admits, 'A geologist would have been delighted with this admirable specimen of the planning powers of nature'; while Knight clings to a cliff, Stephen's narrator writes, 'I clung as firmly as might be to the rocks, and did my best to postpone the inevitable crash.' Both writers describe the thoughts that might pass through the head of a man who believes he is about to die; both texts read like sophisticated variations on the old maxim that pride comes before a fall.

Stephen's biggest influence appears to have been on Hardy's narrative voice. In his story, Stephen's narrator describes himself as a 'double character' who both experienced these events and is now commenting on them, and this is subtly developed in Hardy's narrative. During the passage we are considering, for example, we see things from Knight's point of view, but also observe them from a coolly ironic distance, so that phrases like 'elephantine form' and 'crocodilian outlines' are written in a slightly fussy style that prevents us from getting too worried on Knight's behalf. Hardy would later point out in his memoir that on stage 'actors never see a play as a whole and in true perspective, but in a false perspective from the shifting point of their own part in it'. In this passage from *A Pair of Blue Eyes*, his narrative voice skilfully plays different perspectives off against each other.

This playing with perspective is also reflected in Hardy's manipulation of time. Later we learn that the action described here takes only four or five minutes to unfold if measured by the clock, which for quick readers is roughly how long the whole episode would take to get through. Fictional time is far more flexible. When we read a novel like *A Pair of Blue Eyes*, events that might take millions of years to unfold in chronological time can be compressed into a handful of sentences; conversely, events that might take a matter of seconds to happen in real life can be unpacked in a far more leisurely manner. A novel is a time machine that works even more efficiently than the one discussed in Chapter 18 because, as we saw earlier with Austen's description of the thoughts that chase each other through Emma Woodhouse's head when Mr Knightley proposes to her, it is capable of speeding time up, slowing it down, pausing its forward momentum, or sending it spinning backwards. And here we might notice how Hardy's writing is full of narrative tricks that allow us to measure the imaginary ticking of a clock against Knight's experience of events. For example, he often appears to reach the end of a sentence before extending his syntax with a dash, and ends other sentences with a question mark that allows these thoughts to reverberate far beyond their immediate contexts. Even Hardy's list of the prehistoric animals whose fossil remains are embedded in the cliff ('the mastodon . . . the megatherium . . . the myledon') makes it sound as if Knight has been waiting for millions of years rather than a few minutes.

Hardy's original form of publication added to this sense of narrative suspense, because the chapters featuring Knight's dilemma were spread out between two separate issues of *Tinsleys' Magazine*. February's instalment included an illustration that showed Knight vainly reaching for Elfride's hand, and a final sentence set out as a separate paragraph that declared melodramatically (and near-tautologously) 'Knight felt himself alone in a terrible loneliness'. Hardy's readers then had to wait a whole month before discovering how this situation would be resolved, as Elfride successfully rescues Knight by using her underclothes to fashion an improvised rope. It was a publishing decision that wittily played on the literal meaning of 'suspense', the Latin root of which means 'to hang', just as the reader picking up the story where it left off was like a faint echo of Knight's stubborn grip on the cliff.

Hardy's narrative also demonstrates something more fundamental than this. It reminds us that usually what keeps us reading isn't just habit or a desire to escape temporarily into a parallel world. It's the basic human impulse to learn what will happen next. In Chapter 26 I listed some of the needs that writing can help us satisfy, chief among which was *wanting to know*. This is what brought Hardy's original readers back to his novel after a month's gap, just as it brought the original cinema audiences of *Chitty Chitty Bang Bang* back to their seats after queuing for ice cream. It also forms a large part of what keeps us going from one day to the next: a nagging sense of curiosity, a never-satisfied need to follow the yellow brick road and see where it leads. As a character points out in Tom Stoppard's play *Arcadia* (1993), 'It's wanting to know that makes us matter.'

Books can satisfy this basic human urge, but they can also nurture and refine it, as we've already seen when looking at a number of other literary works. What a novel like *A Pair of Blue Eyes* does is to take our desire to know – a desire that might include what will happen next, how the hero will respond, and maybe even why we should care – and shift it to the very centre of our attention.

Chapter 30

SYMBOLS

IF WE'RE LESS SURPRISED by Knight's escape than Hardy's original readers, it's probably because in the intervening years such scenes have become almost as familiar to cinema audiences as red velour seats and popcorn. After the original cliffhanger endings of film serials like *The Perils of Pauline* (1914), some of which were filmed on the rugged New Jersey coastline, the most famous example is probably the climax of Alfred Hitchcock's thriller *North by Northwest* (1959), which involves Kendall (Eva Marie Saint) clinging to Mount Rushmore by her fingertips before Thornhill (Cary Grant) pulls her to safety. There are dozens of other examples, including the 1993 film *Cliffhanger* which ends with the hero (played by a muscle-bulging Sylvester Stallone) engaged in a bloody fist fight with a criminal on top of a wrecked helicopter that is hanging off the edge of – you guessed it – a cliff. 'Remember, shithead, keep your arms and legs in the vehicle at all times,' Stallone quips, as he leaps to safety shortly before the helicopter topples to the ground and explodes in a satisfyingly large fireball.

Hardy's writing is never this broad, but it does contain a number of moments where his characters are treated like playthings who can be plunged into danger or whisked to safety with a few strokes of his pen. For example, his later novel *Tess of the d'Urbervilles* leaves the reader in little doubt over the heroine's likely fate. When Tess gets into a horse-drawn carriage that is identified as a 'trap', or meets Alec by the d'Urberville family tomb and reads her own surname inscribed in stone, we appear to have entered a world where the character's free will is repeatedly overwritten by the needs of the plot. Even ordinary objects turn out to be part of an inescapable tragic design.

Such objects are usually described as 'symbols', which we could think of as fragments of the world whose usual meaning is thickened when we come across them in a literary text. Consider how a writer might use a tool like a spade. If we go to the garden centre and ask for a spade, we expect to be given a wood and metal implement we can use to dig holes in the ground. A spade is a spade. By contrast, when Seamus Heaney writes in his poem 'Digging' about memories of his father slicing open the soil to discover some new potatoes, or his grandfather cutting neat chunks of turf until Heaney's head is filled with 'The cold smell of potato mould, the squelch and slap | Of soggy peat, the curt cuts of an edge | Through living roots', the spade has clearly drifted away from its straightforward usefulness as a horticultural tool. Instead it has become a symbol of what links Heaney to the history of his family and the Irish nation as a whole, as he picks up his pen and declares 'I'll dig with it', substituting a modern work of literature ('Digging') for traditional back-breaking labour (digging). The object has become charged with an idea.

Similarly, when Gertrude Stein writes 'Rose is a rose is a rose is a rose' in her poem 'Sacred Emily', her point is that when a rose appears in a literary work it usually signifies far more than just a delicately perfumed flower. Depending on the context, it can be used to think about the unique qualities of an individual ('That which we call a rose | By any other name would smell as sweet' Shakespeare's Juliet tells herself when she realises that Romeo is a member of the rival Montague family), mourn the transience of life (in Oscar Wilde's fairy tale 'The Nightingale and the Rose', a nightingale dies to find a rose for a student, who ends up tossing it into the street 'where it fell into the gutter, and a cart-wheel went over it'), or celebrate what is fresh and perfect (in Robert Burns's most famous poem, his love is compared to 'a red, red rose | That's newly sprung in June'). And context is everything when it comes to symbols. A skull in a mortuary is likely to be viewed chiefly as an anonymous body part, whereas when Hamlet is in the graveyard and holds up the skull of Yorick, the clown he used to play with as a boy ('Alas, poor Yorick'), it immediately becomes a symbol of mortality, the loss of childhood innocence, the death of comedy (or perhaps the persistence of black comedy, given how many jokes Hamlet goes on to make at Yorick's expense), and much more besides. When we look at it, we see an object that seems to exist in the real world and simultaneously in the world of metaphor.

Such writing consoles us with the thought that life will always reveal its concealed meanings if we are prepared to unpeel its surfaces and investigate what lies beneath. Sometimes these symbols are as obvious as a crash of cymbals – *North by Northwest* ends with Thornhill pulling Kendall, now his wife, onto the upper berth on a train as it enters a tunnel, which even Freud might consider a bit unsubtle as a visual clue about what they will be getting up to on their honeymoon – and sometimes they are more suggestively ambiguous. It isn't just that A means B (that is allegory rather than symbolism); depending on who is reading a work, and what experiences they bring with them, A could also mean C, or D, or E, or a whole alphabet of ideas combined in a single image.

Some of the most interesting examples appear in literary works where it's not immediately clear whether something is to be interpreted symbolically or not. That's especially true in the case of short stories. When we read a novel our attention may be snared by particular episodes, but we always feel the engine of plot tugging us onwards. By contrast, because a short story gives us far fewer words to consider, we are likely to read them with an especially careful eye. Sometimes short stories are written in a style that rewards this level of scrutiny, as we saw in earlier discussions of 'The Dead' (Chapter 2) and 'Prince Hat Underground' (Chapter 19). These are narratives where ordinary fragments of experience can be irradiated with significance, where potentially everything matters. Yet they also typically feature characters who misread the situations in which they find themselves, and in these circumstances the use of symbolism can also show us what they are unable to see.

Katherine Mansfield's short story 'The Garden Party' was first published in 1922, the same year as Joyce's *Ulysses* and T. S. Eliot's *The Waste Land*. Whereas those works deal with life in a sprawling modern city (respectively Dublin and London), at a first glance 'The Garden Party' appears to have a much narrower focus. In the opening pages we are introduced to the Sheridan family, well-to-do New Zealanders who have invited their equally well-do-do friends to enjoy some drinks and nibbles in their garden. (If their house seems unusually realistic, that's probably because it's based on the one Mansfield's family moved to in Wellington when she was a teenager: 'a big, white-painted square house' with a billiard room and a tennis court in the garden.) Workmen have put up a marquee, the piano has been relocated, some huge bunches of lilies have been delivered to the house, and the family's daughter Laura has delightedly tried on a new hat. Soon the guests start to trickle in:

> The band struck up; the hired waiters ran from the house
> to the marquee. Wherever you looked there were couples

strolling, bending to the flowers, greeting, moving on over the lawn. They were like bright birds that had alighted in the Sheridans' garden for this one afternoon, on their way to – where? Ah, what happiness it is to be with people who all are happy, to press hands, press cheeks, smile into eyes.

'Darling Laura, how well you look!'

'What a becoming hat, child!'

'Laura, you look quite Spanish. I've never seen you look so striking.'

And Laura, glowing, answered softly, 'Have you had tea? Won't you have an ice? The passion-fruit ices really are rather special.' She ran to her father and begged him. 'Daddy darling, can't the band have something to drink?'

And the perfect afternoon slowly ripened, slowly faded, slowly its petals closed.

'Never a more delightful garden-party . . . ' 'The greatest success . . . ' 'Quite the most . . . '

Laura helped her mother with the good-byes. They stood side by side in the porch till it was all over.

'All over, all over, thank heaven,' said Mrs Sheridan. 'Round up the others, Laura. Let's go and have some fresh coffee. I'm exhausted. Yes, it's been very successful. But oh, these parties, these parties! Why will you children insist on giving parties!' And they all of them sat down in the deserted marquee.

'Have a sandwich, daddy dear. I wrote the flag.'

'Thanks.' Mr Sheridan took a bite and the sandwich was gone. He took another. 'I suppose you didn't hear of a beastly accident that happened to-day?' he said.

'My dear,' said Mrs Sheridan, holding up her hand, 'we did. It nearly ruined the party. Laura insisted we should put it off.'

'Oh, mother!' Laura didn't want to be teased about it.

'It was a horrible affair all the same,' said Mr Sheridan. 'The chap was married too. Lived just below in the lane, and leaves a wife and half a dozen kiddies, so they say.'

An awkward little silence fell.

An unspoken question that hovers over any short story is why the writer has chosen to work in such a concentrated narrative form. One answer is that it forces them to think with extra precision about what should be included and what is better left unsaid. This can be as much an ethical as a literary matter. For example, in Zadie Smith's novella *The Embassy of Cambodia* (2013), a modern fable about low-paid workers in London, when the narrator admits that 'there is something to be said for drawing a circle around our attention and remaining within that circle', and wonders 'how large should this circle be?', she is not only reminding us that any act of writing involves choosing to describe this rather than that, or these people rather than those. She is suggesting how tempting it is to apply similar blinkers to our own lives.

Mansfield's story offers two different responses to this question of how large the circle of our attention should be. The first is the selfish perspective of her characters, whose thoughts don't appear to stretch much further than how delightful the garden's flowers are or how much they have enjoyed the passion fruit ice creams. The second is a much wider perspective that slides around the first and sometimes collides with it head on.

Let's consider how this works in the extract reproduced here. The smooth rhythms and internal echoes of 'what happiness it is to be with people who all are happy, to press hands, press cheeks, smile into eyes' introduce us to a self-absorbed social world, where 'All over, all over' refers to the garden party alone. But there is another world. The 'beastly accident' that Mr Sheridan mentions is an event that has already occurred out of sight (even the reader only learns about it second-hand), after the horse of their neighbour Mr Scott has shied at a traction engine and thrown him off, killing him instantly. Presumably Mr Sheridan is being thoughtless rather than witty when he refers to an accident involving a horse as 'beastly' – a word that joins schoolyard and drawing room, and gains an extra edge of mock-sophistication from the story's New Zealand setting – but as we weigh up how we should feel about the bright, brittle world he represents, already we can sense Mansfield's finger pressing down on the scales.

Later Laura visits the victim's family to bring them a basket of party leftovers and pay her awkward respects. (This is another reworked fragment of memory: when Mansfield was a teenager, a young workman living in the lane behind her house was killed on the same day Mansfield's family was giving a summer party, and one of her sisters was asked to take the man's relatives some food while still wearing her party dress and hat.) The family lives in a 'disgusting and sordid' lane of cottages, which are located just a few hundred yards away from the glamorous scene of Laura's garden party, but might as well be on a different planet. Instead of an extensive garden filled with delicious things to eat and drink, the area's 'garden patches' contain 'nothing but cabbage stalks, sick hens and tomato cans'. Here Laura meets Mr Sheridan's grieving widow, who looks nothing like those party guests who were happy to 'press cheeks' and 'smile into eyes': instead the widow's face is 'puffed up, red, with swollen eyes'. Finally, Laura stumbles into the bedroom where the dead man is lying. 'What did garden parties and baskets and lace frocks matter to him?' she asks herself. 'While they were laughing and while the band was playing, this marvel has come to the lane. Happy . . . Happy . . . All is well, said that sleeping face. This is just as it should be. I am content.' Laura responds with a 'loud childish sob', and says the first thing that comes into her head: 'Forgive my hat.' It turns out that a life can be finished even more quickly than a sandwich. All over, all over indeed.

If the victim's mode of death hints at symbolism – a horse panicked by a traction engine, tradition destroyed by modernity – many other details in this passage work in a similar fashion. Read in the light of Laura's later discovery, it is full of glancing references to transience. Flowers and ices are ephemeral, doomed to fade or melt, just as a marquee is only a temporary structure. Similarly, the afternoon comes to a close like a flower shutting itself up, while the guests are compared to 'bright birds' – and we discover from other stories in this collection how vulnerable birds are to having their beauty stolen: one character preserves the 'black feather boa' her mother used to wear, another sports 'a white hat with purple feathers'. Laura's own hat is described as 'becoming', because it makes her look pretty and shows what else she is becoming, namely a younger version of her mother, but as a black hat with a black ribbon it is also associated with death, like a fashionable *memento mori*. Finally, 'on their way to – where?' reminds us that we are all ultimately travelling to the same destination, even if some of us will have a more comfortable journey there than others.

All of these tiny details combine to suggest that the people who are happily drifting through this world are unaware of its hidden workings. Another feature that connects to Mansfield's symbolism – one that is easy to miss, not least because it is a kind of absence – is her use of ellipses. This was a popular feature of writing in the period, used by novelists like Joseph Conrad and Ford Madox Ford to signal that there was more to be said than they were able to put into words, or that any attempt at self-expression was vulnerable to cracking apart at the seams. (This is also the period when 'dot dot dot' started to be used as an alternative to 'et cetera'.) Ellipses are used throughout 'The Garden Party', but in this passage they are concentrated into a short paragraph that offers a selection of comments from the party's guests, either because they are happy to restrict themselves to a few fragments of polite chatter, or because we are eavesdropping on them as they pass by and can only tune into their conversations for a second or two: 'Never a more delightful garden-party . . . ' 'The greatest success . . . ' 'Quite the most . . . ' Usually a set of ellipses indicates that something has been left out. Here they draw attention to what is out of sight and, for the society figures who are attending this garden party, also out of mind, such as the life of the poor, and by implication everything else that allows people like themselves to lead the leisured and decorative lives they do. (Laura has written on the flag that is stuck into the sandwich her father eats, but a servant has made the sandwich itself.) None of this is discussed out loud, but it continues to resonate in the passage's 'awkward little silences'.

At the end of the story, a weeping Laura stumbles out of the cottage and meets her brother at the corner of the lane. 'Isn't life', she stammers, 'isn't life—', and there she stops, overwhelmed by the fact that the dead man looked 'Happy . . . happy . . . ' What are we supposed to make of this?

When we reach the end of a short story like 'The Garden Party' it's tempting to reach for grand conclusions, perhaps because we are keen to prove that we have paid more careful attention to its events than many of Mansfield's characters appear to have done. 'What Laura discovers is that in the midst of life there is death', we might decide, or 'The moral of the story is that it can take something awful happening to another person for us to appreciate our own good fortune.' What we aren't given is enough information to know whether our conclusion is the right one. Because short stories are by definition short, they tend to be radically selective in terms of what they include and what ends up on the writer's equivalent of the cutting-room floor. For this reason, we usually assume that *what* we are being told matters. But in the case of a short story like 'The Garden Party' we aren't told *why* it matters. Even when we are presented with those repeated ellipses we are left to join the dots ourselves.

That's one reason why Mansfield's symbolism is so powerfully effective. It keeps drawing our attention to small narrative details like the huge bunches of lilies (a flower traditionally associated with death) but doesn't give us enough information for us to be sure we have understood them correctly. In fact, there may not be a correct way to understand them, any more than there is only one valid interpretation of Wordsworth's poem about daffodils. Instead, we are presented with a story that keeps saying one thing but doing something different. Why does it repeatedly refer to objects such as flowers and ices? Because they are more significant than some of the other things that could have been described in their place, such as wheelbarrows or garden gnomes. How do we know they are significant? Because traditionally they are symbols of transience. So what is the effect of Mansfield's interest in what Baudelaire's essay on 'The Painter of Modern Life' once described as 'the fleeting forms of beauty in the life of our day'? Among other things, perhaps a reminder that some fleeting forms can last much longer if they find their way into a story as good as this one.

How to Move On

Chapter 31

GROWING UP

WRITERS DON'T HAVE TO invent elaborate fantasies in order to bend life's usual rules. Many of the books I grew up reading only made sense if I was prepared to accept that they already existed at an odd angle to the world I knew. For example, some of the most popular series were flagrantly careless with chronology. The hero of Richmal Crompton's Just William books would always remain a scruffy, tousled eleven-year-old boy, just as Enid Blyton's Famous Five would never become the Famous Four because of a fatal camping accident. In each case, the author's fictional world remained as fixed as a painting, which was an oddly reassuring thing to realise as I added a new pencil line to my bedroom doorframe every birthday, and the piles of books on my floor continued to grow.

When I was slightly older, it turned out that this sort of fictional stasis was also true of adult characters like P. G. Wodehouse's Jeeves and Wooster. To open any one of these books was to enter another world where very little seemed to change from one story to the next. First appearing in 1915, Wodehouse's characters continued to feature in stories of country houses and open-topped motor cars until his last completed novel in 1974, by which time if Jeeves had aged like an ordinary human being he would have been over a hundred years old. Actually, there is every indication that he is not a human being. According to the bumbling Bertie Wooster, Jeeves 'shimmers' and 'glides' like a 'healing zephyr', with only an occasional quiet cough or raised eyebrow to betray the fact that he possesses a physical body at all. In other respects, he is more like a *deus ex machina* who has assumed a human form. However messy the situations Wooster gets himself into, Jeeves is always there to help clear things up; the world they live in is essentially a form of pastoral, where the sun will always shine and serious adult concerns like money and marriage can be treated more like a children's game.

Many other stories have been used by adult writers to imagine recapturing the lost world of childhood. Some of these stories are so popular they have been written more than once. For example, Thomas Anstey Guthrie's 1882 novel *Vice Versa*, a comic caper in which an enchanted Indian stone causes a father and son to swap bodies, leading to a respectable businessman going back to school and a teenage boy running his father's company in his place, was rewritten by Mary Rogers in 1982 as *Summer Switch*. (Rogers had previously written *Freaky Friday*, a version of the story in which a mother and daughter swap bodies, which was later the source of the 1976 Disney film starring a teenage Jodie Foster.) In some ways these characters are living out what reading allows us to do every day: swapping bodies with someone else and enjoying the freedom that comes with being temporarily older or younger than we are.

Instead of playing a child's and an adult's perspectives off against each other, occasionally writers try to combine them into a single fictional voice. The passage from *Housekeeping* discussed in Chapter 17 provides a good example of this narrative double act. It's the sort of writing that does not need to describe explicitly what growing up feels like in order for us to share in this feeling as we read, as Ruth's account reveals her childhood innocence while also showing how it is creased with the ironies of hindsight.

But perhaps the most famous example of a character who asks us to think about the relationship between a child's and an adult's view of the world is the boy who never grew up: the hero of J. M. Barrie's *Peter Pan*. Even if we haven't read it, this is a story many of us think we know. Since his first stage appearance in 1904, Peter Pan has starred in countless theatrical productions worldwide, played by both male and female actors, and in at least ten major films. Barrie's story has been turned into science fiction (in Steven Spielberg's 1982 film *E.T.*, a mother reads her daughter the episode in which Tinker Bell is brought back to life, shortly before her son does something similar for his extraterrestrial friend), a fable about modern gay life (it is repeatedly referenced in the US version of TV drama *Queer as Folk*, where the gorgeous but narcissistic Brian is reassured that he will 'always be young, and always be beautiful', and is fondly nicknamed 'Peter' by a female friend he calls 'Wendy'), and even a source of queasy pornography in which Wendy does far more than merely tuck in the Lost Boys at night. *Peter Pan* has inspired the creation of several statues, a type of rounded collar, a ballet, items of merchandise that range from cuddly toy crocodiles to glow-in-the-dark Tinker Bell costumes, a girl's name ('Wendy' was Barrie's posthumous tribute to a little girl who could not pronounce her r's and so referred to him as her 'fwendy'), a brand of peanut butter, a Disneyland ride, a way of alluding to socially immature adults and a 190-metre-long Scandinavian car ferry. As the most famous modern example of the *puer aeternus* (eternal boy) of classical legend, he has stubbornly resisted all invitations to grow up, even as his cultural presence has become ever larger. Appropriately for a character whose name forms the root of many other words indicating shared or universal values (pantheon, panoply, panorama, pansexual, pantheism), Pan is everywhere.

So it can be something of a shock to return to Barrie's original play and discover that it is far stranger than we might have expected. This is especially true of the scene depicting the death of Captain Hook, the pirate who has spent much of the story pursuing Pan all over Neverland with moustache-twirling menace. After Hook captures Wendy and the Lost Boys, Pan tracks him down to his ship for a final showdown:

> HOOK 'Tis some fiend fighting me! Pan, who and what art thou?
> (*The children listen eagerly for the answer, none quite so eagerly as Wendy*)
> PETER (*at a venture*) I'm youth, I'm joy, I'm a little bird that has broken out of the egg.
> HOOK To't again!
> (*He has now a damp feeling that this boy is the weapon which is to strike him from the lists of man; but the grandeur of his mind still holds and, true to the traditions of his flag, he fights on like a human flail. Peter flutters round and through and over these gyrations as if the wind of them blew him out of the danger zone, and again and again he darts in and jags*)
> HOOK (*stung to madness*) I'll fire the powder magazine. (*He disappears they know not where*)
> CHILDREN Peter, save us!
> (*Peter, alas, goes the wrong way and Hook returns*)
> HOOK (*sitting on the hold with gloomy satisfaction*) In two minutes the ship will be blown to pieces.
> (*They cast themselves before him in entreaty*)
> CHILDREN Mercy, mercy!
> HOOK Back, you pewling spawn. I'll show you now the road to dusty death. A holocaust of children, there is something grand in the idea!

(*Peter appears with a smoking bomb in his hand and tosses it overboard. Hook has not really had much hope, and he rushes at his other persecutors with his head down like some exasperated bull in the ring; but with bantering cries they easily elude him by flying among the rigging.*

Where is Peter? The incredible boy has apparently forgotten the recent doings, and is sitting on a barrel playing upon his pipes. This may surprise others but does not surprise Hook. Lifting a blunderbuss he strikes forlornly not at the boy but at the barrel, which is hurled across the deck. Peter remains sitting in the air still playing upon his pipes. At this sight the great heart of Hook breaks. That not wholly unheroic figure climbs the bulwarks murmuring 'Floreat Etona,' *and prostrates himself into the water, where the crocodile is waiting for him openmouthed. Hook knows the purpose of this yawning cavity, but after what he has gone through he enters it like one greeting a friend.*)

The script is full of stage directions that would be only minimally helpful for an actor or director, but it does remind us that fundamentally theatre is a form of play, and one of the things it is especially good at playing with is time. The crocodile is a pun as well as a character – it is a croco*dial* – because it has previously swallowed a clock, with the result that until now Hook has always been able to hear it coming, like a scaly embodiment of the march of time. But the crocodile's appearance also reminds us that on the stage, as we've already seen on the page in several other literary examples, ordinary chronological time is overlaid by a special form of story time in which the clock can slow down, speed up, run backwards, or freeze according to the needs of the play.

In the case of director Dion Boucicault's original production of *Peter Pan*, this was underpinned by the fact that whenever the play was revived things remained largely unchanged from one year to the next. The same sets and costumes were recycled long after they had become shabby and threadbare; the same bits of stage business were carefully copied. Even when Hook was given a new jacket, it was a theatrical tradition that the patched-up jacket of the actor who originated this role, Gerald du Maurier, should be worn on at least one night of each run. Yet even *Peter Pan* could not be altogether insulated from the ticking crocodile of time. 'When the lost boys seem to be growing up, Peter thins them out,' warns Barrie's narrator in his prose version of the story *Peter and Wendy* (1911), and the young actors playing these parts quickly discovered that a similar rule – less lethal, but just as permanent – was applicable to them too. Every December they would be measured before the start of rehearsals, and ejected from the cast if they had grown too tall. Only then could they appreciate the latent menace of that phrase 'the lost boys'.

Yet although *Peter Pan* continues to return in new theatrical productions every Christmas, Barrie's script remains as hard to pin down as a shadow. The play's tone is especially elusive. As I have already suggested in earlier chapters, usually the tone of a remark helps a listener know how an utterance is being offered and how it should be taken. So, in an ordinary conversation, a sentence like 'You don't say' could be given an edge of excitement ('You don't say!') of boredom ('You don't say . . . '), or of accusation ('You don't *say!*'), and a listener needs to know which of these attitudes is being expressed, or which is most plausible in context, if they are to understand the speaker's intentions. What's true of the relationship between speaker and listener is also true of that between writer and reader. On the page, too, it's the tone of a piece of writing that helps us to determine the writer's attitude towards their subject, towards their audience and even towards their own writing.

In the case of a work like *Peter Pan*, this can involve the writer presenting more than one attitude and allowing these alternatives to knock up against each other on the page. The extract reproduced here measures the simple language of a child ('Peter, save us!') against a far more sophisticated vocabulary ('pewling spawn', 'holocaust', 'yawning cavity'), and includes a subtle grammatical distinction by making Hook not a heroic figure but rather 'not wholly unheroic'. The stage fight brings together elements of slapstick with a burst of blank verse and an allusion to *Macbeth* when Hook cries out 'I'll show you now the road to dusty death', as if he is hoping finally to turn himself into a tragic hero. The recognition of Peter Pan as an 'incredible boy' is a gasp of wonder, but also a reminder that he requires a childlike suspension of disbelief from the audience if he is to seem fully alive as a character – literally so when he flies around and we have to remind ourselves not to look for the wires holding him up.

In *The Little White Bird*, the 1902 novel in which Peter Pan made his first appearance, he is described by Barrie as a 'Betwixt-and-Between' creature, part boy and part bird. Tonally, this extract from the play version is similarly 'Betwixt-and-Between'. Stage directions such as 'They cast themselves before him in entreaty' have a melodramatic edge, but they are slightly over-pitched, and so make the children's actions seem something of a joke; 'again and again' carries a touch of free indirect style, but without letting us know whether it is tapping into Pan's glee or Hook's despair. The overall effect when we read this scene is for us to feel encouraged to recapture the innocent excitement of playing a game, while repeatedly being reminded of the rules.

Barrie devoted much of his life to trying to achieve a proper balance between a child's and an adult's perspective, and often found himself toppling backwards. Having reached his full height of five feet when he was seventeen years old, later photo-graphs show him wearing an overcoat that was several sizes too large for him, as if he was still secretly hoping to grow into it, and he was often accompanied by a St Bernard dog that made him look proportionately even smaller. For many years after he had adopted the boys for whom he originally invented the story of Peter Pan, he continued to treat adulthood as something he could shrug off like a snake shedding its skin, whether he was playing games of cricket or adopting the persona of a clumsy schoolboy when signing off one letter 'i am your frend J. M. Barrie'.

It's tempting to think that *Peter Pan* might be just as effective in allowing adults to dip back into childhood without having to stay there, even if that isn't quite how Barrie understood the play. 'It is as if long after writing "P. Pan" its true meaning came to me', he wrote in a 1922 notebook. 'Desperate attempt to grow up but can't.' Yet for most of us, opening *Peter Pan* is rather different to entering a little time machine like the one we considered in Chapter 18. Actually, it comes much closer to our experience of reading *The Time Machine* itself. Just as we can read about Wells's traveller whirling into the future while we remain firmly stuck in our own time, so when we read about Peter innocently playing on his pipes we can be transported back to the past – specifically, to a time in childhood when we might have been similarly unconcerned at a spectacle like Hook's misery – while acknowledging that our passport will be revoked as soon as we close the book.

In fact, like many of the literary works we have discussed so far, reading *Peter Pan* as an adult reminds us how much we enjoy being able to do more than one thing at once, whether this is enjoying the privileges of adulthood while temporarily borrowing the licence of childhood, or laughing at a character like Hook while also feeling rather sorry for him. To borrow the title of a 2014 novel by Ali Smith, it is a joyous lesson in How To Be Both.

Chapter 32

Thinking Differently

WE HAVE SEEN THAT the script for *Peter Pan* is involved in a complicated dialogue with itself, rapidly switching between sincerity and mockery, sentimentality and ruthlessness. In some respects it supports Tom Stoppard's claim, quoted in Chapter 23, that writing plays is the only respectable way of contradicting oneself. But plays aren't unique in their ability to take up more than one position on a subject. In fact, as the examples in several other chapters have shown us, this imaginative flexibility might be considered as one of the defining qualities of literature. As John Carey has pointed out in his fine book *What Good Are the Arts?* (2005), literature 'operates not just to delight like painting or music or dancing, but to question everything including itself'. It does this not only by scrutinising and modifying what has already been written, as a new sonnet might make us look again at all the earlier sonnets it is responding to, but by having the freedom to include several competing attitudes towards its own central ideas. For while books may include challenges to many aspects of our lives, they begin by challenging themselves. They encourage a questioning attitude by first demonstrating it in their own way of going about things.

This might be viewed as a social and political matter as

much as an aesthetic one. As I also pointed out in Chapter 23, according to the Russian critic Mikhail Bakhtin the novel is a literary form that is particularly open to different viewpoints, stitching them together into a creative patchwork or 'polyphony' and thereby turning itself into a little model of pluralism. The ability of a novel to look at a subject from more than one point of view can also be concentrated into short stories. As we have already seen, these often dwell on moments in ordinary lives rather than events of global importance, but in focussing on such moments they ask us to think carefully about the relationship between size and significance. That is, when we read in Joyce's 'An Encounter' (another of the stories collected in *Dubliners*) about two truants meeting someone who explains in lascivious detail how much he enjoys whipping naughty boys, or in Chekhov's 'The Beauties' about a man who catches a glimpse of a beautiful woman on a railway station platform, these events might not be crucial to anyone beyond the characters themselves, but as we read about them they are still capable of filling our heads to the exclusion of everything else.

Let me give you another example, this time from a short story written by the American author Edith Wharton. First published in 1908, a year after Wharton and her husband had settled in France, where a friend observed her enjoying her new bohemian lifestyle in one of Paris's grandest hotels, 'smoking cigarettes, surrounded by her little literary court, exchanging *mots* with them', 'The Pretext' introduces us to someone who leads a far more conventional life back home. This is a middle-aged woman named Margaret Ransom, who lives in a New England university town where her husband is a law professor. Into this claustrophobic world comes a 'stray young Englishman', Guy Dawnish, who is put under her husband's care and, as his surname indicates, seems to offer her the promise of a fresh start, or at least a suggestion of one. Finally there is an opportunity for her 'cramped' and 'narrow' life to open up like a flower.

There are many questions simmering under the surface of this story, not least because its events are mostly seen through Margaret's eyes, and she is painfully unsure about the nature of her developing relationship with this charming visitor. Is he unaware of her attraction towards him, or does he feel the same way about her? Is the interest he appears to take in her a way of masking his true romantic intentions, or is it merely proof of his good manners?

Things finally reach a climax, or rather an ambiguous anticlimax, one evening when Guy leads Margaret to a secluded spot by the river. He seems to be on the verge of making a grand declaration, yet as he breaks the 'reverberating silence' between them and confesses 'there's something I've been wanting to tell you', he never quite utters the words she longs to hear:

'You've been so perfect to me,' he began again. 'It's not my fault if you've made me feel that you would understand everything—make allowances for everything—see just how a man may have held out, and fought against a thing—as long as he had the strength . . . This may be my only chance; and I can't go away without telling you.'

He had turned from her now, and was staring at the river, so that his profile was projected against the moonlight in all its beautiful young dejection.

There was a slight pause, as though he waited for her to speak; then she leaned forward and laid her hand on his.

'If I have really been—if I have done for you even the least part of what you say . . . what you imagine . . . will you do for me, now, just one thing in return?'

He sat motionless, as if fearing to frighten away the shy touch on his hand, and she left it there, conscious of her gesture only as part of the high ritual of their farewell.

'What do you want me to do?' he asked in a low tone.

'*Not* to tell me!' she breathed on a deep note of entreaty.

'*Not* to tell you—?'

'Anything—*anything*—just to leave our . . . our friendship . . . as it has been—as—as a painter, if a friend asked him, might leave a picture—not quite finished, perhaps . . . but all the more exquisite . . . '

She felt the hand under hers slip away, recover itself, and seek her own, which had flashed out of reach in the same instant—felt the start that swept him round on her as if he had been caught and turned about by the shoulders.

'You—*you*?' he stammered, in a strange voice full of fear and tenderness; but she held fast, so centred in her inexorable resolve that she was hardly conscious of the effect her words might be producing.

'Don't you see,' she hurried on, 'don't you *feel* how much safer it is—yes, I'm willing to put it so!—how much safer to leave everything undisturbed . . . just as . . . as it has grown of itself . . . without trying to say: "It's this or that" . . .? It's what we each choose to call it to ourselves, after all, isn't it? Don't let us try to find a name that . . . that we should both agree upon . . . we probably shouldn't succeed.' She laughed abruptly. 'And ghosts vanish when one names them!' she ended with a break in her voice.

This passage contains six actual questions, but a giant invisible question mark hangs over the whole conversation. In some respects it works like one of those nineteenth-century trick pictures that contained two different images in a single composition: children happily playing together whose heads also form the dark sockets of a skull, or a young Cinderella who becomes an old Fairy Godmother when her head is turned upside down. Read from one angle, the conversation between Margaret and Guy is a tactful romantic encounter in which little needs to be said because they already perfectly understand each other. But read again in the light of what we discover later on (the revelation that Guy has formed 'an unfortunate attachment' to an unknown American woman, and used it as an excuse to break off his existing engagement to an English heiress), it is also a scene of tragicomic misunderstanding in which these silences register the awkward distance between them rather than their intimacy.

Again we see ellipses being used to hint at how much isn't being said, or possibly what can't be put into words, and here they are supplemented by a whole armoury of other literary devices, including dashes, pauses, and even the breaks between each paragraph. If Wharton's prose offers us the narrative equivalent of a trick picture, it's also similar to the unfinished portraits she describes here, enabling her to put us in Margaret's position of frustrated longing while showing how Guy understands that he can produce the illusion of being in love without actually lying.

It seems that Henry James gave Wharton the idea for her story in a gossipy letter dated 7 January 1908 ('The Pretext' was drafted a few weeks later), some months before she told him about her own frustrating love affair with a younger man that had been drifting on for more than a year, and scenes like this one are written in just the sort of delicately evasive style James himself might have appreciated. The more we are told, the less we can be sure about. Margaret's desire not to say 'It's this or that' at first makes it seem as if two alternatives are being offered ('would you like chicken or fish?'), but the rest of this conversation reveals 'or' to be the sort of choice that upon closer inspection isn't really a choice at all. Thus when Guy turns away from Margaret, is he overcome by joy, or embarrassment, or neither? Similarly, is his 'tenderness' mentioned because he recognises that he loves her, or because he suddenly realises that he can use her as an excuse to break off his engagement to another woman? Even the movements of their hands reaching for each other could be seen as a softened hint at mutual desire or an expression of something far less sensual, like a mother reaching for her child's hand when crossing the road.

Some of this can be put down to how Wharton stitches her story together. As we've seen in previous chapters, usually the verbal patterns in a piece of writing show us what connects its ideas, yet here Wharton's patterns appear to make things vaguer rather than more certain. When Guy says 'you would understand everything—make allowances for everything . . . a man may have fought against a thing' and she replies with 'one thing in return . . . Anything—*anything* . . . leave everything disturbed', we are not told whether they are referring to the same 'things' or talking at cross purposes, and consequently we too are not given enough information to decide whether 'It's this or that'.

What's more, our interpretation can change over the years. In Chapter 5, I pointed out that the outlines of children's stories like *Alice's Adventures in Wonderland* continue to move around in our heads long after we first read them, and the same is true of books we encounter much later in life. When I first read 'The Pretext' I was roughly Guy's age, and concluded that he was an English Romeo trying not to hurt the feelings of his would-be American Juliet. Then I reread the story when I was closer to her age, and suddenly it looked very different. Now it was an exploration of the small humiliations that accompany a lopsided love affair, and a recognition that because such an infatuation will never lead anywhere, Margaret can happily brood over it forever. (We are told later that this scene by the river has given her 'a secret life of incommunicable joys' she hoards like treasure.)

What hadn't changed in the time between these two readings was my admiration of Wharton's willingness to give her readers the freedom to decide for themselves what she was doing. It's hard to overestimate the importance of this kind of freedom, not least because we experience it so rarely in other aspects of our lives. If we read a work report, we expect to be given some bullet-point conclusions or a set of recommendations to put into practice; if we attend a lecture or a conference speech, we expect to listen to a number of ideas that we can adopt or reject in our own time. By contrast, a story like 'The Pretext' doesn't tell us *what* to think. It helps us learn more about *how* to think. At the end of it some readers will decide that Margaret's life has been ruined by a thoughtless adventurer, others will be convinced that she had a lucky escape and a few will be unable to make up their minds. What they will all be able to agree upon is that they have experienced a freedom of choice that is sadly absent from this character's life.

Ultimately, what kind of story is 'The Pretext'? A romance? A social comedy? A tragedy of unfulfilled ambitions? In some ways it is all of these and more, and it therefore shows us how difficult it is for us to fix our thoughts and feelings into just one narrative with neat edges; it reminds us how often life spills over the stories we construct to make sense of it.

Chapter 33

ENDING

'THE PRETEXT' ENDS WITH Margaret's sad realisation that Guy 'had used her name to screen someone else – or perhaps merely to escape from a situation of which he was weary'. Yet this discovery doesn't entirely remove the ambiguity of Wharton's title. Although Margaret may indeed have given her would-be lover an excuse to get out of an unwanted marriage, he has also given her the opportunity to dream about a romantically exciting alternative to her respectable life in Wentworth, opening up a counterfactual escape hatch in her head.

This is far messier than the ending some of Wharton's readers might have wanted – one that would have answered all of her story's questions and resolved all of its difficulties. But as her friend Henry James pointed out in a notebook entry on *The Portrait of a Lady* (1880–81), explaining his decision to leave the story of his heroine Isabel Archer similarly unresolved, 'The *whole* of anything is never told'. Consequently, novels that try to tie everything up with a neat bow can seem disappointingly artificial, as if the weight of the earlier pages had crushed the life out of the few remaining to us. For E. M. Forster, this was the worst thing about a badly written ending: it took a structure that had magically transformed a small flat object into a three-dimensional world, and promptly squashed it flat again. 'Why is there not a convention which allows a novelist to stop as soon as he feels bored?' he asked in *Aspects of the Novel* (1927). 'Alas, he has to round things off, and usually the characters go dead while he is at work.'

Some of the most successful novels manage to avoid this problem by being far more open-ended. Dickens's *Bleak House* is cut off in mid-sentence as Esther Summerson explains that 'they can very well do without much beauty in me, even supposing—', ending on a word that goes to the heart of the whole storytelling enterprise (at a basic level, all stories are attempts to explore the creative possibilities of 'just suppose') and a dash that leaves that thought hovering in mid-air. Woolf's *To the Lighthouse* (1927) ends with the painter Lily Briscoe saying 'It is finished' and drawing a line in the centre of her canvas, but the last we see of Mr Ramsay is him springing out of his boat towards the lighthouse, not arriving there. His leap hangs over the edge of the novel, the final full stop here working more like a button marked 'Pause'.

Few contemporary authors are as playful as Julian Barnes in wondering whether a narrative can ever be considered complete, particularly when it comes to our own lives. That's partly because he recognises how hard it is to grasp the past: in his early novel *Flaubert's Parrot* (1984), it's compared to a greased piglet being released into a hall full of students, where it 'squirmed between legs, evaded capture, squealed a lot' and made fools out of anyone who tried to pin it down. But it's also because we all carry around an unreliable narrator inside our heads in the form of our own memories.

Barnes's novel *The Sense of an Ending*, which won the Booker Prize in 2011, reflects on how this might affect our ability to trust the stories we tell about ourselves. The title appears to be a nod in the direction of an influential work of literary criticism first published in 1967, also entitled *The Sense of an Ending*, in which Frank Kermode analyses our attempts to make time meaningful by turning it into a story with a beginning, middle and end, like a giant version of a clock's *tick* [pause] *tock*. As tick leads inevitably to tock, Kermode argues, so the shapeless one-thing-after-another quality of chronological time can be made significant through the imposition of an ending, which in the case of an ordinary human life takes the form of our inevitable death. This is the looming full stop that helps us make sense of everything else we might do.

The twist in Barnes's novel is that the most important death occurs before the narrator has even begun to tell his story. This is the suicide of a brilliant young man named Adrian, an act that eventually draws everything else into its gravitational orbit. The narrator, Tony Webster, is not dead, but he is starting to suspect that he might as well be after decades where he has 'just let life happen to him'. Formerly one of Adrian's schoolfriends, he is now a cautious man in his sixties who receives an unexpected bequest from the mother of his college girlfriend Veronica. As he pieces together different fragments from his past – a weekend stay in the house of Veronica's family, her later relationship with Adrian, the revelation that there was a child – he repeatedly tries and fails to find closure. His emails to Veronica are mostly ignored; he is divorced from another woman, but keeps drifting back to her for company and advice; he imagines his daughter saying of him 'Yes, he's retired now, still fossicking around with those mysterious "projects" of his, doubt he'll ever finish anything . . . '

The central example of this pattern of incompleteness is Tony's attempt to understand Adrian's suicide. This comes several years after 'a steady, unimaginative boy' at their school had hanged himself after getting his girlfriend pregnant, leaving a note that read simply 'Sorry, Mum'. Now Tony tries to persuade himself that unlike this banal ending Adrian's life was somehow perfected by his death:

I don't envy Adrian his death, but I envy him the clarity of his life. Not just because he saw, thought, felt and acted more clearly than the rest of us; but also because of when he died. I don't mean any of that First World War rubbish: 'Cut down in the flower of youth' – a line still being churned out by our headmaster at the time of Robson's suicide – and 'They shall not grow old as we that are left grow old.' Most of the rest of us haven't minded growing old. It's always better than the alternative in my book. No, what I mean is this. When you are in your twenties, even if you're confused and uncertain about your aims and purposes, you have a strong sense of what life itself is, and of what you in life are, and might become. Later . . . later there is more uncertainty, more overlapping, more backtracking, more false memories. Back then, you can remember your short life in its entirety. Later, the memory becomes a thing of shreds and patches. It's a bit like the black box aeroplanes carry to record what happens in a crash. If nothing goes wrong, the tape erases itself. So if you do crash, it's obvious why you did; if you don't, then the log of your journey is much less clear.

Or, to put it another way. Someone once said that his favourite times in history were when things were collapsing, because that meant something new was being born. Does this make any sense if we apply it to our individual lives? To die when something new is being born – even if that something new is our very own self? Because just as all political and historical change sooner or later disappoints, so does adulthood. So does life. Sometimes I think the purpose of life is to reconcile us to its eventual loss by wearing us down, by proving, however long it takes, that life isn't all it's cracked up to be.

We learn at the start of the novel that Adrian's surname was Finn, which comes close to being another example of a cratylic name (the Latin word *finis*, meaning 'the end', also gives us many English words including final, finish and finale), but also indicates how the narrator tries to deal with his old friend's death. Instead of confronting it head on, he allows memories of Adrian to break the surface of the text from time to time, like a shark's fin, before sinking out of sight again. This passage too shows Tony's efforts to evade the truth. For example, in the opening paragraph, his words are like the pieces of a jigsaw puzzle he is trying to put together, but there are several pieces missing, and he imagines they will complete a different picture to the one they eventually do. 'Later . . . later', he explains, 'there is more uncertainty, more overlapping, more backtracking, more false memories', where the ellipsis is just one example of the sort of narrative sidestep Tony repeatedly makes, as he moves around the secrets from his past like a climber carefully avoiding potholes and crevasses. Indeed, as his narrative develops, we gradually come to realise how little he understands that the comforting version of Adrian's death he has carried around for many years is a fiction of his own making. Although he admits in the novel's opening paragraph that 'what you end up remembering isn't always the same as what you have witnessed', he is so unreliable a narrator even he doesn't seem to know what really happened.

An aside in Barnes's slightly earlier work *Nothing to Be Frightened of* (2008) casts some light on what is going on here. 'We talk about our memories,' he writes, 'but should perhaps talk more about our forgettings, even if that is a more difficult – or logically impossible – feat.' Later in *The Sense of an Ending* we discover what Tony has forgotten, whether by chance or by design. Adrian fathered a child, and the mother was not Veronica, his girlfriend, but Veronica's mother. This shock discovery makes us reassess much of what Tony has previously told us, including the possibility that Veronica's mother had also tried to seduce him during that awkward family weekend, with some details of his account, such as him masturbating into a sink in the guest bedroom, or the mother throwing away a broken egg when making breakfast, being the result of his memory concealing or distorting the truth.

We never discover for certain what happened (Barnes's novel is like a whodunnit where the detective closes his notebook and exits the room before revealing who the murderer is) but we are given some clues in this passage that Tony's version of events is at best partial. For example, his description of memory as a thing of 'shreds and patches' is an allusion to the motley worn by the figure of Vice in medieval morality plays (when Shakespeare's Hamlet refers to his usurping uncle as 'a king of shreds and patches' he is also comparing him to this traditional bogeyman figure), which may indicate that his conscience is far more troubled than he likes to make out. And throughout the narrative he puts his theory of 'shreds and patches' into practice. When he tells us about the times in history when 'something new was being born' or admits that 'life isn't all it's cracked up to be', he is offering us unassimilated fragments of his own past that edge towards being confessions – Adrian's son, broken eggs – and then back away again, by taking a handful of facts and disguising them as metaphors.

The slipperiness of memory is revealed in how some words seem to slither around on the page whenever they are repeated. The most self-conscious examples are Tony's variations on 'meaning': 'I don't mean . . . what I mean . . . that meant'. Like a greased pig, the harder he presses down on this word the further it seems to slip from his grasp.

It's a conclusion that applies to many other literary works besides Barnes's novel. Throughout this book, I have tried to show that the meaning of such a work is always flexible, uncertain, open to change. That isn't only because your reading and my reading will never perfectly coincide, any more than two separate lines of print will ever meet. It's also because the relationship between a reader and a book is much like any other relationship. Even after many years you never quite know what to expect from it.

In his version of *The Sense of an Ending*, Kermode writes that he is concerned with 'making sense of the ways we try to make sense of our lives', and Barnes's novel reminds us that this struggle is never fully resolved. That's why his ambiguous final sentence, 'There is great unrest', is so touchingly lifelike, as it could indicate that Tony has finally worked out what happened all those years ago, or that he remains as clueless as ever. Indeed, like many of the other works discussed in this book, *The Sense of an Ending* shows us that making sense isn't a process that has a straightforward end, like making a cake. It's an ongoing challenge.

Epilogue

What Next?

WHAT HAPPENS WHEN we stop reading? In his essay 'Journées de Lecture' ('Days of Reading'), first published in 1905 as an introduction to his French translation of John Ruskin's *Sesame and Lilies*, Marcel Proust recalls that when he was absorbed in a book as a child it was almost impossible to break the author's spell. Nothing could deflect his attention, not a 'troublesome bee' nor the sound of church bells in the distance that 'might have warned me that time was passing' if only he was listening to them rather than to the voices in his head. On the evenings when he was coming to the final chapters of a book, he remembers relighting his candle after his parents had said goodnight, and reading in bed while the outside world was 'steeped in silence' and 'the dark yet blue sky was full of stars'. Finally, he writes, 'the last page had been read, the book was finished', although alongside the satisfaction of completing the story inevitably there was disappointment that it had come to an end. 'Was there no more to the book than this, then?'

It's a good question, and not only in terms of the finite number of pages that any book contains. As I have been suggesting, literary works like those we have been considering can entertain us with fictional accounts of what did happen and equally with what might happen if the usual rules of reality were relaxed; they can distract us from our lives by temporarily putting us inside someone else's head, or let us try out new thoughts and feelings so that we can decide which ones we would like to adopt as our own. Is that all?

Proust's response is that although we might go to a writer looking for answers to some of life's most difficult questions, the most any book can provide us with is the resources to search for these answers within ourselves. 'It is one of the great and wonderful characteristics of good books . . . that for the author they may be called "Conclusions", but for the reader "Incitements"', Proust explains. 'We feel very strongly that our own wisdom begins where that of the author leaves off, and we would like him to provide us with answers when all he is able to do is to provide us with desires.'

Sometimes these desires will lead us back to the same book for another reading, as I discovered when returning to Edith Wharton's 'The Pretext' after a gap of many years – and indeed as I have tried to show when assessing a number of other works throughout this book. That might seem surprising to anyone who assumes a literary text is drained of interest once we know what happens inside it, just as some cinemagoers don't understand why anyone would want to sit through a popular film like *The Sixth Sense* or *The Usual Suspects* once they know the key plot twist. Actually, a strong case could be made for thinking that we never read the same book twice. John Carey points out that how we read will always be affected by what we have read in the past, as we build up networks of associations in our minds and plug every new work into this private field of reference: 'Our past reading becomes part of our imagination, and that is what we read with.' Even a book we know practically by heart will look slightly different each time we open it, just as we never see exactly the same face each time we look in a mirror. When we read a book we have read before there is always more to see, more to say.

As I explained in Chapter 28, when noting the popularity of fictional sequels and modernisations, this is something that authors themselves have long recognised. Sometimes it is an impulse that can be seen working its way through a literary career. For example, seven years after *The Sense of an Ending*, Julian Barnes published another short novel, *The Only Story*, and his choice of title was veined with irony for readers who recognised some of the buried connections between these two works. The main narrative focus of *The Only Story*, an affair between a nineteen-year-old student and a forty-eight-year-old housewife, is like a novel-length extension of the discovery that lies at the heart of *The Sense of an Ending*, while Barnes also plants some more specific echoes with which to tease his readers. In both novels an older woman gives £500 to the narrator, and both are partly set in a sleepy part of London's stockbroker belt with 'tile-hung' houses and a church called St Michael's. Both narratives also pursue themes that can be found in many of Barnes's other novels, such as the elusiveness of the past and the infinite permutations of that little four-letter word 'love'. Yet when we read either work, these literary connections will be overlaid by the more private associations we bring with us. For me these might include memories of growing up in a place very similar to the one Barnes is gently satirising, or the hastily pencilled notes I made in the margins as I read both novels for the first time. Your associations will probably be different. That is how each reading of a novel, in the sense of merely understanding the printed words, becomes a *reading*, in the sense of a critical response to how (and how successfully) it works.

Do such activities have any effect on the rest of our lives? One answer to this question is given by Dickens's David Copperfield, as he recalls the excitement he felt as a boy after discovering a shelf of his late father's books tucked away at the top of the family home. Soon he is treating them as a parallel world he can escape into whenever he needs some respite from his miserable childhood. He impersonates the heroes, making himself Tom Jones one day and a bold sea captain the next; he transforms the world around him by turning every barn in the neighbourhood and every stone in the church into a piece of improvised scenery for whatever he is reading about. Above all, he assuages his loneliness by means of a 'glorious host' of new friends populating his imagination. 'When I think of it,' he writes, 'the picture always rises in my mind, of a summer evening, the boys at play in the churchyard, and I sitting on my bed, reading as if for life.' Later David gets into trouble by treating his pretty but unsuitable first wife Dora as a character from a fairy tale with whom he can live happily ever after, and there's an early indication in this scene of him reading on his bed that real life is far more complicated than any story. David is not 'reading for life', as someone might read to enrich their own existence or try to discover a better alternative, but 'reading *as if* for life'. Already there is a warning that books and the real world might not map perfectly onto each other.

Nor should we assume that reading is bound to improve us in other ways. In previous chapters I have outlined some of the evidence that suggests it can have a beneficial effect on our brains and general sense of well-being, and it would be good to be able to report that this was a simple case of cause and effect, so that the more books we read the more impressive we will be in other respects. Unfortunately, there is no guarantee that reading will make someone a more sympathetic and morally nuanced thinker, or even more interesting to talk to, no matter how much time they devote to it.

To take a famous example, Joseph Stalin was a voracious reader, and as a young man he devoured the classics of European literature alongside canonical works of political theory. By the time of his death, he had amassed a personal library of some 25,000 volumes stamped with 'Biblioteka I. V. Stalina' – the Library of J. V. Stalin – and claimed to read 500 pages a day. (It may not be a great surprise to learn that he also had a habit of failing to return books he had borrowed from the library.) He was an unusually active reader, using pencils, coloured crayons, and fine-nibbed pens to annotate the books that most interested him, with some of his less complimentary comments including 'waffle', 'gibberish', 'nonsense', 'rubbish', 'fool', 'scumbag' and 'ha ha'. Yet few people would claim that Stalin's bookishness made him a more kindly or thoughtful individual; a historian who has studied his reading habits concludes that although books undoubtedly provided Stalin with solace and intellectual nourishment, they also 'helped insulate him from the inhumane realities accompanying his violent pursuit of utopia'. Plainly here was a reader who failed to see that it wasn't only when opening a work of fiction that he held other people's lives in his hands.

Yet while reading isn't likely to be enough on its own to improve someone's life in strictly measurable terms, or allow us to claim that good readers are also good in other ways, the examples we've been looking at do show that it can give us new ideas to think about and extra resources to think with. Even if we aren't able to treat these books in the manner that Clark Kent treats telephone boxes, entering them as one person and exiting them as someone else, when we finally raise our eyes from the page we may still discover that we have re-entered the world at a slightly different angle. That's certainly been my experience. Over the decades, some of the literary works I've been discussing in these pages have become as familiar to me as my own heartbeat, while others are more like new friends I still need to become better acquainted with. But they all have one thing in common: they make me feel more alive when I am reading them, and better equipped to deal with life outside books when I finish the last page.

Proust recalls his boyhood self on a cold day 'walking, stamping my feet, running along the paths, whenever I had just closed the book, exhilarated by having finished my reading, by the energy accumulated by my immobility'. If this captures the coiled-spring energy of a child who has been sitting still for a long time, it's also a good description of the effect that novels, poems, plays and other forms of literature can have on adult readers, as we close a book and realise that it has opened up the world to us in a new way. As George Eliot points out in *Middlemarch*, 'Every limit is a beginning as well as an ending.'

A Note on Sources

Prologue: Learning to Read

The anecdotes by Patrick Leigh Fermor, Doris Lessing and Judith Kerr about learning to read are drawn from *The Pleasure of Reading*, ed. Antonia Fraser (1992, repr. London: Bloomsbury, 2005). Maryanne Wolf's account of how other children learn to read may be found in *Proust and the Squid: The Story and Science of the Reading Brain* (Cambridge: Icon Books, 2008), and I. A. Richards's comment that this is a process that continues into adulthood in *How to Read a Page* (New York: W. W. Norton & Co., 1942). John Sutherland discusses the rising tide of print in *How to Read a Novel: A User's Guide* (London: Profile Books, 2006). Virginia Woolf's comment is taken from her lecture 'How Should One Read a Book', later repr. as an essay in *The Common Reader: Second Series* (London: Hogarth Press, 1932). William Empson's comment about growing old is reported by Christopher Ricks in *The Force of Poetry* (Oxford: Clarendon Press, 1984). Nietzsche's description of himself as 'a teacher of slow reading' may be found in *Daybreak: Thoughts on the Prejudices of Morality* [1881], trans. as *The Dawn of Day* by John McFarland Kennedy (New York: The MacMillan Company, 1911). For more recent defences of slow reading, see Carl Honoré's *In Praise of Slowness: How a Worldwide Movement Is Challenging the Cult of Speed* (San Francisco: Harper, 2004), John Miedema, *Slow Reading* (Sacramento, CA: Litwin Books,

2009), and David Mikics, *Slow Reading in a Hurried Age* (Cambridge, Mass.: Harvard University Press, 2013).

1. Welcome

The long passage by George Orwell is taken from *Nineteen Eighty-Four* [1949] (Harmondsworth: Penguin, 1983), and his essay 'Why I Write' [1946] is from *Why I Write* (Harmondsworth: Penguin, 2004). For more on the context of Orwell's novel, see Dorian Lynskey, *The Ministry of Truth: A Biography of George Orwell's 1984* (London: Picador, 2019). Martin Amis's welcome to a new reader is taken from *Inside Story* (London: Jonathan Cape, 2020). For more on literary beginnings, see Edward W. Said, *Beginnings: Intention and Method* (New York: Basic Books, 1975), and A. D. Nuttall, *Openings: Narrative Beginnings from the Epic to the Novel* (Oxford: Clarendon Press, 1992).

2. It's the Little Things

Christina Rossetti's 'A Christmas Carol' is quoted from the poem's original publication in *Scribner's Monthly* 3 (January 1872), and James Joyce's short stories are quoted from *Dubliners* [1914], ed. Jeri Johnson (Oxford: Oxford World's Classics, 2000). Adrienne Rich's observation on the force field of a poem is taken from *What Is Found There: Notebooks on Poetry and Politics* (New York: W. W. Norton & Co., 1994). Chekhov's letter to his brother is printed in *The Unknown Chekhov: Stories and Other Writings Hitherto Untranslated*, trans. Avrahm Yarmolinsky (New York: Noonday Press, 1954).

3. One Moment

Wordsworth's 'Daffodils' is quoted from *Poems in Two Volumes* [1807], ed. Helen Darbishire, 2nd edn. (Oxford: Clarendon Press, 1952), and

Dorothy Wordsworth's journal entry may be found in *The Grasmere and Alfoxden Journals*, ed. Pamela Woof (Oxford: Oxford World's Classics, 2008); my information about the events of this day is drawn from Fiona Wilson, *The Ballad of Dorothy Wordsworth* (London: Faber & Faber, 2021). Woolf's phrase 'moments of being' is taken from her essay 'A Sketch of the Past' [1939–40], repr. in *Moments of Being: Autobiographical Writings* (London: Pimlico, 2002). Nigel Molesworth's scornful view of poetry is drawn from Geoffrey Willans and Ronald Searle, *Down with Skool!: A Guide to School Life for Tiny Pupils and Their Parents* (London: Max Parrish, 1953).

4. *What Do You Mean?*

A. E. Housman's poem is quoted from *The Poems of A. E. Housman*, ed. Archie Burnett (Oxford: Oxford University Press, 1997); for some biographical context see Peter Parker, *Housman Country: Into the Heart of England* (London: Little, Brown, 2016). The ambiguity of 'Let him have it Chris' and the tonal uncertainty of 'I don't think you could have done it better' are both discussed by Christopher Ricks in *T. S. Eliot and Prejudice* (London: Faber & Faber, 1988). The deliberate ambiguity of language used by men who could be sounding each other out for something more than a conversation is outlined by Graham Robb in *Strangers: Homosexual Love in the Nineteenth Century* (London: Picador, 2004). William Empson's comment on maintaining oneself between contradictions is taken from a note to his poem 'Bacchus', repr. in *William Empson: The Complete Poems* (Harmondsworth: Penguin, 2001).

5. *Pictures*

Lewis Carroll's writings are quoted from *Alice's Adventures in Wonderland and Through the Looking-Glass*, ed. Hugh Haughton (Harmondsworth: Penguin, 2003). Claud Lovat Fraser's rejected illustrations to *A Shropshire Lad* are reproduced in a special edition of the poem published by The Hayloft Press in 1995, and Housman's comments are taken from Archie Burnett (ed.), *The Letters of A. E. Housman*, 2 vols. (Oxford: Clarendon Press, 2007). Francis Spufford's claim about reading in childhood is made in *The Child That Books Built: A Life in Reading* (London: Metropolitan Books, 2002).

6. Eat Me

Patience Agbabi's 'Eat Me' is quoted from her collection *Bloodshot Monochrome* (Edinburgh: Canongate, 2008), Mark Strand's 'Eating Poetry' may be found in his *Collected Poems* (New York: Alfred A. Knopf, 2016), Francis Bacon's 'Of Studies' in *The Essays* (Harmondsworth: Penguin, 1985), and William Carlos Williams's 'This Is Just to Say' in *Selected Poems* (New York: New Directions Pub., 1968). In this chapter I also quote from Roald Dahl's *Charlie and the Chocolate Factory* [1964] (New York: Penguin, 1998), while Leigh Hunt's comment on 'The Eve of St Agnes' is repr. in G. M. Matthews (ed.), *John Keats: The Critical Heritage* (London: Routledge, 1971), and F. R. Leavis's claim about cottage-trees is included in *The Common Pursuit* (London: Chatto & Windus, 1952). The notes about photocopiers and prom are taken from the website www.foundmagazine.com. Don Paterson's aphorism about poems as memory machines is included in *The Book of Shadows* (London: Picador, 2004).

7. Conversations

The long passage by Sally Rooney is taken from *Normal People* (London: Faber & Faber, 2018). I discuss Lewis Carroll's stammer in *The Story of Alice: Lewis Carroll and the Secret History of Wonderland* (London: Harvill Secker, 2015). William Hazlitt's essay 'On the Conversation of Authors' is quoted from Vol. 7 of A. R. Waller and Arnold Glover (eds.), *The Collected Works of William Hazlitt*, 12 vols.

(London: J. M. Dent & Co., 1903), and his earliest meeting with Coleridge is discussed in his 1823 essay 'My First Acquaintance with Poets'. The anecdote of Proust's encounter with Joyce is included in Alain de Botton's *How Proust Can Change Your Life* (London: Picador, 1997). Keats's encounter with Coleridge is described in a letter to George and Georgiana Keats (February 14, 1819), repr. in *The Letters of John Keats, 1814–1821*, 2 vols., ed. Hyder Edward Rollins (Cambridge, Mass.: Harvard University Press, 1958). Henry Green's 1950 BBC radio talk 'A Novelist to His Readers' is repr. in *Surviving: The Uncollected Writings of Henry Green*, ed. Matthew Yorke (New York: Viking, 1993), and his comments on fictional prose as a 'gathering web of insinuations' and 'a long intimacy between strangers' are made in his memoir *Pack My Bag: A Self-Portrait* (London: The Hogarth Press, 1952). George Eliot's claim that art is 'the nearest thing to life' is made in her article 'The Natural History of German Life' (1856), repr. in *Selected Essays, Poems and Other Writings*, ed. A. S. Byatt (Harmondsworth: Penguin, 1990).

8. Points of View

The long passage by Zoë Heller is taken from *Notes on a Scandal* (London: Picador, 2003). Wayne C. Booth discusses the figure of the unreliable narrator in *The Rhetoric of Fiction*, rev. edn. (Chicago: University of Chicago Press, 1983).

9. The Nearest Thing to Life

The long passage by Jane Austen is taken from *Emma* [1815] ed. John Mullan (Oxford: Oxford World's Classics, 2022). The creative use of punctuation is discussed by, among others, John Lennard in *But I Digress: The Exploitation of Parentheses in English Printed Verse* (Oxford: Clarendon Press, 1991). D. H. Lawrence's essay 'Why the Novel Matters' is repr. in his *Selected Essays* (Harmondsworth: Penguin, 1981).

10. What's in a Name?

The long passage by Anita Loos is taken from *Gentlemen Prefer Blondes* [1925] (Harmondsworth: Penguin, 1999). Hegel's comment on the comic spirit is contained in *Hegel's Aesthetics: Lectures on Fine Art*, trans. T. M. Knox (Oxford: Oxford University Press, 1975).

11. My Family and Other Animals

The long passage by Virginia Woolf is taken from *Flush* [1933], ed. Kate Flint (Oxford: Oxford World's Classics, 2008); Flint's introduction to this edition also discusses Woolf's broader interest in animals. Craig Raine's poem is quoted from *A Martian Sends a Postcard Home* (Oxford: Oxford University Press, 1979); and the passage about Laska hunting snipe is quoted from Leo Tolstoy, *Anna Karenina*, trans. Marian Schwartz (New Haven: Yale University Press, 2014). Thomas Nagel's essay 'What Is It Like to Be a Bat?' [1974] is repr. in *Mortal Questions* (Cambridge: Cambridge University Press, 1979), and William Empson's observations on how 'dog' has been used as a metaphor in literary texts are contained in *The Structure of Complex Words* (London: Chatto & Windus, 1951). Viktor Shklovsky's essay 'Art as Technique' is repr. in David Lodge (ed.), *Twentieth Century Literary Criticism: A Reader* (London: Longman, 1972). The importance of smell to writers and artists is discussed by Constance Classen, David Howes and Anthony Synnott in *Aroma: A Cultural History of Smell* (London: Routledge, 1994).

12. Keeping It Real

The long passage by George Eliot is taken from *Adam Bede* [1859], ed. Carol A. Martin (Oxford: Oxford World's Classics, 2008), and the passage from *The Water-Babies* is quoted from the edition ed. Robert Douglas-Fairhurst (Oxford: Oxford World's Classics, 2013). John

Updike's comment about giving 'the mundane its beautiful due' may be found in his Foreword to *The Early Stories: 1953–1975* (New York: Alfred A. Knopf, 2003). Adrienne Rich's poem 'A Valediction Forbidding Mourning' is repr. in her *Selected Poems 1950–2012* (New York: W. W. Norton & Co., 2018). The historical context of George Eliot's political views is provided in Kathryn Hughes, *George Eliot: The Last Victorian* (London: Fourth Estate, 1998).

13. Making It New

Wendy Cope's 'The Orange' is quoted from *Serious Concerns* (London: Faber & Faber, 1992), and her other poems are in the collection *Making Cocoa for Kingsley Amis* (London: Faber & Faber, 1986). Coleridge's claim about *Lyrical Ballads* may be found in his *Biographia Literaria* (1817), and Shelley's claim about poetry in general is from *A Defence of Poetry*, written in 1821 and first published in 1840. For Ezra Pound's comment, see his collection of essays *Make It New* (London: Faber & Faber, 1934). William Empson's discussion of 'and' is contained in *Seven Types of Ambiguity* (London: Chatto & Windus, 1947).

14. Foreground and Background

Arthur Conan Doyle's 'The Boscombe Valley Mystery' and 'A Case of Identity' are repr. in *The Penguin Complete Sherlock Holmes* (London: Viking, 2009), and the original publication context is discussed in Mike Ashley, *Adventures in the Strand: Arthur Conan Doyle and the Strand Magazine* (London: The British Library, 2016). Flaubert's story is repr. in *Three Tales*, trans. A. J. Krailsheimer (Oxford: Oxford World's Classics, 2009). Virginia Woolf's *Orlando* [1928] is quoted from the edition ed. Rachel Bowlby (Oxford: Oxford World's Classics, 2008). Joseph Conrad's remark is contained in his 'Preface' to *The Nigger of the 'Narcissus'* [1897], ed. Allan H. Simmons (Cambridge: Cambridge University Press, 2017). Georgia O'Keeffe's comment about seeing is cited in Elizabeth Hutton Turner, *Georgia O'Keeffe: The Poetry of Things* (Washington DC: Phillips Collection, 1999). Roland Barthes's essay 'The Reality Effect' [1969] is repr. in *The Rustle of Language*, trans. Richard Howard (Berkeley: University of California Press, 1989).

15. Atmosphere

The long passage by Charlotte Brontë is taken from *Wuthering Heights* [1847], ed. John Bugg (Oxford: Oxford World's Classics, 2020), and Virginia Woolf's essay on the novel is repr. in *The Common Reader: First Series* (London: Hogarth Press, 1925). The uses of fog in literature and film are discussed by Christine L. Corton in *London Fog: The Biography* (Cambridge, Mass.: Harvard University Press, 2015). Ruskin's observations on the 'pathetic fallacy' are repr. in *John Ruskin: Selected Writings*, ed. Dinah Birch (Oxford: Oxford World's Classics, 2009). Shakespeare's interest in the weather as a theatrical and psychological resource is outlined in Gwilym Jones, *Shakespeare's Storms* (Manchester: Manchester University Press, 2014).

16. Wandering and Wondering

The long passage by Jan Morris is taken from *Trieste and the Meaning of Nowhere* (London: Faber & Faber, 2001). The comment by Jonathan Raban is taken from *Soft City* (London: Hamish Hamilton, 1974). Joyce's comment about Dublin is quoted in Frank Budgen, *James Joyce and the Making of Ulysses* [1934] (Bloomington: Indiana University Press, 1960). Woolf's essay 'Literary Geography' is repr. in *The Essays of Virginia Woolf, Vol. 1: 1904–1912*, ed. Andrew McNeillie (London: Hogarth Press, 1986); the different approaches taken by Joyce and Woolf are helpfully compared by Jeri Johnson in her essay 'Literary Geography: Joyce, Woolf and the City', *City*, Vol. 4, No. 2 (2000).

17. There's No Place Like Home

The long passage by Marilynne Robinson is taken from *Housekeeping* (London: Faber & Faber, 1981). Dickens's letter is repr. in *The Letters of Charles Dickens, Vol. 3: 1842–1843*, ed. Madeline House et al. (Oxford: Oxford University Press, 1974). Philip Larkin's 'Home Is So Sad' and 'Poetry of Departures' are quoted from Archie Burnett (ed.), *The Complete Poems of Philip Larkin* (London: Faber & Faber, 2012), and the biographical context may be found in Andrew Motion, *Philip Larkin: A Writer's Life* (London: Faber & Faber, 1993). Henry James's preface is repr. in *The Portrait of a Lady* [1881], ed. Roger Luckhurst (Oxford: Oxford World's Classics, 2009).

18. Imaginary Worlds

The long passage by Margaret Atwood is taken from *The Handmaid's Tale* (London: Jonathan Cape, 1986). 'Writing Utopia' is quoted from Margaret Atwood, *Writing with Intent: Essays, Reviews, Personal Prose: 1983–2005* (New York: Carroll & Graf, 2005). H. G. Wells is quoted from *The Time Machine* [1895], ed. Roger Luckhurst (Oxford: Oxford World's Classics, 2017), and Aldous Huxley from *Brave New World* [1932] (London: Vintage, 2007).

19. Once Upon a Time

'Prince Hat Underground' is quoted from Kelly Link, *White Cat, Black Dog* (London: Head of Zeus, 2023). C. S. Lewis's article 'Sometimes Fairy Stories May Say Best What's To Be Said' was originally published in the *New York Times* (18 November 1956). Bruno Bettelheim is quoted from *The Uses of Enchantment: The Meaning and Importance of Fairy Tales* (New York: Alfred A. Knopf, 1976). Angela Carter's letter is quoted in Robert Coover's introduction to Angela Carter, *Heroes and Villains* [1969] (Harmondsworth: Penguin, 1998). Max Weber's comment on the 'disenchantment' of culture is made in *The Sociology of Religion* [1922], trans. Ephraim Fischoff (London: Methuen & Co., 1965).

20. Accidents

The long passage by Charles Dickens is taken from *Nicholas Nickleby* [1838–39], ed. Paul Schlicke (Oxford: Oxford World's Classics, 2008). W. H. Auden's comments on rhyme are made in his essay 'Writing', repr. in *Selected Essays* (London: Faber & Faber, 1956). My remarks on Racine in this chapter draw on Clive Scott's study *The Riches of Rhyme: Studies in French Verse* (Oxford: Clarendon Press, 1988). Keats is quoted from *The Letters of John Keats, 1814–1821*, 2 vols., ed. Hyder Edward Rollins (Cambridge, Mass.: Harvard University Press, 1958), and Joyce is quoted from *Finnegans Wake*, ed. Robbert-Jan Henkes, Erik Binder-voet and Finn Fordham (Oxford: Oxford University Press, 2012).

21. Order

The passages by Virginia Woolf are taken from 'The London Scene' [1931], repr. with other essays in *The London Scene* (London: Daunt Books, 2013), *Mrs Dalloway* [1925] (London: Vintage Classics, 2016), and *The Waves* [1931] (Harmondsworth: Penguin, 2019); her letter is quoted by Jeri Johnson in 'Literary Geography: Joyce, Woolf and the City', *City*, Vol. 4, No. 2 (2000). Bret Easton Ellis is quoted from *American Psycho*, new ed. (London: Picador, 1998). Michel Foucault's comments may be found in *The Order of Things: An Archaeology of the Human Sciences* (London: Tavistock Publications, 1970). Aracelis Girmay's 'Elegy in Gold' is contained in her collection *Kingdom Animalia* (Rochester, NY: BOA Editions, Ltd, 2011). Coleridge's comment on prose may be found in *Table Talk of Samuel Taylor Coleridge* (London: Routledge, 1884). For more on literary lists, see Francis Spufford's *The Chatto Book of Cabbages and Kings: Lists in Literature* (London: Chatto & Windus, 1989) and Chapter 1

('Lists') of Eric Griffiths, *If Not Critical*, ed. Freya Johnston (Oxford: Oxford University Press, 2018).

22. Feelings

Carol Ann Duffy's 'The Love Poem' is quoted from *Rapture* (London: Picador, 2005). For more on mirror neurons, see Marco Iacoboni, *Mirroring People: The Science of Empathy and How We Connect with Others* (New York: Farrar, Straus & Giroux, 2008). William Empson's comment about feelings is made in his essay 'Teaching Literature' [1934], repr. in *Argufying: Essays on Literature and Culture*, ed. John Haffenden (London: Chatto & Windus, 1987).

23. Arguments

Hamlet's soliloquy (with modernised spelling) is taken from the First Folio text [1623], widely available online. Monty Python's sketch 'Argument Clinic' is repr. in *Monty Python's Flying Circus: Just the Words*, 2 vols. (London: Methuen, 2019). Mikhail Bakhtin's essays on fiction are repr. in *The Dialogic Imagination: Four Essays*, trans. Michael Holquist and Caryl Emerson (Austin: University of Texas Press, 1981). Clive James's comment on line endings is contained in his essay 'Larkin Treads the Boards', repr. in *Somewhere Becoming Rain: Collected Writings on Philip Larkin* (London: Picador, 2019), and Empson's claim on the writer as a 'go-between' may be found in his introduction to *Coleridge's Verse: A Selection*, ed. William Empson and David Pirie (New York: Schocken Books, 1973).

24. Mind the Gap

Elizabeth Bishop's poem 'O Breath' is quoted from *Poems* (Chatto & Windus, 2011); for some biographical context, see Brett C. Millier,

Elizabeth Bishop: Life and the Memory of It (Berkeley: University of California Press, 1993). Peter Ustinov's anecdote is included in his memoir *Dear Me* (London: William Heinemann, 1977). The passage by Charlotte Brontë is taken from *Jane Eyre* [1847], ed. Margaret Smith (Oxford: Oxford World's Classics, 2019). Adrienne Rich's comment on breaking a silence is contained in *What Is Found There: Notebooks on Poetry and Politics* (New York: W. W. Norton & Co., 1994). Peter Robinson's poem 'Cleaning' is quoted from his collection *This Other Life* (Manchester: Carcanet Press, 1988).

25. Body Matters

Ivor Gurney's poem 'Pain' is quoted from his *Collected Poems*, ed. P. J. Kavanagh (Manchester: Fyfield Books, 2004); some context is provided by Kate Kennedy in *Dweller in Shadows: A Life of Ivor Gurney* (Princeton and Oxford: Princeton University Press, 2021). The research on reading conducted by Avni Bavishi, Martin D. Slade and Becca R. Levy of the Yale University School of Public Health ('A Chapter a Day: Association of Book Reading with Longevity') is published in *Social Science and Medicine* 164 (September 2016). For more on literature and empathy, see Maja Dijikic, Keith Oatley, Sara Zoeterman and Jordan B. Peterson, 'On Being Moved By Art: How Reading Fiction Transforms the Self' in *Creativity Research Journal* 21:1 (2009), and Peter Bazalgette, *The Empathy Instinct: How to Create a More Civil Society* (London: John Murray, 2017). My discussion of pain draws especially on Elaine Scarry, *The Body in Pain: The Making and Unmaking of the World* (Oxford: Oxford University Press, 1985). Virginia Woolf's essay 'On Being Ill' [1926] is repr. in her *Collected Essays*, 4 vols. (London: Hogarth Press, 1967–72). Sigmund Freud's essay 'Thoughts for the Times on War and Death' is included in Vol. XIV of the Standard Edition of Freud's works ed. James Strachey (London: Hogarth Press, 1957).

26. Good and Bad Sex

The long passage by Laurence Sterne is taken from *A Sentimental Journey* [1768], ed. Tim Parnell and Ian Jack (Oxford: Oxford World's Classics, 2008), and the work's critical reception is described in Alan B. Howes (ed.), *Laurence Sterne: The Critical Heritage* (London: Routledge, 1995). The biographical context may be found in Ian Campbell Ross, *Laurence Sterne: A Life* (Oxford: Oxford University Press, 2001). *Sons and Lovers* [1913] is quoted from the Oxford World's Classics edition ed. David Trotter (2009). For more detail on the neurological processes involved in reading, see Jaak Panksepp, *Affective Neuroscience: The Foundations of Human and Animal Emotions* (New York and Oxford: Oxford University Press, 1998), and Norman H. Holland, 'Literature and Happiness', *PSYART: A Hyperlink Journal for the Psychological Study of the Arts* (2007). Adam Phillips's comment is taken from his essay 'On Flirtation', in *On Flirtation* (London: Faber & Faber, 1994). Paul Valéry's claim is made in an essay published in *La Nouvelle Revue Française* in March 1933 about his poem 'Le Cimetière marin' ('The Cemetery by the sea'). George Saunders discusses Tolstoy's story in his book *A Swim in a Pond in the Rain* (London: Bloomsbury, 2021).

27. The Attraction of Repulsion

The long passage by Bram Stoker is taken from *Dracula* [1897], ed. Roger Luckhurst (Oxford: Oxford World's Classics, 2011). Christopher Ricks's account of blushing may be found in *Keats and Embarrassment* (Oxford: Clarendon Press, 1974), and the symptoms of tuberculosis are discussed by Susan Sontag in *Illness as Metaphor* (New York: Farrar, Straus & Giroux, 1978). Erving Goffman's argument about the self's 'territorial preserve' is from *Relations in Public: Microstudies of the Public Order* (New York: Basic Books, 1971). On the psychology of disgust, I am drawing on Paul Rozin's

'A Perspective on Disgust', *Psychological Review* 94 (1987), Mary Douglas, *Purity and Danger: An Analysis of the Concepts of Pollution and Taboo* (London: Routledge & Kegan Paul, 1966), and William Ian Miller, *The Anatomy of Disgust* (Cambridge, Mass.: Harvard University Press, 1997).

28. Ghost Hunting

In Memoriam [1850] is quoted from Christopher Ricks (ed.), *The Poems of Tennyson*, 3 vols. (London: Longman, 1987). My discussion of clichés in *Dracula* draws on Christopher Ricks's argument about Samuel Beckett in *Beckett's Dying Words* (Oxford: Clarendon Press, 1995). Oscar Moore's description of dancing in a disco is taken from *PWA: Looking AIDS in the Face* (London: Picador, 1996). Queen Victoria's response to Tennyson may be found on the Royal Collection Trust website www.rct.uk. Larkin's poem is quoted from Archie Burnett (ed.), *The Complete Poems of Philip Larkin* (London: Faber & Faber, 2012). Martin Heidegger's comment is contained in *Poetry, Language, Thought* (New York: Harper & Row, 1971).

29. Suspense

The long passage by Thomas Hardy is taken from *A Pair of Blue Eyes* [1872–73], ed. Alan Manford (Oxford: Oxford World's Classics, 2009); the biographical context may be found in Florence Emily Hardy, *The Life of Thomas Hardy* (1928–30, repr. London: Palgrave Macmillan, 1962). Sergei Eisenstein's essay 'Dickens, Griffith, and the Film Today' is repr. in his collection *Film Form: Essays in Film Theory*, ed. and trans. Jay Leyda (New York: Harcourt, Brace & World, 1949).

30. Symbols

Katherine Mansfield's 'The Garden Party' [1922] is quoted from *The Garden Party and Other Stories* (Harmondsworth: Penguin, 2007); the biographical context may be found in Claire Tomalin, *Katherine Mansfield: A Secret Life* (London: Viking, 1987). Other works referred to in this chapter include Thomas Hardy, *Tess of the d'Urbervilles* [1891], ed. Simon Gatrill (Oxford: Oxford World's Classics, 2008), Seamus Heaney, 'Digging' in *Death of a Naturalist* (London: Faber & Faber, 1966), Gertrude Stein, 'Sacred Emily' in *Geography and Plays* (Boston: The Four Seas Company, 1922), Zadie Smith, *The Embassy of Cambodia* (London: Hamish Hamilton, 2013), and Charles Baudelaire, 'The Painter of Modern Life' [1863], repr. in *The Painter of Modern Life, and other Essays*, trans. and ed. by Jonathan Mayne (London: Phaidon, 1964). A detailed discussion of the uses of ellipses in narrative may be found in Anne Toner, *Ellipsis in English Literature: Signs of Omission* (Cambridge: Cambridge University Press, 2015).

31. Growing Up

The narrative and theatrical versions of *Peter Pan* discussed in this chapter are quoted from Robert Douglas-Fairhurst (ed.), *The Collected Peter Pan* (Oxford: Oxford University Press, 2019); further biographical context may be found in Andrew Birkin, *J. M. Barrie and the Lost Boys* (London: Constable, 1979).

32. Thinking Differently

Edith Wharton's 'The Pretext' is quoted from *The Hermit and the Wild Woman and Other Stories* (London: Macmillan & Co., 1908); the biographical context may be found in Hermione Lee, *Edith Wharton*

(London: Chatto & Windus, 2007). John Carey's claim is made in *What Good Are the Arts?* (London: Faber & Faber, 2005).

33. Ending

The long passage by Julian Barnes is taken from *The Sense of an Ending* (London: Jonathan Cape, 2011). Henry James's comment is reproduced in *The Notebooks of Henry James*, ed. F. O. Matthiessen and Kenneth B. Murdock (Oxford: Oxford University Press, 1947). E. M. Forster's warning is contained in *Aspects of the Novel* (London: Edwin Arnold, 1927). Other works referred to in this chapter are Charles Dickens, *Bleak House* [1852–53], ed. Stephen Gill (Oxford: Oxford World's Classics, 2008), Virginia Woolf, *To the Lighthouse* [1927], ed. David Bradshaw (Oxford: Oxford World's Classics, 2008), Julian Barnes, *Flaubert's Parrot* (London: Jonathan Cape, 1984) and *Nothing To Be Frightened of* (London: Jonathan Cape, 2008), and Frank Kermode, *The Sense of an Ending: Studies in the Theory of Fiction*, new ed. (Oxford: Oxford University Press, 2000).

Epilogue: What Next?

Proust's essay 'Days of Reading' is repr. in *Against Sainte-Beuve and Other Essays*, trans. John Sturrock (Harmondsworth: Penguin, 1988). Other works referred to in this chapter are Julian Barnes, *The Only Story* (London: Jonathan Cape, 2018) and Charles Dickens, *David Copperfield* [1849–50], ed. Nina Burgis (Oxford: Oxford World's Classics, 2008). My information about Stalin's reading habits is drawn from Geoffrey Roberts, 'Joseph Stalin: Bloody Tyrant and Bookworm', *Irish Times* (20 September 2016).

Acknowledgements

For their advice, encouragement and inspiration at various points during the research and writing of this book, I am indebted to Stig Abell, Mac Castro, Sophie Duncan, Eric Griffiths, Geri Halliwell-Horner, Seán Hayes, Natalie Haynes, Simon Horobin, Roddy Howland Jackson, Tabitha Jones, Martha Kearney, Laurie Maguire, Dan Mallory, David Milner, Andrew Motion, Sam Plumb, Luc Rosenberg, Michal Shavit, Helen Small, Peter Straus, Gill Woods and Julian Yarnold.

The author and publisher are grateful for permission to quote from the following works:

Patience Agbabi, 'Eat Me', from *Bloodshot Monochrome* (London: Canongate, 2008); Craig Raine, 'A Martian Sends a Postcard Home', from *A Martian Sends a Postcard Home* (Oxford: Oxford University Press, 1979), courtesy of the author; Wendy Cope, 'The Orange', from *Serious Concerns* (London: Faber & Faber, 1992); Philip Larkin, 'Home Is So Sad', from *The Whitsun Weddings* (London: Faber & Faber, 1964); Carol Ann Duffy, 'The Love Poem', from *Rapture* (London: Picador, 2005), reproduced by permission of Macmillan Publishers International Ltd, text copyright © Carol Ann Duffy, 2005;

Index